THE GENTLE GENERAL

SUNY Series in American Labor History

Robert Asher and Amy Kesselman, Editors

Other books in this series include:

THE GENTLE GENERAL

ROSE PESOTTA
ANARCHIST AND LABOR ORGANIZER

ELAINE LEEDER

STATE UNIVERSITY OF NEW YORK PRESS

Published by
State University of New York Press, Albany

For information, address State University of New York Press,
State University Plaza, Albany, N.Y. 12246

Production by M. R. Mulholland
Marketing by Fran Keneston

Library of Congress Cataloging-in-Publication Data

Leeder, Elaine J.
    The gentle general : Rose Pesotta, anarchist and labor organizer /
Elaine Leeder.
        p.   cm. — (SUNY series in American labor history)
    Revision of the author's thesis: The gentle warrior (Ph.D.)—
Cornell University, 1985.
    Includes bibliographical references and index.
    ISBN 0-7914-1671-2 (CH : acid-free). — ISBN 0-7914-1672-0 (PB :
acid-free)
    1. Pesotta, Rose, 1896-   . 2. Trade-unions—United States—
Officials and employees—Biography. 3. Women anarchists—United
States—Biography. 4. Labor movement—United States—History—20th
century. 5. International Ladies' Garment Workers' Union—History.
I. Title. II. Series.
HD6509.P47L44   1993
331.88'092—dc20
[B]   92-43028
                                                                CIP

10 9 8 7 6 5 4 3 2 1

To the Memory of
Ida and Samuel Sneierson
and
Sophie Leeder

CONTENTS

ILLUSTRATIONS

CHRONICLES OF A GADFLY: OVERVIEW OF ROSE PESOTTA'S LIFE HISTORY

1896	20 November, born in Derazhnya, Russia, as Rachelle Peisoty.
1909–12	Attends Rosalia Davidoff's private girls' school.
1913	October, leaves home for the USA with her grandmother; arrives 24 November, 1913; name changed to Rose Pesotta during immigration procedures.
1914	Joins Local 25 of the ILGWU.
1914–24	Works at the sewing machine as a seamstress.
1919	20 December, Theodore Kushnarev deported on the *Buford*. Father is killed by General Petlura in Derazhnya.
1922	Attends the Bryn Mawr summer school.
	Fall—researches Sacco and Vanzetti case for Local 25; meets with them and begins to speak on their behalf around the country.
1924–26	Attends the Brookwood Labor College.
1926–33	Works as a seamstress in NYC.
1924–28	Works and writes for the *Road to Freedom*.
1927	22 August—Sacco and Vanzetti executed.
1930	Attends the Wisconsin summer school.
1933	Sent to Los Angeles as an organizer by the ILGWU.
1934	May—elected as the only woman vice president of the ILGWU (the third woman ever elected).
	Sent to Puerto Rico to organize seamstresses.
1935	January—sent to Seattle to organize.
	Fall—sent to Milwaukee on emergency assignment.
	Late fall to early 1936—sent to Buffalo to organize seamstresses.
1936	February–March—sent to Akron to organize rubber workers with CIO; becomes involved with Powers Hapgood.
	April—goes to South Bend Indiana to help organize UAW convention.
	September—goes to Montreal to organize.
1937	January–February—sent to Flint to organize auto workers for the CIO.

February—back to Montreal for more organizing.

May—reelected to second term as vice president of ILG.

June—Cleveland Knitting Mill strike.

August 2—slashed by razor in Cleveland strike.

October—leaves Cleveland to return to NYC.

December—vacations in Europe and England with Emma Goldman and anarchist friends.

1938   January—Boston.

1940   January—L.A.

1942   February—leaves L.A. to vacation in Mexico. Then back to NYC and the sewing machine.

1944   June—Boston; resigns as ILGWU vice president.

        November—publishes *Bread upon the Waters*.

1945   August—takes job with the Anti-Defamation League of the B'nai B'rith. Travels to Cleveland, Akron, Cincinnati, Chicago, and Detroit.

1946   July—travels to Norway to participate in summer school of Worker's Education Association; also visits Poland to see effects of World War II.

        November—resigns from ADL and goes to work as seamstress in New York City.

1949   January—goes to work as the Midwest regional director for the American Trade Union Council of the Histadrut.

        4 February—Powers Hapgood dies.

1950   Visits Europe and Israel.

        Begins writing *Days of Our Lives*.

1955   Marries Albert Martin (Frank Lopez).

1958   *Days of Our Lives* published.

1965   6 December—dies in Miami, Florida.

        9 December—buried at Mount Moriah Cemetery, New Jersey.

PREFACE

As I approached the modest home on a tree-lined street in Levittown, New York, I knew that I had come to the right place. Waiting for me in the driveway, propped up against a chair, was a framed original photograph of Emma Goldman and boxes of photos and letters of Rose Pesotta. They had been neglected in this garage for thirty years, mildewing with the passing of the rains and seasons, untouched by anyone since Pesotta's death in 1965. Dorothy Rotker, Rose's niece had kept these mementos, having sent a substantial portion of other materials to the New York Public Library Rare Books and Manuscripts Division just after Rose's death. Now she was graciously giving the remaining materials to me, with the hope that I might share them with the public and, eventually, pass them on when I was finished using them.

Sifting through the hundreds of photographs, I found Rose from her early days in the garment district, through her labor college days and her exciting career as a labor organizer, and then on into her middle years and later life. There were original letters from her lover Theodore Kushnarev, including a vivid description of his life on Ellis Island and then his deportation with other anarchists in 1919 on the *Buford*. The letters were so passionate that I felt the fire burning between the two, later feeling the pain as time and circumstances separated them, the victims of political repression.

My odyssey into Rose Pesotta's life was completed. I had come full circle: from the day in 1981 when I first heard Rose's best friend, Clara Larsen, speak fondly of Rose at a labor history workshop on immigrant anarchism at the Tamiment Institution to this hot summer day in 1987 in Levittown. In between I had spent countless hours reading the archives at the New York Public Library, the Tamiment, and the International Ladies' Garment Workers' Union, and interviewing Rose's friends and colleagues. Now was the time to again revise what I had written as a dissertation and make Rose known to the public—particularly to feminists, labor historians, and activists who might benefit from her experiences.

Before leaving the Rotker home, I inquired about one more memento which Rose had cherished since 1927, when it had been given to her by Bartolemeo Vanzetti just before his execution. Vanzetti had carved a penholder for her, a holder made of ivory with an "exquisite design," intricate in detail and carefully executed. Dorothy handed me the pen, indicating that I should have it so that the anarchist connection would carry to yet another generation. I walked away from that day rededicated to my mission: to tell the story of Rose and her friends—their lives and trials as anarchists, as labor activists, and as keepers of the revolutionary tradition to which they had dedicated their lives.

It is time for a new generation to experience, recognize, and appreciate Rose Pesotta. Her name is familiar to labor historians because of her recently reissued autobiography *Bread upon the Waters*. But Rose Pesotta was more than a labor leader. She participated in prerevolutionary activities in Russia, the resurgence of the garment workers' industry, women's labor colleges in the 1920s, the effects of the growth of Communism, labor activism and organizing in the 1930s, and the anarchist movement. She was part of most major progressive activities that were popular during her time and she actively intervened and participated in quite a few of them. Additionally, Rose experienced the effects of gender politics personally as well as in the labor movement generously, as well as the virulent factionalism of unionism in the 1920s and 1930s.

Rose Pesotta spoke for the masses of workers who toiled in the sweatshops. Her people were the powerless and voiceless in the sea of political turmoil of her era. Rose was able to identify and articulate the concerns of the common person, and, accordingly, she related well to and was esteemed by, all with whom she came in contact. For a decade she organized garment workers, but long after those active years she continued to work for war refugees, for victims of government persecution, for minorities and for women. Her voice was most heard as that of a labor organizer, but her anarchism and and later ideological evolution carried her on long after her most public years. For this, Rose's story is one of importance and interest to those outside of labor history as well. Rose Pesotta was a common woman, an immigrant, well educated, and dynamic. Her biography brings to life eras that many of us know of only vaguely and speaks to us because it is the life of one of us, the common worker, struggling to make it in a difficult and demanding world. This is the story of a woman born in pre-revolutionary Russia, an immigrant in New York City, a radical, a labor organizer, a world traveler, and a dedicated activist and friend. A woman who was absolutely pioneering in her work and her personal life.

In these years, Rose Pesotta has become my role model and spiritual mentor. Through her I have learned the ideology of anarchism, but also—and far more importantly—the courage to go on, even in the face of enormous loss, failure, and pain. Rose Pesotta was a difficult woman for some, admired by many and close to very few, but she was also a survivor, a woman with a revolutionary vision who continued to live that vision to the end.

As one approaches a study of Pesotta's life, a number of questions and themes emerge that will be explored throughout this work. The first and overriding theme is that of Rose as a woman fighting actively throughout her life against patriarchy and the dominant social order of a male-dominated hierarchy. Rose fought against it all her life, and the question becomes how such a woman could survive and deal with the qualities of such a system. As we shall see, Rose struggled valiantly, winning sometimes and losing often in the battle. Her struggle began in her family of origin, continued in the labor movement, occurred in her personal relationships with men, through the writing of her autobiography, and ceased only at the end of her life. As a result of this battle, a minor theme is that she lived as a lone woman in the struggle against domination by father, lovers, bosses, and union executives. Pesotta, unusual in her day and time, became a Joan of Arc who ran her life and her work like a Gilbert and Sullivan show. This flair and independence are characteristics that will be explored in depth in the coming pages.

Another thematic concern is her ability as an anarchist to deal with a bureaucracy such as the International Ladies' Garment Workers' Union. Pesotta, a vice president and organizer for the union for over ten years, constantly tried to juggle the competing demands of such ideological differences. We will explore the juxtaposition and conflict between the two and attempt to understand whether it is possible for someone to be an officer and an anarchist at the same time. We will also assess whether Pesotta was co-opted by the union, or if she was able to remain the philosophical anarchist she alleged herself to be.

Third, the nature of being a survivor, against all odds, is a theme that pervades Pesotta's life. As we shall see, under the most adverse conditions she was able to find a means to deal with whatever problems presented. Rose Pesotta always seemed to persevere against all odds and to counter the negative elements that attempted to do her harm. In the end, perhaps, overcome by illness and harshness from her two movements, she eventually succumbed, but not without years of struggling and valiant efforts to organize and to fight back.

In this book I will explore the nature of Rose Pesotta's life: I will try to understand who she was, where she came from, what she did, and the significance of her activities in relation to women of her era. I will look closely at one union within the larger labor movement, as well as at what occurred to one woman within it. I will also explore the nature of the anarchist movement and its role during the eras under consideration.

Although Pesotta did not lead any major institution, nor remain

public beyond her ten years in office, the reader will find her of interest
for a number of important reasons. Pesotta had a complicated personality,
one not easily explainable and certainly not diagnosable, based on the
evidence and material available. Nonetheless, watching her in operation,
seeing how effective she was while still being lonely and alone in the
world, makes for an unusual case study. Additionally, she had quite a bit
to say about many of the important events of her era and participated
actively in more than a few of them. She explored issues such as race
relations, male and female dynamics and inequality, friendships, romance, politics, and political theory. Her life experience led her through
the factional wars of the union as well as the formation of the CIO and
the building of union bureaucracy. For these reasons, her story is an
interesting one to follow and makes her both a role model and a catalyst
for thinking about a number of contemporary and relevant issues.

I make no claims to have written the definitive work on Pesotta's
life, I try merely to begin an exploration of an important life and to
document the activities of a woman who left a wealth of material and
information. Lessons from her life may be of use to a current generation
of activist women, historians, and sociologists. Pesotta still speaks to
those who are confronting questions that were prominent in her day and
remain so today: gender relations, the nature of bureaucracies, racism,
ethnic conflict, and how one deals with war. The answers to some of
these, perhaps, may be found in the telling of the story.

ACKNOWLEDGMENTS

A work of this length takes years to complete. Over that period of time, countless individuals have touched my life and aided me in many ways. It is impossible to mention all the librarians, archivists, scholars, and secretaries whose assistance has brought this biography to fruition. However, there are a few people who stand out in their support and counsel. First my gratitude to Amy Kesselman and Robert Asher of the SUNY Series in American Labor History for seeing the merit of my work, for taking the raw material and helping me hone it into a publishable manuscript. Without them this book would still be languishing on my shelf. Ruth Meyerowitz was most helpful in suggesting contemporary feminist historical works to include in the most recent revision, as was Harold Troper with his insights on Jewishness and Pesotta's later life evolution.

Perhaps the greatest thank-you goes to Dorothy Owens, Ithaca College manuscript editor. Her generosity in time, editorial suggestions, and pure encouragement gave me the energy to go on when times were very bleak. Without her this book would not exist. Richard Polenberg of Cornell University's History department was crucial in his first recommending that I study Pesotta and then in his careful and insightful mentoring. Richard Strassberg of Cornell's Industrial and Labor Relations Documentation Center was invaluable in suggesting sources and helping me gain access to crucial archives. Alan Hahn of Cornell's Human Service Studies helped me understand Pesotta's life in the context of social-movement theory. David Porter of Empire State College proved to be the kind of colleague and friend who reemerges regularly, as he helped me think through the handling of various editorial and intellectual difficulties. Paul Avrich served as an inspiration and role model as an anarchist historian. Grateful acknowledgement is also made to the Rare Books and Manuscripts Division of the New York Public Library, Astor, Lenox and Tilden Foundations for permission to quote from the correspondence of Rose Pesotta to Mary Donovan Hapgood.

A number of Rose Pesotta's friends and family members provided me necessary information about the lost details of her life. Clara Rothberg Larsen fed me Friday-night dinners as she told me wonderful stories of her lifelong friendship with Pesotta. Valerio Isca shared his writings on Rose and the anarchist community. Dorothy Rubin Rotker, Elias Rotker, and Edward Rotker were remarkable in giving me all of the remaining letters, photos, films, and memorabilia, which will eventually be donated to the appropriate archives. Jack Hochman shared his love of his aunt and contemporary ILGWU information, while Fanya Bimbat told of her sister and their family life in the Ukraine. Thanks to Gus Tyler for permission to quote extensively from his eulogy on Rose Pesotta.

Certainly my family and friends have been part of this odyssey from the beginning, aiding as they could. David and Abigail Leeder were patient as I traveled for many summers gathering material for this book. Anne Marie Gallonio provided me with a wonderful Cape Cod retreat in which to devote myself to the revisions. Cleo Gorman, Ron Ackerman, Barbara Adams, Carla Golden, David and Deena Schwartz, Larry Reverby, Lin Nelson, Peter Kardas, Craig Longley, Bob Armstrong, Connie Tuttle, Carol Ehrlich, and Sandra Pollack all remained loyal and generous friends during the twelve-year process from start to finish. Each added, in her or his way, to my support system and provided the encouragement and nurturance I needed to continue.

Finally I wish to thank various academic institutions for their support of this project. The Ithaca College Sociology department provided me with a stimulating and freeing environment in which to work and to teach the materials that are part of this book. The Provost's Office at Ithaca College granted me a summer research stipend, which allowed me to travel for interviews and supported me for three months of study. The Semester at Sea Program from the University of Pittsburgh joyously celebrated with me and gave me a group of colleagues and friends I will always remember.

Although this book has been touched by many people, I alone am responsible for its contents and its interpretations. The person I am most grateful to is Rose Pesotta, a woman whose life has become the measure against which I judge myself and my work. Rose Pesotta was a woman far ahead of her time and an iconoclast at that. In the years of working on her life, I have come to see different aspects of her life with varying understandings, based on what was happening in my own life. It was Pesotta's dictate, to go on in face of all adversity, that has been my true inspiration. It remains my life goal.

1

Early Life

I must find a way out.

The Russian Pale during the late nineteenth century was an isolated area, inhabited by Jews who had been legally authorized to settle there by the Czars. They made up 12 percent of the entire population of the area. Just prior to the assassination of Alexander II, in 1881, four million Russian Jews—about one-half of the entire world Jewish population—were confined to an area consisting of twenty-five northern and western provinces out of a total of eighty-five provinces making up the empire (see figure 1).[1] The Jews had been dislocated from crowded urban areas as a result of pogroms that were organized in massacres of helpless people.

Progressively more restrictive governmental measures were instituted, including expulsions from villages, censorship of the press, and mandatory conscription of Jewish children, sometimes for as long as twenty-five years. Almost 94 percent of all Russian Jews were confined to an area of about 386,000 square miles between the Baltic Sea and the Black Sea.[2] Once there, they were confronted with severe deprivation and hardship. Allowed to engage only in commerce and crafts and barred from owning land, the Jews were considered citizens but had a second-class status within the population. They also sometimes worked in factory production, carpentry, plumbing, and other trades, while struggling to survive within a culture of raw and painful poverty.

Living in small, all-Jewish villages in semirural areas known as "shtetls," thousands of which dotted the provinces of the Pale, most Jews had few ties with other Russian citizens. Under constant threat of violent attacks and pogroms from the outside world, these communities were united against the hostilities that could engulf them at any moment. The Jews lived in fear for their lives. And yet these villages were a world all their own, which provided emotional sustenance and community sup-

FIGURE 1

Map of the Pale

Reprinted by permission of the publishers from *The Promised City: New York Jews, 1870–1917* by Moses Rischin, Cambridge, Mass.: Harvard University Press, Copyright © 1962 by the President and Fellows of Harvard College.

port. They pulsated with the activity of daily life, including trading, education, and cultural pursuits.

The shtetls were vibrant communities oriented to otherworldly values. Jewish religious traditions, learning, and practices structured daily existence. They also provided hope for a better life and for a spiritual strength with which to cope with the atrocities regularly confronting them. Religious orthodoxy attempted to isolate the Jew from the external world, promising individual salvation and immortality, as well as the coming of the Messiah, who would protect and redeem His people. Religion also provided the structure for a communalism, uniting all against the petty harassment of the peasantry, the official terrorism of the czar and cossacks, and the acidic winds of modernism blowing from the West. In carrying out religious tenets, voluntary self-help organizations called *hevras* were organized by Jews to aid the sick, raise funds for the needy, and educate the poor. These groups, in addition to the synagogues, were the mainstays of the shtetls, providing a unifying community force.[3]

Religious traditions dictated every aspect of life in the shtetl. They decreed that men be scholars, thinkers, and teachers, while women confine their concern to home and family. Men received importance and honor from this noble undertaking, and it was entirely acceptable for a man to spend all day in the shul studying and praying, while his wife cared for the home and earned the money to support the family. Religious education was reserved exclusively for the men, while the women were expected to be observant and to set examples of reverence for the children and the community. Women were the responsible parties who carried the obligations. Honor and prestige for all came from performing *tsedaka*, acts of social responsibility. Although there were exceptions, these were norms of behavior to which the community generally adhered.

The period just prior to the turn of the twentieth century was an unsettling one, and despite rigid norms, the shtetl was far from stagnant. Into these closed communities, new and innovative ideas inevitably spread. The *Haskalah*, or Jewish Enlightenment, called for the modernization of custom and thought in order to gain for the Jews equality with their Russian neighbors.[4] Modern ideologies were disseminated, from the *yeshivas* (schools) in the cities, where some Jews congregated, to even the most backward villages, by traveling students who educated the Jewish youth. Many of these young people often grasped eagerly at the new ideas and movements. While governmental persecution and repression were the norms, revolutionary ideas were brewing, and Jews excitedly formed new political organizations to implement them. Traditions were challenged, and new ideas flourished. Thousands of Jewish immigrants left the Pale in search of a better way of life.

Into this world of transition Rachelle Peisoty (Rose Pesotta) was born on 20 November 1896. She was the second eldest of eight children, reared in Derazhnya, a small railroad town in the Ukraine. According to Rose, who wrote of her early years in her autobiography *Days of Our Lives*, life in this shtetl was idyllic, her upbringing peaceful and plentiful.[5] Although Jews did not generally fare well there, her family was an exception. Her parents owned and operated a small shop they inherited from Rose's great-aunt Sheba, who obtained it as a result of a change in one of the czar's edicts. The property also included a share of an inn and some land in town. In the store they sold flour, nuts, dates, and other staples of the Russian diet. Wealthy enough to hire a peasant girl to help out, the family could afford to have clothing made by seamstresses, and each child was outfitted completely for the Passover holiday.

As the family was atypical, so the village itself seemed somewhat insulated from the turmoil raging beyond its limits. Jews, Poles, Ukrainians, Armenians, and Germans all lived side by side. Ethnic conflict had little influence on Rose's early childhood.[6] Among Rose's fondest memories was her *cheder* (school) teacher, "Kalman the melamed, the schoolmaster in the elementary cheder who was a *shlimazel*, or luckless one." She warmly described Judith, the ancient shroud maker, and Mendel, the tailor, who once worked on Sarah Bernhardt's gown and who had actually held his hands in hers. Her memories of childhood were charming and simple.

According to family folklore, the Peisoty family reverently observed every orthodox Jewish tradition. Indeed, the parents were so orthodox that the children's shoes were hidden on the Sabbath to ensure that none of them would break the rules of the day of rest. The family also prayed together every morning.[7] Rose's mother, Masya, shaved her head and wore a wig or *shaitel* (head wrapping) in order that she not be attractive to men other than her husband. The oldest boy in the family, David, was catered to by the sisters because, according to Jewish tradition, the son will say prayers (*kaddish*) for the dead parents. His status within the family is a prestigious one, especially as only a male can carry on the family name. Her father wanted boys and was displeased that six out of his eight children were daughters. Esther was the oldest child, then came Rose, Marishka (Miriam), Hannah, David, Luba, Abraham (Yoseler), and Fanya, who was born after Rose emigrated. Two other children died in infancy.

The girls were less favored than the sons, being expected to do the housework and to prepare for the Sabbath. They cared for each other while Masya, their mother, cared for the shop. The eldest girls were responsible for the youngest, and all of the children were deeply involved with each other. They shared religious observances, sang in four different languages and danced the native style of each culture, and participated in public festivities. Rose's description of her childhood is filled with vivid images such as frolicking naked in the big river that ran through the town: "No one in Derazhnya owned a swim suit. We went into the water without either suit or self-consciousness. Though we disrobed in separate bath houses, boys and girls lined up together and dived into the river from the flume near the millwheel. We tried to outdo one another in water stunts."[8] She recollects public parties that became community celebrations. She remembers competing against local boys, demonstrating courage and initiative, qualities she felt served her well throughout her life. Her recollections were of prosperity and happiness.

But all was not bliss in Derazhnya. Rose's father was a dynamic, unconventional man, yet strict and somewhat rigid.[9] Isaack Peisoty was a well-respected member of the community. He married Masya, his second cousin, when he was twenty-six and Masya was sixteen; they had inherited the store at the death of Aunt Sheba. Isaack was not much of a businessman and spent a great deal of his time organizing self-help groups in the community, leaving Masya to do most of the hard work. Isaack set up a matsoh co-op during the Passover holiday, when it appeared that the matsoh bakers were going to exploit the Jewish consumers in the region.[10] Later he was the president of the *aksia* (free loan association). In addition, because he was educated in both the Talmud and secular education, he often acted as a lay doctor in the community, dispensing herbs and medicines. He was well loved by the locals, whom he treated with generosity and respect. According to Rose's eldest sister, Esther, however, Isaack was not quite as kind to his own children. Although Rose never spoke of this in her writings, Esther felt that both she and Rose were forced to leave home because of Isaack's autocratic behavior. Esther decided to leave home with her beau, Abraham Rubin, who was emigrating to escape the draft. She felt rejected by her father and wanted to escape his old-fashioned, authoritarian ways. When Isaack took Esther to the German border as she was about to leave for the United States, he merely turned to her after the long trip, looked at her directly, said, "Take care of yourself," and walked away. Esther never saw her father again and, some seventy years later, cried as she told the story.[11]

Rose's autobiography is replete with details such as having been spanked for poor penmanship while learning the alphabet in Hebrew and Russian. She also describes her brother David's special treatment. He was given better foods at the table because her father's attitude was that girls

FIGURE 2

Peisoty family, circa 1913, Derazhnya, Ukraine.

Hannah   Rose   Luba   Miriam   David

Masya
and
Yoseler

Isaack

Photo courtesy of Fanya Peisoty Bimbat.

were not worth bothering with. If Rose felt any resentment, however, she successfully succeeded in repressing it. She romanticized her family in all of her writings and avoided any criticism of her father. Instead, she remembered fondly reading to him as he lay ill in bed, while he instructed her in pronunciation and the historical background of what they were discussing. Rose portrayed herself as a dutiful daughter who thrived in the warm, nourishing atmosphere of the family and the shtetl.

Education was of the utmost importance to Jews, and the Peisoty family was no exception. Rose was first educated, as were her sisters, at home. By the time her education was completed, Rose was proficient in four languages. Yiddish, the language of the shtetl, was spoken at home. It was the language of wandering and life in exile. Hebrew was taught to all Jews as the language of prayer. It was the holy language through which one studied the Torah or sacred book. Ukrainian, Rose's third language, was the one that most Jews used in commerce and interaction with neighbors. Finally, Rose was taught Russian in order that she might read the classics and scholarly books. She enjoyed Russian folk songs and, in fact, sang easily in all four languages.

From 1909 to 1912 Rose attended Rosalia Davidoff's private girls' school near her home.[12] Her stay there, however, was interrupted by an accident that resulted in her father's subsequent illness and forced Rose to leave the private school. Thereupon, she received tutoring at home and read extensively in her father's library. Her tutors were former students of the *yeshiva*, who had learned of the ideas of the *Haskalah*. These young men traveled around the countryside, itinerant educators, passing on political and economic teachings as they roamed.

> My sister Esther had met these students and had been fired by the contacts she made in Odessa, and presently she joined a circle in Derazhnya which was part of the democratic section of the movement designed to replace the despotic tzar and all his feudal rule with a democratic system of government. Meetings of the group were held in several places—in the cemetery at the edge of town, in backroom workshops, and in a few homes. Esther took me along to some of these meetings and found a special use for me. I served as a carrier of leaflets. Being padded with them, I felt like a walking barrel. That was a precaution in the event of arrests, the theory being that a child could run away without being searched.[13]

According to Esther, Rose really did not know what she was carrying; she was inveigled into the work because she was young and immature.[14]

Rose's political education began with her reading of revolutionary pamphlets her father had hidden in the attic and with her sister Esther's introduction to the radical circle. Esther, one year older than Rose, visited Odessa during the summer of her fifteenth year.[15] Odessa, a port city on the Black Sea, was teeming with art, theater, fashion, and new ideas. Once, after returning from her trip, Esther began to speak of evolution and revolution. Rose remembered her father saying, "Stop that kind of talk at once. If there's any such talking to be done in this house, I'll do it. Comb out that silly looking pompadour and take off those stilts before you break an ankle. Give the children their supper and put them to bed."[16] Isaack, a self-proclaimed Bundist and political activist himself, refused to allow political talk to go on openly in his home.[17]

Although Rose's father kept revolutionary pamphlets in his attic, he squelched any discussion at home, fearing for the family's safety. His fear was justified. Radicals were being persecuted by the authorities, and many were on the run to avoid incarceration. Since the assassination of Czar Alexander II in 1881 by revolutionaries, all reforms were curtailed, and a period of absolute repression had taken hold. It was not the time to be a visible activist. But these forces did not dampen the girls' excitement and dedication to the movement. By age fourteen, in 1912, Rose joined the radical underground democratic circle and adopted an outlook that was to shape her life's work. These radical groups had begun to emerge under the reign of Alexander II, who had instituted modest liberal reforms, diminished censorship, and heightened expectations for greater improvement. When these hopes were not met with actions, various theoreticians and propagandists united to agitate for greater social change.

During the last two decades of the nineteenth century and the first decade of the twentieth, Jews found themselves torn by conflicting claims. A new world, in the guise of radical movements or cultural progress, conflicted with hallowed Jewish traditions. Jews were bombarded with socialism, Zionism, and other major secular ideologies.[18] The strength of the family and the community organizations was being eroded, and the shtetl was losing its young people. Discussions of class struggle and revolution abounded. Socialism was stirring the masses, and many Jews felt compelled to join the revolutionary movements that were organizing to destroy the empire.

Among them was Rose, who saw herself as continuing in the tradition of the great revolutionaries who preceded her. She read the works of Mikhail Bakunin, the noted anarchist revolutionary and theoretician whose ideas were to influence her significantly. Bakunin, a believer in direct action, found his way to many of the barricades in Europe's revolutions. She studied Alexander Herzen, a leading figure in nineteen-century

Russian radicalism. Herzen's ideas formed the ideological core of Russian revolutionary tradition: He detested and feared capitalism, abhorred the bourgeoisie and had contempt for the middle-class way of life, and wrote of the revolutionary potential of the Russian people. She also read of Vera Figner, a terrorist active in the Narodnaya Volya (People's Will) movement, as well as other notable Russian women activists. Rose read voraciously of the historical antecedents for the movements that she joined, studying and familiarizing herself with committed revolutionaries who were imprisoned or exiled for their work.

Rose was also quite aware of the countless heroines who distributed propaganda, ran printing presses, smuggled arms, and fought for social reforms in Russia. These "new Jewish women" were Rose's role models; and at a young age, she tried to emulate them.[19]

> Most fascinating of them were the women who had abandoned their well-cushioned life, and donning simple peasant garb, went *V Narod*—to the populace. Notable among them were Sophia Perovskaya, Sophia Bardina, Essie Helfman, Vera Figner, and at the turn of this century, Maria Spirindonova and Catherine Breshkovskaya, whose names are world renowned, and millions of others who went into exile and to their doom unknown, unsung, and undefended.[20]

Rose participated eagerly in the democratic circle, which was also a secret society. She often read to the illiterate members of the group, met with revolutionaries who were traveling incognito through her village, and discussed world events with her allies. Her political activism and her growing intellectual curiosity took their toll on her dedication to traditional daughterly roles. She admitted,

> I went on doing the household chores and taking care of the children, but I began to believe I was leading a humdrum life. Esther's letters made me restless. My only escape from it was that I followed closely the current events in the daily and weekly papers.[21]

Rose led a double life—respectful on the one hand, rebellious and radical on the other. She began to question life as she knew it, remaining close to her family, yet striving for independence and identifying with those outside her family sphere. It was just a matter of time before this contradiction would be addressed.

The moment of decision came when Rose was betrothed, without her knowledge, to a neighborhood boy. Fifty years later Rose was to vividly remember that moment.

One morning, we were seated around the samovar at the breakfast table, and I was feeding the newest baby tapioca in milk. The other youngsters were smacking their lips and dipping their toasted cinnamon buns in hot cacao. Marishka, always whimsical, took a mouthful and burst into uncontrollable laughter, spattering liquid on all within range.

"What's the matter with you?" I wanted to know. "Are you crazy or what?"

"You're getting married!" she exploded, pointing at me.

"What are you talking about?"

"It's the truth. You're getting married. Dad said so last night."[22]

It appears that Rose's younger sister overheard her parents planning to marry off Rose to a neighbor's son just returned from the army. Rose recalled, "I had a few words with the young man and concluded without hesitation that he was 'not my type.' A feeling of outrage and revolt against this high-handed plan took possession of me. I determined that come what might, no such marriage would take place."

Later that night, she read aloud to her democratic circle recently smuggled revolutionary pamphlets. She was inspired by the vision of a just society, in the writings of young women like herself who could have chosen marriage and a traditional lifestyle but did not.

If I accepted my parents' plans, it would mean my marrying this returned soldier, keeping house, bearing children and getting lost in the narrow life of a market town, as had most of the girls I knew. They never had a thought outside their homes. The idea of such a future appalled me. All day, automatically attending to my tasks, I kept repeating to myself: "I must find a way out, I must find a way out. I must find a way out."[23]

Rose considered all her options. "I pondered the question of running away, of becoming a member of the revolutionary party. And if I did this, I would be pledged to take any order that might be given, doing whatever task was assigned to me, though it might lead to incarceration and the long trek to the Siberian wasteland. I weighed the possibilities: the service I might render to the people and the consequences to myself if things went wrong, as had happened so often with militant workers in the underground movement."[24] After considerable soul searching, Rose secretly wrote to her sister Esther, who emigrated to the United States just a few years before. "Next morning I wrote her a long letter, pouring out my heavy laden heart. I set forth all the reasons why she must help me without delay, cautioning her not to mention to our parents that I had written her about my problem. 'Tell him you're lonesome for the family and want your sister with you. . . . Promise that if I don't like it in the United States you'll pay my return passage home. Please do it right away.'"[25] Rose felt so trapped, so desperate, that she resorted to a suicide threat "to make certain that Esther would not dismiss these pleadings lightly, I ended with a threat that she could not ignore. If I did not hear from her favorably, I would take carbolic acid and end it all."[26]

Although Rose was determined to escape the trap of an impending forced marriage, she decided to escape in a socially acceptable manner. In choosing between revolutionary activities and doing what many of her neighbors and friends had already done—moving to the United States under the guidance and protection of a family member, Rose picked the limited rebellion; she was attracted to revolution, but turned to her sister instead to save her from what was planned for her. Rose was pragmatic in this decision, much as she turned out to be later in her life. She extricated herself from a difficult situation carefully and within the reconcilable boundaries. She might have had revolutionary leanings, but she did not choose the revolutionary path; instead, she was a radical with clear limits. She would not engage in illegal or out-of-bounds solutions; she determined to find a way out, but in a manner that her family could accept and to which they could reconcile themselves. After all, her sister did the same thing several years before her.

Her father treated his eldest daughters unyieldingly, first Esther and then Rose, yet Rose was not angry with him. She spoke of him fondly and with only warm memories. Her youth was filled with some boredom and drudgery, but, as she said, it was unheard of for her to be directly disobedient.[27] In this, Rose's story contrasts markedly with the manner in which her later role model and close friend Emma Goldman recalls the departure from her own authoritarian father. Goldman, unlike Pesotta, portrays herself as a "'lonely and unhappy waif,' surrounded by 'hard and cold stone cliffs,' comforted only moments by servants, subject to the whims of her parents and loved by an older half sister who was herself little better than a galley slave."[28] She remembers feeling unwanted by her father and desiring always to escape the authoritarian patriarch's violent outbursts of temper. When Goldman's sister Helene prepared to leave Russia in 1885, Emma, who decided she could not bear losing her sister and wanted to run from her father, staged a dramatic scene: "[I] pleaded, begged and wept. Finally, I threatened to jump into the Neva, whereupon he yielded."[29]

Both Goldman and Pesotta wanted to escape the fate that awaited them if they were to remain at home; however, Pesotta chose to do so quietly, with planning and cunning, whereas Goldman agitated and created a scene. This difference in style played itself out continually during the lives of these two seemingly similar anarchist women. Pesotta chose to work within the union and within acceptable social institutions and mores, whereas Goldman went outside norms and institutions. In fact, although they came from similar origins, because of dissimilar upbringings and life circumstances their lives played out in quite disparate ways.

Pesotta's father might have been authoritarian; however, he was also an educated, well-respected leader in his community. Pesotta looked up to him and appreciated his accomplishments. Obviously, there was warmth and respect between them. He taught her to read and to think and encouraged her intellectual capacities, quite unlike what Goldman's father had done. To meet her own needs, Rose carefully orchestrated a plan that her father could not oppose, which was a pattern she was to repeat in later relationships with men in authority. She might disagree with them, but she would carefully create situations in which she could reach her own ends with as little confrontation as possible.

Rose proceeded with her thoughtfully laid plan:

> And to guard against our letter carrier, Israel Sunshine, getting any hint of my appeal, I mailed the letter at the railway depot, handing it to a man in the mail car of a westbound train. At home I began to calculate how long it would take for me to receive an answer. Five days for mail to cross Polish Russia, Austria, and Germany and then about two weeks to New York, allowing for delay in the departure of a steamship for that city. 'Esther will act promptly,' I told myself, 'so I ought to have a reply in six or seven weeks.'[30]

As she waited for a reply, Pesotta quelled her anxiety by having her palm read by a clairvoyant, who told her that there was "a dispatch on the way to you. Something you have been expecting impatiently. Don't worry. It is coming soon and it will gladden your heart. . . . All will end the way you wish."[31]

In just four weeks, a large envelope from the United States arrived. The letter and the steamship ticket to New York via Antwerp, Belgium, greatly disturbed her mother and father. They felt that Rose was abandoning them, and they feared that she was dissatisfied with them and her life in Derazhnya. It took nine months for her parents to give permission for Rose to leave; they finally agreed only when Isaack's mother decided to also go to the United States. Rose was ecstatic; no forced marriage would occur, and a new life was to begin.

Rose was clearly moving in a radical life direction. She began to ally herself with others who believed that freedom could come as a result of dramatic social upheaval; she wanted a social order based on equality for all. Her father had already taught her about caring for humanity by his own charitable works in the community. The familial kinship of her home life, with its warm, friendly environment, prefigured the radical ideal she would later develop. But by his patriarchal behavior, Rose's father also created a need in her to fight back against perceived unjust authority with cunning and careful planning, a pattern of response to authority that was to manifest itself continuously in her life. Through the nurturance and warmth of a loving community and home life and the constrained rebellion against what she saw as a potentially mundane existence that would have been hers, Rose's psychological script was set for a lifetime of dedicated political activity. But it took much more to turn Rose into the committed radical she was to become.

From the assassination of Alexander II to the outbreak of World War I, almost one-third of all East European Jews emigrated to the United States.[32] In October 1913 Rose joined the thousands making the voyage. Once again she did what was acceptable. She escaped, but did so cautiously under the watchful eye of her grandmother. Her father accompanied both Rose and Babushka (her grandmother) to the German border, as he had Esther.[33] Isaack, fearful of Rose's being abducted and forced into prostitution by "white slavery," provided protection and guidance by accompanying her. In fact, his fears were justified: There was a growing incidence of prostitution in the immigrant Jewish community at the time. In New York City from 1913 to 1930, 17 percent of the arrested prostitutes were Jewish, out of an entire population that was nearly one-third Jewish.

At the border, Rose realized that she would probably never see her father again, and the two of them cried in each other's arms. She parted from him saying, "Father dearest, forgive me and please take care of yourself."[34] "In the last instant, as I looked up at him, he seemed all at once to have grown older. I stopped a moment, irresolute, then I forced myself to walk on, straight ahead. I had made my choice; there could be no turning back. The gate closed behind me, shutting out my past."[35]

Rose and her grandmother traveled in style. They bought second-class passage on the ship *Finland* from Antwerp, unlike most Russian immigrants, including Esther, who were forced to go in steerage. They carried with them a teakettle, tea, food, bedding for Esther, blankets imported from Vienna, and a Caucasian wall rug with an image of a life-size tiger set against a black background.[36]

In her little bag Rose carried ten ruples (or five American dollars). Rose made acquaintances on the ship and began to enjoy her newfound freedom tremendously. Her second-class ticket even allowed her to enter New York without having to go through Ellis Island. At this time, during immigration procedures, her name was changed to Rose Pesotta. She was met at the Twenty-third Street dock by her sister, who immediately took her to the Ninety-eighth Street apartment east of Fifth Avenue. Rose was about to embark on a new life. She did so in a comfortable and well-attended style, a style that was to remain characteristic for her all her life. Rose chose to leave the oppressive quality of her father's decision making. She had, for the first time, confronted patriarchal authority and had won. She had made her escape.

Between 1881 and 1914, close to two million Jews came to the United States, most of them from Eastern Europe. They were, for the most part, members of family units who came to live with each other. Relatives followed relatives. The migration was also generally a movement of young people. By the time Rose joined the ranks, many who were well educated were emigrating.[37] Rose was part of the later immigrant group, arriving between 1905 and 1914. They were exposed to the reawakening of Jewish consciousness and enlightenment.[38] Although members of an ethnic group in flight, they arrived with an astute knowledge of politics and Jewish culture that was to influence their adjustment to American society. They came, as did Rose, with hope for a new life and with a dedication to making that ideal a reality.

2

THE NEW LIFE

It is ever so hard to die for the cause,
yet it is far more difficult to live for it.

—T. Kushnarev

The New York Rose entered on Thanksgiving Eve in 1913 was a vigorous metropolis, crammed with people and ideas, and alive with commerce and industry. Although she and her family did not live on the Lower East Side, where most immigrant Jews previously settled, her orientation and peer groups were centered there. Most immigrants lived in overcrowded slums, yet Rose describes her sister Esther's fourth-floor walk-up on Ninety-eighth Street as spacious, clean, well furnished, and rich in marvels.[5] It had steam heat, gas lights, and a gas range, as well as a bathroom with actual plumbing, all of which amazed Rose. Only 8 percent of all Jews were lucky enough to live with such amenities.[2] Esther even had a Victrola with a morning-glory horn and fine recordings of classical and popular music. She did well, having gone to work immediately in the needle trades. Her husband, Abraham Rubin, had fared well as a typesetter.

By the time Rose arrived, the number of Jews living on the Lower East Side was declining, and by 1916 only 23 percent of the city's Jews lived in that area, the majority dispersing to other parts of the city. By 1915 Jews constituted almost 28 percent of the New York City population and made their influence known in culture and industry.[3] Although there was a slow and gradual improvement in their standard of living and conditions of work, life for a large number of Jewish immigrants remained difficult.[4] Most lived in slums and were overworked, thereby becoming susceptible to serious illness, breakdown, and suicide. Tuberculosis was a problem, and the housing situation was considered scandalous; tenements were not fireproof, and they were overcrowded and filthy. The conditions under which most immigrants lived were squalid and abysmal. Within the clutter of buildings, people, and pushcarts, daily life was an assault on the senses: smelly, noisy, and abrasive. As late as 1910, Manhattan had 2,500 six-story walk-ups, 14,797 basement apartments, and 25,753 tenement rooms without windows. It was hard to win the battle against dirt and illness.[5]

Work conditions were equally deplorable. Most Jewish immigrants were employed in the garment industry, and the fate of most Eastern Europeans was tied to this trade. Between 1889 and 1899 the growth of that industry was two to three times more rapid than growth in other industries.[6] The women's clothing industry showed the sharpest growth, coinciding with the upsurge in Jewish immigration. The garment industry was primarily owned by an earlier generation of German Jewish immigrants, and this new generation of Jews found it easier to work for other Jews than for Gentiles. Some had come to the United States with tailoring skills. Much of the production took place in sweatshops, which were large, unventilated tenement rooms packed with workers, work tables, and sewing machines. Shop floors were grimy and bathrooms rare. Workers put in long hours and were plagued by speedups and arbitrary and difficult shop foremen. By 1914 the hourly wage for male workers was thirty-five cents. Needless to say, women earned far lower wages than men.

Rose's entrance into this community was relatively unremarkable. Soon after she arrived, her sister enrolled her in an English night-school class for foreigners. Tiring of the method of teaching used there, Rose created her own innovative approach. At the Harlem branch of the public library on East Ninety-sixth Street, Rose found her favorite Russian authors, including Tolstoy, Turgenev, Gorky, and Dostoyevsky. She first read them in Russian and then turned to the English version of each novel and read the translated text with the Russian fresh in mind. She also read the daily papers and magazines and tried to pick up useful phrases. Within a few months, Rose had taught herself her fifth language.[7]

Rose soon found a job as a seamstress, making shirtwaists as Esther had before her. She learned the job the hard way, changing positions regularly, because many of the shops were shut down—sometimes overnight. She acquired speed and skill quickly. Her first job was with Bloom and Millman on West Eighteenth Street as a section worker on middy blouses. She earned only six dollars for a forty-nine-hour workweek, and there were no employment benefits. Rose joined the Waistmakers Local 25 of the International Ladies' Garment Workers' Union (ILGWU) soon after entering the industry.

In 1909, just four years before Rose's immigration, Rose's sister Esther participated in an event that was to have an enormous impact on the garment industry and the climate for labor agitation in the United States. During the "Uprising of the Twenty Thousand," shirtwaist makers, most of them teenage Jewish women, went on strike, protesting sexual discrimination and class exploitation characterized by a myriad of abuses and humiliation; they were charged for needles, power, and supplies, taxed for their chairs, and made to pay for clothes lockers. Conditions were unsafe and unsanitary.

Local 25 was quite small at that time, with only a hundred members and four dollars in its treasury.[8] Nonetheless, a general strike was called, and most shops in the shirtwaist trade shut down. The most outstanding organizers and participants were the young women themselves, who won the admiration of the general public. Previously unorganized workers, who had seen themselves only as short-term workers on their way to marriage, became active and involved unionists. The fledgling Local 25 grew to ten thousand members, and when the strike finally ended after two months, significant improvements were seen in working conditions.

Indeed, the Uprising of the Twenty Thousand has also become an important event in the history of women in labor. It has been analyzed from various vantage points by labor historians; and feminist historians are currently viewing it as an important example of cultural ideals for women interacting with the reality of working women's lives under capitalism.[9] The strike was an example of public activism by women who earned the approval and admiration of their communities. Nonetheless, it is also an example of how paternalism and patriarchal attitudes reaffirmed women's secondary status in the workplace and in the labor unions themselves. The strike opened an era of Jewish labor activism and militancy for women that later provided a vehicle for Rose's political and ideological development.

Another event that influenced the industry in which Rose worked was the Triangle Shirtwaist Fire. On 25 March 1911 one of the largest garment shops in the city, the Triangle—not far from Washington Square on Greene Street—caught fire, and 146 workers, mostly Jewish and Italian young women, were burned to death. The doors of the shop were locked to prevent stealing, and the remaining exits were blocked by sewing machines. Doors opened in, because the stairs were too narrow to have them open out. There were no provisions for fire safety and only one fire escape, far below where most of the women worked. Many of the young women jumped to their deaths rather than be burned alive in the inferno. The conditions at Triangle, even after the uprising, were significantly dangerous. There was only a partial settlement there, and the demand for adequate fire escapes and open doors had not been met, the result of which was the loss of 146 lives.[10]

The fire had a strong impact on the entire population of the city. It brought together many of the political issues of the time and particularly affected Jewish immigrants, many of whom had family or friends in the industry. Many identified with the victims because they, too, worked in similar conditions. The fire gave impetus to the unionization movement and helped to swing public sentiment to the side of the labor movement.[11] Naturally, Rose learned of this event from her sister Esther, who had been working in the industry at that time. The fire left its lasting impression on Esther and the entire garment industry. When Rose immigrated two years later, her sister informed her of the horror. By then the industry began to institute reforms to prevent future similar tragedies.

Women's participation in unions prior to the uprising had always been notoriously minimal. Before the unionization drive in the clothing trades, only about one in fifteen women in the work force belonged to a union, compared to one in five men,[12] although almost 20 percent of the entire work force was women. Their low union participation was related to a number of factors: family expectations concerning the behavior of women, the nature of the trade unions themselves, and limited opportunities for them in the work force. The union leadership tended to discourage women as workers and did not take them seriously. In fact, they were kept out of the unions for fear that they would displace male workers. Even when the women were the most militant, as with the Uprising of the Twenty Thousand," the general assumption was that they would become wives and mothers and eventually leave the work force. It was also assumed that they did not belong in the work force or in unions. The outcome was that women were isolated from the male workers, and those women who did organize themselves into unions were often turned down by the parent organizations. Even in the clothing industry, where many of them became devoted to unionization, they were forced to retain their second-class status within the union. The union leaders did not believe that women were a "fighting force" and were also afraid of the women's different and separate needs. The union was not eager to address women's issues. At best, the union was ambivalent, knowing full well that they needed the growing numbers of women as bargaining tools against the owners, but hoping at the same time that the women would leave the work force.[13]

Discrimination against women in labor had always existed. For example, in 1913, just before Rose's arrival, a "Protocol in the Dress and Waist Industry" was instituted. It was the first agreement between labor and management negotiated by outside parties. In it, sexual discrimination was formalized by reserving the highest-paid jobs for the men. The hierarchy within the garment industry put cutters, who were men only, at the top; pressers, an exclusively male trade, made the next-highest sal-

aries, with ironers following. Women's jobs, which included drapers, join-
ers, examiners, and finishers, were all significantly lower paid. Even men
and women who did the same work were paid differentially.[14] Nonetheless, some gains were instituted for women. Unions were able to use the
grievance procedure of the protocol to charge foremen and employers
with sexual harassment. This, plus the instituting of sanitary provisions,
showed marked progress.[15]

The union looked out for the men primarily and only secondarily
addressed the needs of the women, who made up the majority of workers
in the industry. Nonetheless, the women in the clothing trades were
devoted unionists, believing that unions were their only hope. Many of
the women outdid the men in their militancy and on the picket line and
at outdoor meetings. Rose participated in many such events soon after
coming to this country. She became an active member of Local 25, and
later Local 22, as a dressmaker, where she met many comrades who were
to become her lifelong friends. As a member of Local 22, Rose met Clara
Rothberg, with whom she began to attend demonstrations and meetings.
"Rose and I would work all day at the sewing machines and then march
on the picket lines from 1:00 a.m. to 5:00 a.m. and then return at 7:00
a.m. to a full day of work in the shop." Police routinely broke up such
rallies and arrested picketers. Clara remembers running through the
streets with Rose to avoid arrest. They both believed that conditions
were deplorable and that the only hope for change lay with their union.
She remembers: "We earned peanuts! We had to do it; there really was no
choice for us." They were so devoted to the union that Clara fondly
recollects, "Right after my wedding, we went back to the picket lines. My
husband and I didn't have time for a honeymoon."[16]

As early as 1914, Rose was also attending night-school classes held
by her union's education department. Local 25 was the first to establish
such a program, in which the young workers could study English and
subjects of "social significance."[17] Rose took classes in history, politics,
physical fitness, and art, and participated in discussion groups. She felt
that it was there that she began to gain poise and self confidence. In fact,
it was with this group that Rose first took outings beyond the city limits.
She began to attend Unity House, which at that time was a Catskill
Mountain union vacation retreat. She continued to visit this center after
it moved, first to Bear Mountain and then to the Poconos. First a center
and then a resort hotel where union members could vacation together,
Unity House offered classes, as well as concerts, plays, and recreational
activities.

For a very short time, Rose even tried the nursing profession. With
employment being scarce in the garment industry, she felt nursing might

earn her a livelihood and be a more appropriate field for her. In the winter of 1917, Rose spent a few months in training at Manhattan State Hospital on Ward's Island in the East River working with mental patients. It was a spartan life, as she described it: "the arduous toil, twelve hours a day, and for meals in the main dining room, [I] lived in a room adjacent to the ward, [with] meager pay."[18] She started as an attendant for sixty women, making beds and trying to keep the place clean. She dressed the patients, combed their hair, and washed them. Eventually, she moved on to taking temperatures and doing first aid. She even had to supply her own uniforms, which she had made in her previous garment shop. Rose hoped that in three years she would become a full-fledged nurse.

Her free time was severely restricted to only thirty-six hours off every two weeks, during which she tried to contact her colleagues who were active in political work. In February 1917, when the Russian Revolution broke out, Rose was ecstatic but felt extremely isolated from her comrades, who were active in the garment industry building support for the revolution. She asked herself, "Why am I staying here among these derelicts when over in Russia a new society is being born? There must be some better way to help the Russian people now that our dream is being realized."[19] Rose was just twenty years old and wanted to be actively involved in the revolutionary excitement. The last straw came when her supervisor insisted that she work night duty when she was supposed to attend a farewell dinner for a group of émigrés who were to sail the next day to Russia. She attended the meeting instead, having lost all patience with the dull, irksome duties and the wearisome hours of student nursing.

On 26 March 1917, Rose joined an enthusiastic audience at the Harlem River Casino on 127th Street and Second Avenue, listening to Leon Trotsky, Nikolai Bukharin, and others speak with eloquence, confidence, and conviction concerning the workers' free society in Russia. The farewell party was attended by approximately eight hundred guests, mostly Russian and German radicals. Trotsky spoke on the causes of the war and the February Revolution in Russia and the provisional government that followed. Emma Goldman was also there and found him to be eloquent and lucid, although she disagreed with everything he said.[20] Rose, however, remembers, "Like a refrain, in their speeches I recall the words: 'The land, the peasants, the factories to the workers, equal rights for women and minority groups.'"[21] Shortly afterward, she quit her nursing course and returned to the garment industry, so that she might get back into the political arena.

Rose's political work and contacts were quite important to her during her early years in New York, and it was through these people that

FIGURE 3

Rose Pesotta, Milton Rubin, and Esther Rubin, New York City, circa 1918.

Photo courtesy of Dorothy, Elias, and Edward Rotker.

she was recruited to the anarchist movement. Soon after her arrival, she met a number of political activists who believed in anarchism. They educated her to the current issues with which they were dealing. Rose's readings had already led her in their direction. Having found a number of activists in the shops, she soon felt at home among them. She began to attend meetings and to participate in their social and political activities.

During her studies in Russia, Rose encountered the names of Peter Kropotkin, Mikhail Bakunin, and Pierre Joseph Proudhon. She had also been brought up with deeply ingrained concepts of social justice and community in her home in Europe. When she found inequality and injustice in this country, she felt compelled to act, as she had in Russia. She was attracted to the movement's ideas and to the people in it and soon became a dedicated member.

Rose's sister Esther remembers that soon after coming to the United States, Rose began to socialize with anarchists and left Esther's home to live with her comrades at the Clara de Hirsch Home for Girls, at three dollars a week—the home, a shelter for immigrant women, was operated by the National Council of Jewish Women and funded by the Baron de Hirsch Fund. During this period, New York was a hotbed of radicalism. Young immigrants were immersed in unionism, political study, and agitation. There was a blend of radicalism and romanticism in the activities that kept Rose occupied. The young people worked together and studied by day, held meetings and played together by night. Many immigrants joined a variety of radical organizations, all having visions of the just society they did not find upon arriving on America's shores. "Frustration paved the way for new political faiths, as it already had in the old country."[22]

Between 1910 and 1919, there was an upsurge of radicalism in the United States, including socialism and a growth of interest in anarchism. Socialists argued for a form of government run by the workers, while anarchists believed in the abolition of government and the creation of a society based on liberty for all individuals. Anarchism has a long and colorful history in both Europe and the United States, but has never been a widely popular political ideology. Espousing the abolition of the state, some anarchists have engaged in violent activities, but many anarchists, like Rose and her colleagues, were nonviolent and based their actions on humanistic and idealistic values. Anarchists were concerned for others and believed that individuals could best decide how to live their own lives. Anarchists favored the use of direct action such as general strikes and boycotts, as well as the use of political propaganda. They believed that the poor and powerless would bring about necessary social change, but not through reformist means such as the ballot. Generally, anarchists were atheists, believing that the idea of God was used by the church to maintain its own authority, and that religion was a tool for containing massive social change. Social change, it was argued, would come through revolution and through the establishment of small, leaderless communes and work groups that would have the power to determine for themselves how they will operate. The incipient trade union movement offered anarchists an opportunity to apply their beliefs, hoping that workers would take over and control the workplace. And Rose came to believe, with her friends, that revolution in the United States would occur through an uprising of the workers, hopefully through unionism. Thus, many anarchists, as well as other socialists, were active in the trade union movement. There were conflicts about how these unions would operate, but generally anarchists supported the unions, although some saw no hope at all for the unions.

In the United States, anarchism had its base in the large immigrant populations that arrived after 1865, of which Rose was a part. Many immigrants came to this country expecting to find work and hope for building a new life; what they found instead was a continuation of the discrimination they had experienced at home, but in a less violent and blatant form. Because Rose and her colleagues were forced to work in sweatshops for minimal pay and to live in squalid tenements, they had few resources to mobilize a revolution. They hoped that the labor movement would provide that vehicle.

Early in anarchist history in the United States, an important event occurred that was to greatly affect the anarchists, including Emma Goldman and much later Rose Pesotta. A strike was called on 1 May 1886, and one hundred thousand workers marched in Chicago to demand an eight-hour workday. On 3 May, a demonstration was called at McCormick Harvester for better working conditions. There, one worker was killed by Harvester guards. The next day there was a small demonstration to protest the killing. It was a peaceful demonstration that had been called by labor organizers, some of whom were identified as anarchists. A bomb went off, and seven policemen were killed. The police reacted by killing several demonstrators and wounding two hundred. Eight anarchists were tried (although none of them were there the day of the demonstration), and seven were sentenced to death. Later, four were hanged for the crime, one committed suicide, and two sentences were commuted to life. Years after, those not executed were pardoned. Many believed that the men who died were killed for their ideas—ideas that were threatening to the elite who controlled society.[23]

The Haymarket Massacre, as it has come to be called, as well as the resulting executions, brought notoriety to the anarchist movement.

Many people who had never heard of anarchism were moved to action by the heroism and strength of the martyrs. Although the eight-hour-day movement was stopped for a while, the anarchist movement grew and became more active and diverse. The movement used violence, strikes, and other radical tactics, resorting to extraordinary channels in order to influence the larger society. The movement recruited many immigrants to its ranks, some of whom remained active throughout their lives. These recruits had little to offer the movement in the way of financial resources, but gave generously of their time and energy. These people became Rose's friends when she came to the United States in 1913.

One important recruit to the anarchist movement who would significantly influence Rose's life was Emma Goldman. Emma was so moved by what happened in Chicago that she dedicated her life to anarchism, becoming a dynamic speaker on birth control, drama, and anarchist ideals who drew crowds wherever she went. Rose heard Emma speak with her comrade Alexander Berkman in May 1914 at an anticonscription rally at Madison Square Garden. From then on, she saw Emma as a role model and followed her activities closely. Later, a friendship developed between the two, flowering into a close and deep relationship.

Early in her career, Emma Goldman participated in an event that further committed her to the anarchist cause. In 1892 there was a lockout at a Carnegie Steel Plant at Homestead near Pittsburgh. Pinkerton guards were called in, and many workers were killed. Emma's friend Alexander Berkman attempted to assassinate Henry Clay Frick, the plant owner, in retaliation for his having called out the Pinkertons. Emma participated in raising the money for the gun and for Berkman's trip to Pittsburgh. Berkman spent fourteen years in prison for that act, which he called "propaganda by the deed." Much later Rose met Berkman, and although she knew him only peripherally, we shall see that he, too, had a significant personal impact on her. After Berkman was sent to prison, Emma launched publication of an important magazine, *Mother Earth*, which helped anarchists maintain connection with each other. Unfortunately it was destroyed by the authorities during World War I, but not before Rose began to read it and to discuss it in anarchist meetings. It became an important means through which Rose learned about anarchist ideology.

Around the turn of the century, just before Rose emigrated, the anarchist movement was at its height. Various institutions and organizations emerged from the movement, and it gained somewhat an air of respectability in certain radical circles.

One such organization that developed during this period was known as the Modern School. From 1911 to the 1960s there existed a loose federation of schools founded on anarchist principles of education,[24] which included the belief that children should be taught in a healthy physical environment and that they need short and interesting instructional periods. The schools attempted to implement the ideas of Peter Kropotkin, an anarchist theoretician, who combined a respect for children with a belief that education must involve both mind and body. The schools were founded in New York City; in Stelton, New Jersey; and throughout the country. When Rose joined the anarchist ranks, she found herself involved in summer adult education programs at Stelton, which were organized at the school for anarchists seeking education and a summer respite. Leaders of the anarchist movement participated in the schools and often lived at them. Rose visited the schools often, leading workshops and taking training classes among these anarchists.

Other movement organizations that developed included mutual aid societies, such as the Workmen's Circle (Arbeiter Ring) programs, that were both socialist and anarchist. There were also funds established to raise bail for comrades in jail or to help cover legal expenses for victims of government persecution. During its most solid period, the anarchist movement and its adherents were respected and influential. Although there were never vast numbers aligned with anarchism, it did gain some public credibility. In fact, *The Free Voice of Labor*, an anarchist newspaper founded in 1890, maintained a readership until 1977.

However, by the time Rose became active, the anarchists were losing their numbers as the assault against radicalism grew. Government surveillance began, and social controls became much more effective, hindering recruitment to radical causes. Eventually, the mass base of potential supporters among the immigrants became better integrated into society.[25] In the United States, with the advent of World War I, the Russian Revolution, and the growth of antiradical repression, anarchist ideology lost its appeal, as well as many of its members. During the raids, thousands of radicals were rounded up and imprisoned. The No Conscription League, which Emma and Berkman started during the war years, was suppressed in 1917, and many of its members jailed. The February Revolution of the same year drew many anarchists back to Russia; and in late 1919, a series of deportations began to send back to their countries hundreds of active anarchists, particularly those from Eastern Europe and Italy.[26] The culmination of the repression was reached with the A. Mitchell Palmer Raids of 1919–20, which triggered the Red Scare that followed. Rose actually met Emma Goldman while the latter was awaiting deportation at Ellis Island after being arrested in the raids in November 1919 on the first round of arrests. It was five years after Rose first heard Emma speak in 1914. Rose was there to visit her fiancé, Theodore Kushnarev, who was also being deported.

One of Rose's important early contacts in the anarchist movement

was with Kushnarev, who became her first great love and her first experience in disappointment and loss. Kushnarev was one of the radical aliens
rounded up in Russian labor and cultural centers in various American
cities and one of the 249 who were deported on the ship *Buford*. Born 1
May 1896, Theodore Kushnarev was a Russian seaman who came to the
United States in September 1918. He and Rose met in the anarchist circle
soon after his arrival. They fell in love, and Rose was devastated by his
forced departure.[27]

After the deportation, Rose and Kushnarev kept up a passionate
correspondence, and for quite a few years he tried to make his way back
to the United States and to Rose. His first letter in English described the
sadness and pain of his departure on the *Buford*:

> Four o'clock at night. I skip a scene of excitement that I'll never
> forget, men were crying over lost tools, lost savings of hard labor of
> many years, husbands crying for wives, children, lovers for sweet-
> hearts, sons for mothers. Oh Hell! they call us: 'Come on boys.' We
> go. The detectives stand in two rows way down by the ferry.
> Threats, abuse, derision, all and everything is the lot of those who
> were caught by the net of American justice. We are packed on the
> ferry. Soldiers guard us. A war vessel follows us as we leave shore of
> the island of tears and grief and go to the ship. The *Buford*: we go at
> 5:30. At 6:30 the boat began to rock. We were going. . . . No matter
> the hardship of the 27 day trip and the stay at the island which
> lasted months—still our revolutionary fire is still alive.[28]

The letters continued from 1919 to 1925, and for the first few years
the passion between them was alive. In 1920 he wrote:

> But no matter how you feed a heart, if it is "wolfish" it looks toward
> the forest and aiming there too. . . . You may soon hear of me from
> some unknown to yet, yet part of the globe. I shall be on my route
> back. "Toward home" is my battle cry now. . . . Good-by dear until
> the day when we shall meet each other. I embrace you and kiss you
> with my heart kisses.[29]

For a short time, in 1921, Kushnarev was incarcerated by the Communist government. When the "error" was discovered, he was released
and wrote to Rose of the abhorrent conditions of civil war and starvation
in Russia. He thought his imprisonment was an error, but it is possible
that since he was known as an anarchist, there had been, in fact, no error
at all. Anarchists were beginning, at that time, to experience repression at

FIGURE 4

Theodore Kushnarev and Rose Pesotta, New York City (n.d.).

Photo courtesy of Dorothy, Elias, and Edward Rotker.

the hands of the Bolsheviks, who were clamping down on dissidents opposed to their regime. In March of 1921, the sailors of the Kronstadt naval base in the Gulf of Finland near Petrograd revolted against the Bolshevik government. For sixteen days their rebellion held out, before being crushed by the army. Anarchists were falsely alleged to have been leaders, and in the aftermath, a wave of political arrests occurred. Anarchists, including Kushnarev, were rounded up and imprisoned.[30] In a letter from that time, Theodore once again affirmed his undying love to Rose:

> I have pledged my love to you, my heart is yours. . . . When I lived in Petrograd and Moscow, your picture was never off my table nor your name ever off my lips.[31]

But when Rose asked to come back to Russia to aid the revolution, he said:

> Would that I could give you my consent to come to Russia. Oh how glad I would be to see you, to kiss you my love, to press you to my suffering heart. Oh how I need you, your brave spirit, black darling eyes, and a soul of a heroine burning behind them. But be you earth and heavens witnesses, and you goddess of love, my judge, I cannot, for I see no purpose in it. Of course life is being improved upon in Russia everyday. But Russia needs specialists; Russia needs artisans, technical men of art and science, but not bearers of ideas, of which the hungry, cold, sick, famined, and famished people are quite sick, after nearly five (FIVE LONG YEARS) of revolution. . . . Enough of equality, let us have bread.[32]

Without her fiancé's encouragement to join him in Russia, Rose decided to stay in the United States and to work for his return. In 1921 Kushnarev found a job as an interpreter for Herbert Hoover's famine and medical relief program (the American Relief Administration, which operated during 1921–1922), and conditions improved for him. But by 1922, Theodore became ill with typhoid fever, which lingered for years. His ill health waxed and waned and seemed to be exacerbated by the extreme weather conditions and deprivation he and other Russians endured. Some of his letters describe the "hysteria and breakdown" that he suffered from overwork and exhaustion. There were times he yearned for Rose and her support: "A breakdown will surely follow if I do not relax and there is no one to care for me as you did, my love . . . therefore I must run . . . lest I become a nervous wreck."[33] During one of his more

FIGURE 5

Theodore Kushnarev, U.S. Customs Service Identification Card, 5 September 1918.

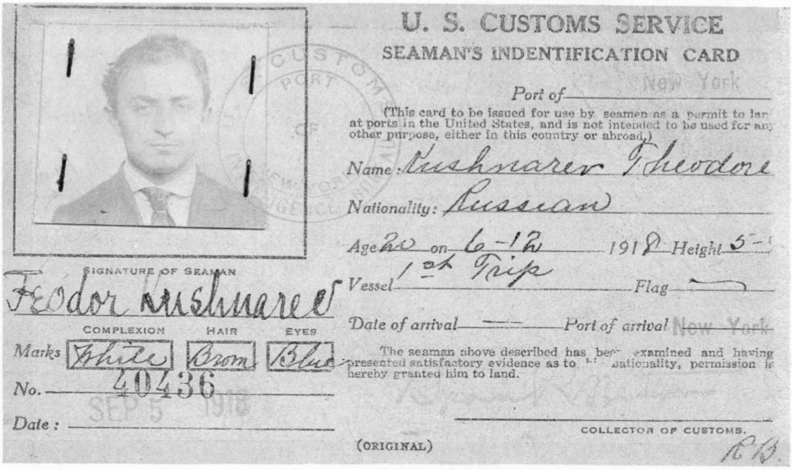
U. S. CUSTOMS SERVICE
SEAMAN'S INDENTIFICATION CARD
Port of New York
(This card to be issued for use by seamen as a permit to lan at ports in the United States, and is not intended to be used for an other purpose, either in this country or abroad.)
Name: Kushnarev Theodore
Nationality: Russian
Age 20 on 6-12 1918 Height 5-
Vessel 1st Trip Flag —
Date of arrival — Port of arrival New York
The seaman above described has bee examined and having presented satisfactory evidence as to nationality, permission is hereby granted him to land.
COLLECTOR OF CUSTOMS.
(ORIGINAL)
SIGNATURE OF SEAMAN
Feodor Kushnarev
COMPLEXION HAIR EYES
Marks White Brown Blue
No. 40436
Date: SEP 5 1918

Courtesy of Dorothy, Elias, and Edward Rotker.

difficult periods, Theodore wrote: "It is ever so hard to die for the cause, yet it is far more difficult to live for it."[34] And regularly, Theodore tried to find legal means of returning to the United States. His letters were passionate and loving. In 1922 he wrote:

> I love you too much to tell you that on paper. I know that I dream of you, very, very often . . . not at night, for I sleep as sound as a buck, but in the day. When I look at a girlish face, that reminds me of you—immediately a picture of your features stands before my eyes—I see your eyes, your chin, your lovely hair, and I wish to kiss them, to press my hungry lips to yours, to embrace you, to lift you up and carry you off to . . . where before the face of nature and God I could tell you all that I keep in my heavy heart and breast.[35]

However, it appears that the loneliness and misery took its toll on Theodore. Rose surmised that he had given his love to another woman and wrote him a bitter letter after he had turned down an offer for a legal six-month visit to the United States. Although her letter is lost, he answered in December 1923.

To me you seem an angel of sympathy and friendliness through and in spite of the severe and bitter lines of your letter. I cannot but thank fortune that to such a woman as you I owe half of the spirit that leads me on to live to work, to struggle, to hope, in the name of a better future.

I say half, for the other half of my heart, my thoughts, my all belongs to another woman. Vera knows that I love you. Now you both know that I love you both.

This is not a paradox. Nor a nice phrase. Two loves are in my heart. And neither can conquer. . . .

You ask me to tell you whether or not you are free from the word you gave me at the hour of my departure. . . . I cannot tell you anything. Let your heart be your prompter. I shall love you as I always did, whether or not you're the wife of another. This is my answer.[36]

His behavior tortured and embittered Rose, who had waited loyally for a reunion with her beloved. It also appears that Kushnarev and Vera had a child, Anne, who was born on 23 January 1924, just one month after he informed Rose of Vera's very existence! Theodore wrote warmly and in friendship, announcing Anne's birth. However, in the same letter, he once again sought Rose's assistance in bringing both himself and now his family into the United States. Although Rose's reply has been lost, we do know that she continued her correspondence with him, but only as a comrade and a friend. Rose was in pain over this scorning of her devotion and love; but even after the birth of his child, Theodore protested his love for her.

In any case I still love you, as I always did. As I always shall. For you're the one I should have loved alone—had life been different.[37]

The Red Scare took its toll on Rose. She had lost the first love of her life, first to Russia, and then to another woman. So although their correspondence continued, gone was the flame, the longing, and the passion. In fact, when Theodore asked her for aid in emigrating to Cuba, Rose flatly turned him down and was angry at his request. By December 1924 Theodore's "ailments" returned, and he described his life as "exile, loneliness, poverty, and all this in a hole of a town."[38] Their letters ended abruptly in July 1925 when he died of typhoid. Kushnarev had finally been making plans to move to Mexico with comrades. He died never having seen Rose again.

Rose suffered another loss as well. In early 1920, soon after Kushnarev's departure, her father was killed by counterrevolutionary forces in Russia. During the years 1919 and 1920, terror reigned in the Ukraine, as anti-Bolshevik and anti-Semitic raids swept the area. As civil war spread, a volunteer army sprang up in the Ukraine that formed as an anti-Bolshevik crusade. The "white terror," as it was called, was far worse than anything perpetrated by the Reds. This gang of terrorists committed the most frightful atrocities on suspected Bolsheviks, socialists, liberals, and democrats. "In August 1919, one General Petlura took to the field with an army of some 40,000 strong, mostly Poles and Galicians ripe for plunder and commenced an offensive against Kiev and Odessa."[39] General Petlura, "half officer and half brigand was a social revolutionary who had been, in turn, dancer, schoolmaster, and bath attendant." He had a policy of pogroms against the Jews, which he was implementing fully.[40] One night in early 1920, General Petlura's army overran Rose's town, Derazhnya. Her father, hearing a pounding on his door, answered it unarmed, carrying salt and bread to greet the visitors. Rose recalled, having been told by family members, "Father opens it, to see who the intruders are, and to reason with them if need be, as he has done at other times like this. Mother is close behind him. Unarmed, he is shot down before he has a chance to speak or raise a hand. He dies as he had lived, unafraid."[41]

Interestingly, Rose's sister Fanya, who was then a three-year-old child living in Derazhnya with the family, tells another version of the story. According to her, the father was trying to protect his two eldest daughters from being taken by the Petlura brigands. They came looking for the girls, and when Isaack refused to reveal their hiding place, a few took him to a room in the home and shot him while the rest of the family was nearby. Whatever the true story, Rose became ill upon hearing the news of his death, and it took months for her to recover from the tragedy. Coming so soon after losing Kushnarev through deportation, this added blow was quite important to Rose's development. The loss of both her father and her fiancé drove Rose to despair, followed by renewed dedication to radical activity. Deep and painful as the losses were, they moved her a significant step toward political and labor activities. She decided to carry on the work that these two most important people in her life had begun. As much as she might have rebelled against her father's authoritarianism, she truly admired his courage and dedication to social causes. His death gave added impetus to her need to rededicate herself to radicalism. Perhaps she wanted to be unafraid, as he had been.

While all this was happening in Rose's personal life, various political splits and factions were forming on the left after the Russian Revolution. Eventually, in the United States, a Communist party was founded, based on the Bolshevik model being implemented in the Soviet Union. Many of Rose's friends became involved with the Communist party. The resulting factional splits caused much turmoil within the labor movement, as sides were taken over the political developments in the Soviet Union.

The 1920s saw a civil war in the garment district. From 1919 to 1928, a fierce battle was waged between the centrist leadership of the ILGWU and the left wing, which organized the opposition. The conflict reflected different ideological roots: The ILGWU administrators believed in a "pragmatic unionism based on 'real' conditions and designed to win maximum benefits for workers without jeopardizing the security of the union organization."[42] Initially the leftists were a few opponents who built a mass movement.[43] Eventually the leftists aligned themselves with the Communist party, following a directive from Russia that all world trade unions should become affiliated with the Red Trade Union International in Moscow or be abandoned. In particular, they began an effort to attract members of the needle trades to their party. Of that era, Charles "Sasha" Zimmerman, Rose's colleague and friend and later a vice president of the ILGWU and a Communist party member, remembers: "Originally the left wing movement was not a Communist movement. It was a movement of dissatisfied garment workers looking for more progressive methods of representation and other reforms to make it better."[44]

The Communists began to take over leadership in a number of important locals and in the hierarchy of the ILGWU, advocating "boring from within." To counter this effort, the centrists then responded by attempting to push the Communists out in a number of confrontational ways: They would not allow new board members of certain locals to be seated; they blocked left-wingers' participation in conferences by challenging their credentials and by bringing charges against elected Communists, claiming that a policy of "dual unionism" was taking place. This resulted in vicious attacks and counterattacks that lasted for the entire decade.

By 1922 the anarchists split ideologically with the Communists when they saw that "the Communists intended to dominate the reform movement and make it subject to outside orders."[45] As an anarchist, Rose felt that the union was devastated by the struggle and that membership in the union diminished markedly because of the fighting; as a result, she became vigorously anticommunist. She saw many of the gains that the union had previously won in the industry lost:

> I see the union go to pieces. Through much of that decade savage internal strife rages within our organization. This is a result of the setting up of the Red Trade Union International in Moscow, designed to take over the labor movement of the whole world and to "liquidate" all the trade unions affiliated with the Amsterdam Inter-

national. Those of us who did not side with that aim watch with apprehension the fast disintegration of all our past aims.[46]

Finally a strike in 1926 completely closed down the industry. After six months, the involvement of over thirty-five thousand workers and the arrest of hundreds, the Communist-led effort was a failure. The employers won favor in the public's eye, and even the most staunch allies of the Communists knew that the effort was lost.[47] At this juncture, the ILGWU administrators formed an alliance with the employers (and their gangsters) and the police to launch an all-out effort to finally purge the Communists.[48] In August of 1928, the left wing and its allies called for a new cloak-and-dressmakers union. They established the Needle Trades Workers' Industrial Union, made up of twenty-five hundred members of the ILGWU radical faction. The centrists were left with the remnants of the union, down in membership by almost half. The result left various factions bitter with each other, and the vestiges of the battle were felt for years to come.

Meanwhile, during all these struggles, Rose worked quietly at her machine. She continued her political work in the union as a member of the anarchist faction and began a career of writing and organizing, using her anarchist ideology as a basis for her work. Earlier, in 1924, Rose spoke publicly at her first ILGWU convention to appeal for funds on behalf of the Red Cross for Political Prisoners in Russia. According to later reports, "While the civil war in Russia was continuing Miss Pesotta said that most American supporters of the Revolution had accepted the need for harsh and disciplinary measures. But now the fact had to be faced that socialists, anarchists, and moderates of all kinds were being imprisoned simply because they disagreed with Bolshevism."[49] Rose's presentation led to a vote of 222 to 25 calling on the Soviet government to release all its political prisoners immediately—a vote that provoked heated debate between the pro- and anti-Bolshevik forces in the union.

Rose's intelligence and personal dynamism were slowly coming to the attention of those in the union hierarchy, especially through her anticommunist activities. Because of her charisma, earlier, in 1920, she was elected to her local's executive board. Although not much is known about her participation at this level of the union, we do know that her tenure did not last very long.

Local 22—to which she belonged—was one of the largest locals in the union. Known as a gateway local, it offered membership to immigrants and newcomers to the city. It was also a militant and active local during the civil war within the union throughout the 1920s. Her involvement included serving on various strike committees. Local 22 was chartered as the dressmakers local, having been severed from Local 25 in an attempt to block Communist takeover—an unpopular decision that actually accelerated Communist insurgency.[50]

Rose emerged as a spokesperson for those in her shop, and her eloquence and education earned her the respect of her peers. Subsequently, she was invited to attend a series of labor colleges that had been formed as part of the workers' educational movement. They were designed to provide education for rank and file members, to develop their effectiveness, and to identify leaders among them. At these schools unionists studied economics and social studies in order to resolve the problems they would encounter as workers and eventual organizers.

In the summer of 1922 Rose joined 104 other young women from around the country at the Bryn Mawr Summer School for Women Workers from around the country. The school was established in 1921 and directed by Hilda Worthington Smith, a former dean of Bryn Mawr; financed by philanthropists such as J. D. Rockefeller, the school ran for seventeen summers. Rose participated eagerly in all the studies, particularly enjoying the eight weeks of reading in the humanities. This was Rose's first taste of formal American education, and she relished it. During the summer of 1924 Rose also attended the Brookwood Labor College in Katonah, New York, where she studied the social sciences under the tutelage of faculty recruited from many notable universities. Brookwood was a bit more progressive and left-leaning than Bryn Mawr had been, although all of the labor schools had as their philosophical basis a belief in social reform.[51] Students were workers from steel mills, coal mines, auto plants, garment industry and textile mills, not only in the United States but also in other countries. One such student was Horst Borenz, a German activist with whom Rose was to become politically and emotionally involved. She continued to be in touch with him through visits and correspondence after he returned to Germany.

Rose was so taken with the labor college that she attended Brookwood again from 1925 through 1926 and then went to the Wisconsin Summer School in 1930. These programs provided social, cultural, and political education and were training grounds for future labor activists. They placed immigrant and working women in an atmosphere of stimulation and creativity. In all these programs, Rose worked at developing her writing skills, as well as gaining theoretical grounding in the social sciences. She developed skills in speaking and negotiating and began to show talent for influencing others to join her cause. Rose was flamboyant, attractive, and naturally outspoken. With her flaming eyes and dark hair, she developed a reputation as a firebrand.

Rose formed many deep and meaningful friendships as a result of

FIGURE 6

After shoptalk at Bryn Mawr summer school (n.d.).

Photo courtesy of Dorothy, Elias, and Edward Rotker.

FIGURE 7

Graduated class of 1925 and first-year class, Brookwood Labor College
(Rose Pesotta front row, second from right).

Photo courtesy of Dorothy, Elias, and Edward Rotker.

her political work. Socially, she was gaining in popularity and was regarded as an attractive and vigorous young woman. She was in a circle of
women who worked in the shops, attended the labor colleges, agitated,
and did political work together. Friends remember her as a dark, somewhat Spanish-looking woman with sparkling eyes and a fiery temper. Her
closest friends were Clara Rothberg and Anna Sosnovsky, who were also
union members. She often entertained her many anarchist friends with
extravagant gourmet meals. Often these anarchist women, in particular,
wanted to transcend conventional social and moral precepts. Many of
them were economically independent of their families. Some lived with
their mates without marriage, and all of them argued that personal autonomy was essential in their lives. Some of Rose's acquaintances engaged in
violent activities, although most did not. All of them, however, accepted
the inevitability of violence as a tactic for social change.[52] They dressed
unconventionally and tried to live nonconformist lifestyles. For Rose, that
meant wearing knickers and boots, hitchhiking around the country while
carrying a knapsack, and having a love affair with a Russian revolutionist.
She befriended Mollie Steimer, a young activist who had been deported
in 1921 after having been jailed for distributing political leaflets during
World War I. They met while participating in anarchist groups and were
to remain lifelong friends.

All of these women shared a belief in the importance of complete
freedom over all else. They believed in sexual varietism (nonexclusive
sexual relationships) and in voluntary motherhood (women's right to
birth control). Some actively confronted discriminatory attitudes within
their unions. These women were iconoclasts and colorful characters with
minds of their own. At the time, they did not have a conscious feminist
identity, but they were certainly aware of the discrimination they were
experiencing in most areas of their lives. They were aware that men and
women were essentially the same psychologically and intellectually and
tried to prove it on the picket lines and at the political meetings. Rose
would later say of this era that it was "a tough job for a woman to prove
she is on par with a man. I had to elbow my way through."[53] They were
an outspoken lot and continued to be so throughout their lives. Sometimes that outspokenness would get them in trouble, as happened to
Rose when she entered the union hierarchy.

By 1928 Rose had been in the United States for fifteen years and had
emerged from childhood into her important adult years. She was a woman who was coming into her own, after experiencing enormous changes
and development through school and organizing. Rose had worked in the
deplorable conditions of the garment industry and had also seen the
second-class status of women in the union. She had heard the fiery

speeches of Emma Goldman in 1914, and had eventually met her famed role model in 1919. She had had the eye-opening experience of being a nurse and had participated in the excitement of supporting the Russian Revolution. She had also been arrested and harassed on the picket lines. Most importantly, Rose had experienced the deportation of Kushnarev in 1919 and the death of her father in 1920, both at the hands of antirevolutionary forces. She had lost her love to another woman, and then to typhoid. These losses seemed to deepen her sense of dedication and commitment. Added to these experiences, she had gained an education at the labor colleges in 1922, 1924, 1925, and 1926, as well as having been educated informally by her anarchist colleagues. She had a vast network of friends and comrades. And with these many forces operating in Rose's life by the late 1920s, the stage was set for a dynamic and exciting career. Rose did not engage in any violent or illegal activity, but she had obviously become radical in orientation by engaging in reading, thinking, and participating in numerous political activities. Although we have no way of knowing where she stood on all the major debates within the political left, she clearly aligned herself with the anarchist ideology and activities of her day. There was no turning back from this radical course of action with the anarchists and the ILGWU. These groups became the main focus of her life's work. Rose had indeed found, as Kushnarev had written her earlier, that "it is ever so hard to die for the cause, yet it is far more difficult to live for it."

3

SACCO AND VANZETTI

Eternal Symbols of a Dream

According to George Woodcock, "What remained of American anarchism during the decades between the wars entered into the condition common to sects that pass their age of militancy, lose the missionary urge and settle down into self contained inactivity."[1] Thousands of anarchists were left in the country, however; Rose and her comrades were part of a core group of dedicated activists who retained their beliefs and did not recognize they were losing their effectiveness. Hoping for the reemergence of their movement, they continued to study, organize, and propagandize. These activists distinguished themselves from others on the left by their inherent distrust of all those in authority. They detested hierarchy and the dominance of any group over another. Although they participated in most major social and political upheavals of their day, they did so cynically with regard to the immediate outcome but continued to foster the belief that human goodness would triumph over domination.

An anarchist network survived, although diminished in numbers. Comrades were in touch with each other in various communities; and, eventually, a new publication, *Road to Freedom*, emerged as an anarchist successor to Goldman's *Mother Earth*. *Road to Freedom*, an outgrowth of the Modern School at Stelton, New Jersey, was the publication arm of the International Group that met in New York throughout the 1920s. Members of various ethnic groups belonged to the International, which met at the Spanish Center located on East Twenty-third street near Lexington Avenue.[2]

Published from 1924 to 1932, *Road to Freedom* kept anarchism alive in the United States during its quiet time. Rose was a writer/secretary for this journal throughout its existence and was one of the few women authors found within its pages. The journal included writings on experimental education, utopian anarchism, working-class organizing, and "propaganda of the deed"[3]—acts of individual resistance to authority. Most of the content in *Road to Freedom* was geared to the immigrant groups for which it was written; these included Italians, Russians, Jews, and Spaniards.

The journal reflected the anarchists' deepening hatred of Communists, Marxists, and socialists, resulting from difficulties in the unions and events in Russia, where the revolution appeared to them to have been betrayed by the Communists. From her exile in Europe, Emma Goldman began to write to her comrades, describing her disillusionment with the Bolsheviks, and *Road to Freedom* printed some of these stories, as well as news about other international anarchist issues. It attempted to remain oriented to the labor movement and to offer a clear picture of contemporary life from an antiauthoritarian perspective. However, it was also eclectic in its content. Sometimes the writing was brilliant, but often it was simply eccentric and unfocused.

Road to Freedom was first edited by Hippolyte Havel, a former editor of *Mother Earth*. Havel, a Czechoslovakian immigrant known for his outrageous costumes, has been called "an anarchist bursting with atmosphere." Described as a small, rotund figure sporting spectacles, goatee, and moustache, his high forehead topped with disorderly black hair streaked with gray, Havel was one of the most notorious and colorful personalities in the movement. He always carried a silver-tipped cane, and his manner and appearance possessed a distinctly Old-World flavor. A friend likened him to a ragged chrysanthemum, yet he was an imposing character with a long and interesting radical history.[4] Havel was succeeded as editor by Walter S. Van Valkenburgh, a less colorful but equally dedicated anarchist and friend of Emma Goldman. Both men later died of alcoholism, demoralized by the failure of their political activities. Clearly the death of these two illustrates the price that radical agitators pay for sacrificing themselves to the struggle. It is something we see over and over within the ranks of dedicated activists.[5]

An issue that filled the pages of *Road to Freedom* throughout the 1920s was the Sacco and Vanzetti case. Most of the writers and all those who remained in the movement, including Rose, were involved in the attempt to save the lives of these two anarchist immigrants. Through her work as a writer/secretary with *Road to Freedom*, Rose met the doomed two. It was, for her, a deeply moving, meaningful, and traumatic experience.

Nicola Sacco and Bartolomeo Vanzetti were arrested in 1920 and convicted of having participated in a robbery and in the killing of two payroll guards in South Braintree, Massachusetts. Vanzetti was also convicted for an earlier robbery attempt in Bridgewater, Massachusetts. Both were Italian immigrants active in the anarchist movement. They maintained that, when arrested, they were attempting to pick up a friend's car so that they could remove anarchist material from other anarchists' homes. They alleged that they feared the material might be confiscated. It was a reasonable fear, since one of their comrades, Salsedo, had recently been arrested and had died in New York City under unusual circumstances (it was suspected that he might have been pushed from a window; it was also alleged that he had committed suicide).[6]

Supporters believed that the two were framed because of their political ideology. Nicola Sacco always maintained that he was convicted and sentenced to death because he was an anarchist. His lawyer William Thompson reported that "at the root of it all [their differences] lay his conviction, often expressed to me, that all efforts on his behalf, either in court or with public authorities would be useless, because no capitalist society could afford to accord him justice".[7] Knowing that anarchists such as Proudhon, Bakunin, and Kropotkin had been jailed for their beliefs, and having no faith in capitalism or its laws, Sacco saw little reason to hope that his situation would be changed through the courts or by authorities.

Instead of seeking help within the "system," Sacco believed that only the anarchist tradition of direct action could save his life. Taking up a theme of Kropotkin, Sacco hoped that action in the streets would force the authorities to free him. When a group of Smith College students demonstrated on his behalf, he applauded their activity and hoped that the demonstrations would continue to grow throughout the United States and Europe. He was disappointed that American workers did not do more to help him.[8] Sacco believed that only friends, comrades, and the "international proletariat" could aid his struggle, not the legal battles that were being waged. Throughout his seven years of imprisonment, Sacco argued that court maneuvers were futile. After his lost appeals, he refused to cooperate in any way with authority. Instead, he was grateful for the "honest friendships" that were shown to him. He felt what he termed "brotherly affection" toward well-to-do individuals (whom he called "members of the ruling class") who came to his aid, but thought that these liberal friends were deluding themselves if they believed that he would receive justice.[9] On the other hand, Sacco only felt anger toward his "philanthropist friends" and those who were using him and his case for their own gain. Sacco believed, as had Bakunin before him, that the only hope for him—a worker and man of the earth—lay with the poor and disenfranchised.

When arrested, Bartolemeo Vanzetti was a fish peddler and an anarchist activist. During his incarceration, he became a philosopher and a writer. Although he, too, believed that he was arrested because of his immigrant status and political activities, he showed more hope than did his comrade. He believed that he was in "merciless hands." But he said, "I will do my utmost to say to my enemy that he is wrong."[10] This statement implies that Vanzetti had faith that, once educated, the capitalist legal system might see justice done. Certainly, throughout his incarceration Vanzetti attempted in every possible way to use legal channels to stop the inevitable. Until the end, he protested his innocence and continued to express confidence in the inherent goodness of human nature[11] and the hope that his cause would be vindicated.[12] After Madeiros, a local hoodlum, confessed to the crimes for which Sacco and Vanzetti were convicted, Vanzetti expected that the appeals process and the lawyers would win his freedom. He also stated that if he had his later lawyer, William Thompson, from the beginning, he most certainly would have been freed.[13] This attitude, too, conveys the anarchist tradition of hope for all humanity, its inherent goodness and ability to change. Certainly both men had been active in the revolutionary brand of anarchism, including participating in a number of bombings prior to their arrest for the Braintree crimes.[14] Anarchism was totally integrated into their lives.

When Rose and her anarchist friends entered the case in 1922, the debate became whether or not to work through the legal system to get the two released. The anarchists were of two minds, as represented by Sacco and Vanzetti's divergent opinions: Either use the enemy's weapon of the courts and legal system to obtain release, or take to the streets in direct action, not bothering to petition those in power. For the most part, the defense committee chose the legal approach. Only later did they turn to more confrontational tactics.

When it appeared that legal maneuvers were failing, Vanzetti once again argued that it was time for him to embrace the anarchist principle of direct action. He went on hunger strikes to tell the Lowell Commission, a special investigating committee established by Governor Fuller, that witnesses on his behalf were being poorly treated. He stated that he was "tired of words" and now wanted the "thunders of the worldwide agitation and protest" to induce the enemy to free Sacco and himself.[15] He wanted the world to "shout not whisper on their behalf."[16] Vanzetti showed gratitude to various writers and to a Chinese student for engaging in the anarchist approach of political propaganda.[17] Like Sacco, he came to believe that mass protest would better aid his situation.

However, as the final legal efforts were being made on their behalf, Sacco and Vanzetti each dealt with the Massachusetts authorities in his respective characteristic manner. Sacco continued his active resistance to authority. Sacco needed freedom or death. For him, commutation of the death sentence would have been no victory at all. He had been a man of nature and had worked with his hands. Unsentenced during most of his imprisonment, he had not been allowed to work. He was tortured by being separated from his work, his wife, and his family. Prison had robbed him of his life, and he chose to die rather than to live half dead.

Vanzetti, on the other hand, had grown and developed in prison. He had done some work as a translator. He had written his memoirs and had been able to work in the prison shops because he had been sentenced for the Braintree robbery. Like many anarchists before him, Vanzetti had used the prison experience to deepen his political thought, to write, and to study. While in prison, he had developed a political following through his writings, which were published in international journals. Because he could live in prison, he fought hard until the end for a commutation of the death sentence. He hoped that if he were not executed, a way would eventually be found to clear his name. Until the end, Vanzetti maintained his hope that justice would prevail, protesting his innocence all the way.

In the fall of 1922, Rose became involved in the Sacco and Vanzetti case.[18] At an ILGWU meeting in Boston, Rose was introduced to Frank Lopez, who was then secretary of the Sacco and Vanzetti defense committee. A Spanish anarchist whom Sacco and Vanzetti's attorney Fred Moore had saved from deportation, Lopez was in charge of propaganda for Spain, South America, Mexico, and Cuba, and shared responsibilities with Mary Donovan for arranging publicity on the case.[19] Later Lopez would become important in Rose's life, emerging once more in the 1950s to become her husband.

Rose was already sympathetic, having researched the case for her Local 25 executive board. She felt that Sacco and Vanzetti were victims of a frame-up and that the case itself was one of "mass injustice." Aldino Felicani, the defense committee treasurer, asked her to act as liaison between the defense committee and the labor movement, particularly the foreign language groups—Russian, Jewish, Spanish, Portugese, and Polish. As a result, for a number of years Rose worked with a local committee in New York City to arrange a series of mass demonstrations at Union Square and around the country. She spoke at large meetings in various steel and coal cities in Pennsylvania and Connecticut. At some of the sessions, she worked with Michelangelo Musmanno, who later became a Pittsburgh judge and a justice on the Pennsylvania Supreme Court. In Detroit, which she visited a number of times, she spoke to small groups of auto workers, mostly foreign born, who appeared with their whole families.[20]

She hoped, as did Vanzetti, that the courts would eventually save them. Believing this, she did enormous agitational and educational work on their behalf. To her, it was not contrary to anarchism to believe in the court system. She hoped that the ultimate truth would vindicate them. She trusted the criminal justice system; and if that failed, she believed in the inherent goodness of human beings to undo this tragic miscarriage of justice.

Because she trusted the criminal justice system, Rose later wrote that she was appalled that Sacco and Vanzetti had been tried in a cage, which she felt served as a message to the jury that they were "dangerous men." In fact, the cage she described was a waist-high metal lattice, slightly higher in the back. To supporters, it looked like a cage; to others, there was nothing formidable or forbidding about it.[21]

One night after Rose had put in several evenings at the defense offices, Lopez informed her that he was going with Fred Moore the next morning to visit both of the prisoners at the Charlestown prison. He offered to take her along. Rose first met Sacco, who was brought into a reception room. He had not yet been sentenced and still hoped to return to his family in Stoughton. He was actively engaged in the study of English, and Sacco seemed to Rose "happy as a lark." He took her into his cell and proudly showed her his collection of English and Italian dictionaries and other books that had been sent by friends and sympathizers. She was impressed by his youth, health, and vitality. At that time, he was receiving considerable physical exercise daily in the prison yard. To Rose, Nicola Sacco was "just another Italian boy, friendly and humorous such as any boy as we might see anytime in our neighborhood in New York."[22]

Before the end of the visit, Nicola's wife, Rosina, came in with their son Dante, who was then nine. Sacco's eyes brightened when he saw them. He was not able to visit with his daughter inasmuch as official rules prevented her from being brought into the jail. His parting words to Rose were from the Russian author Andreyev: "When thousands kill one, it means that one has conquered."

Rose's next visit was with Vanzetti, who was then thirty-five but seemed vastly older. He had been brought in during his lunch hour from work in the tailor shop. They spoke of authors, including Kropotkin, Gorky, Darwin, Tolstoy, and Hugo. Upon parting, Vanzetti gave her a copy of a sketch he had written of himself, *Story of a Proletarian Life*, which was being distributed by the defense committee.

From that time until their death, Rose continued to correspond with the two and passed their words and messages on to other friends. Their letters often thanked Rose for her many visits and for the inspiration she gave them. In one letter Sacco wrote:

My life in prison is monotonous and I am sad away from my family. And yet the faithful ones find the courage. You are among those

faithful comrades. Today I could not help send you the warm salute
of spring. The unexpected visit that you together with Abe Winocur and Fanny Luchovsky kindly [gave] to me certainly pleased
me.[23]

She and other members of the *Road to Freedom* group would visit with
Sacco and Vanzetti and carry messages of support from comrades around
the country. Rose and Havel went as often as they could, sent books and
articles, and kept the two prisoners posted on anarchist activities. In
some of his letters to Rose, Vanzetti even asked her advice regarding the
best way to appeal to Clarence Darrow to take over the case.

Maybe there is some friction between the anarchists and the communists on the committee. The communists wanted Darrow but
the anarchists and friends seemed lacking in determination. . . . I
consulted with Thompson on it and then gave up the idea from my
head at least until the latest motion is filed. I would like to explain
this all to Darrow. . . . I sense something wrong has been done in
this case, the persons concerned to it, and to Darrow.[24]

Whenever Rose visited, she tried to look her best and put on a brave front
for the two. She was cheerful and attractive, and they admired her good
looks and the exuberance she conveyed. "You are getting younger and
more well,"[25] Vanzetti wrote to her after one of her visits.

When in Boston, Rose worked with the defense committee. There
she met Mrs. Elizabeth Glendower Evans, a member of a wealthy New
England family, who had devoted herself to labor causes in the past.
Elizabeth Evans and Anna Davis, another Massachusetts society woman,
had taken on major fund-raising efforts on behalf of Sacco and Vanzetti.
Rose also met Powers Hapgood, at that time a labor organizer from
Indiana, and Mary Donovan, who became secretary of the committee and
Hapgood's wife. After Vanzetti's death, the Hapgoods named their first
child, Barta, for their fallen colleague. The committee work built for Rose
an important support network. Friends of this period remained influen-
tial throughout her life, and the events that were to follow left a lasting
psychological impact on her work. She was constantly shuttling between
Boston and New York, doing agitational work on behalf of Sacco and
Vanzetti and consulting with the committee.

When she could, Rose attended court proceedings on the case.
Once, during a new hearing, she saw the two brought in, in shackles. She
remembers them seated in the locked cage during the recess, surrounded by a dozen uniformed police. They were led back to the jail with
children running after them. Rosina Sacco and her son were seen tagging

along behind the crowd. Rose said, "It would look funny to me had it not been so tragic."

Throughout their correspondence with Rose, Sacco and Vanzetti expressed gratitude for her involvement in the case. They were always glad when faithful comrades visited; and from this, they drew courage. Other letters discussed the legal maneuvers with the Massachusetts Supreme Court and later with the Lowell Commission, which was established by Governor Fuller to determine how he should proceed with the case. Toward the end of the case, some of the letters reflected the despair of both inmates. One stated: "The enemy can imprison, torture, kill some, or many of us, destroy our homes, our poor few books and our institutions, but the enemy cannot destroy ideas, rights, truths or causes."[26]

Rose's sister Esther was living in the Boston area during the time Rose was involved with the case. Many evenings Rose would lead "a pilgrimage" to Esther's home,[27] and comrades would sit for hours discussing the case. Esther overheard many of the details, although she never actively engaged in the debate. She recalls hearing that "Sacco was guilty and Vanzetti was not. The committee wanted Sacco to confess to save Vanzetti's life."[28] The conviction of Sacco's guilt was, of course, speculation on the part of the committee members, but it was an opinion shared by some historians and activists close to the case. There are others who certainly continue to argue the innocence of both.[29] Rose often led the animated discussions in her sister's home. Esther recalls that Lopez would arrive on a motorcycle, distant and aloof. He argued that the case was good political propaganda and should be used by the committee in this way.

In fact, the case did become a propaganda issue. After the appeals appeared to be failing, the gauntlet was taken up by members of the Communist party. There was continual debate within the committee and with Sacco and Vanzetti over handling the Communists' involvement, including discussion as to whether to hand over the defense to the International Labor Defense Committee, which was run by Communists.[30] Eventually, the defense stayed in the hands of the lawyers hired by the anarchists on the committee. Members of the committee felt that the Communists were interested only in the publicity that the case could generate rather than in the plight of the Sacco and Vanzetti. The antagonism between anarchists and Communists continued throughout the case, coinciding with Rose's experiences with the Communists in her union. Although her letters back to Vanzetti have not survived, it seems that her anticommunist position was toughened by what she saw in the Sacco and Vanzetti case.

As the case moved toward its conclusion, Rose continued her

wholehearted commitment to the two. Nonetheless, she was overwhelmed by the horror and inevitability of the outcome. On 9 April 1927, she visited them. They had been sentenced to die on 10 July, but the defense committee was seeking a pardon from the governor. Vanzetti wrote to her after that visit: "I will only say that the State of Massachusetts will do its best to burn us and it would seem too shameful and dangerous, it will do its best to bury us alive and forever in an old fortress. But the optimist may be right and I wrong. Yet do not hope and trust but in yourselves."[31] In that mailing, he included a gift for Rose, a penholder he had carved out of the handle of a toothbrush. It was cylindrical in shape and made of ivory, executed in an exquisite design. Rose treasured the gift for the remainder of her life.

On 1 June 1927, the governor postponed the execution for one month while the Lowell Commission investigated the case. In July, Rose was again taken to the prison to see the two. This time, she was accompanied by the newest attorney, William Thompson. In a Charlestown death cell, she found Sacco unrecognizable. In five years he had changed dramatically. He looked like a ghost, with hollow eyes, and appeared shrunken. His hands were feeble and transparent. His spirit was broken, and he had given up all hope. Vanzetti, on the other hand, had not. His eyes were sunken and he was practically bald. But his handshake was firm and his voice unshaken, his English had improved, and fire flashed from his eyes. To Rose, it appeared that he would "fight to live to the very end."[32] After leaving the two, Rose continued her agitational work on their behalf, returning to New York City to one more time arouse public sentiment and raise funds to help them.

When the Lowell Commission found no reason to commute the death penalty, Rose returned to Boston to await the execution. On 10 August, with her colleagues Carlo Tresca, an Italian anarchist, and Powers Hapgood, along with hundreds of other sympathizers, Rose participated in a mass demonstration at the State House. Many, including Rose, were arrested that day. She recalled that the police had placed a seven-minute limit on picketing. When seven minutes were up, the whole group was placed in custody, with others replacing the arrested to form a new line. The new group would then be arrested seven minutes later. This process continued all day and evening. Those who were arrested would return to the pickets after being bailed out.

At eleven o'clock that night, Rose was one of the many who gathered at the defense offices. The condemned men had already been dressed in the garb they were to wear to the death chamber. At the last minute, Governor Fuller granted them a reprieve until 22 August.

The next day found Rose back in New York arranging a mass demonstration and radio broadcasts. She worked on sending out appeals to important individuals to pressure Fuller, and she remained in telephone contact with the Boston group. She worked with little sleep, feeling feverish and desperate. However, all the efforts were in vain, and on 22 August 1927, at midnight, Sacco and Vanzetti were executed. Rose was not in Boston at the time.

On the following Sunday a double funeral was held. According to Rose, Vanzetti's prophetic words were borne out: The police did not permit the cortege to pass the State House. Thousands marched through the streets, many weeping and wearing armbands reading "Remember Justice Crucified." Fifty thousand people watched from the sidewalks. Ten thousand made it to the Forest Hills Cemetery, although only one hundred were allowed in the chapel, Rose among them. Mary Donovan gave the funeral oration, and then those who wanted to were allowed into the crematorium to look through a glass plate at the bodies being burned. According to Clara Rothberg's recollection, Rose and Clara were among the very few present when the two caskets were burned.[33] The experience seared itself into Rose's mind.

That same evening, at midnight, Rose left Boston and remained away from that city for nearly five years. The cremation scene haunted her continually. She said: "August 22, 1927—when they were executed—stands as the blackest day in the history of Massachusetts. For years afterward, I stayed away from Boston."[34] Later Rose wrote poetry about the chapel in Little Italy where the funeral of Sacco and Vanzetti was held.

> That funeral chapel in the heart of little
>   Italy has never seen so many flowers
> with such flaming inscriptions.
> Only those linked with the cause of
>   social justice
> Deserve such gifts.
> There in two coffins side by side
>   their wrists no more in chains
> Lie my two comrades
>
> .   .   .   .
> An electric current has turned their pale faces blue
>
> .   .   .   .
> Their eyes are closed eternally
> The lips will bid goodbye no more
>
> .   .   .   .
> Gazing at my two murdered comrades I
>   recall the days

When they were young and free
Goodbye my robust brave comrade Sacco.
Same to you good comrade Vanzetti
I kept my promise, I came. . . . but
   only I alone could see you.[35]

Because her life, her work, her thoughts, her friends, and her soul
were caught up with Sacco and Vanzetti, Rose's participation in the case
remained important the rest of her life. Hers was a deeply personal,
wrenching experience. She knew these men as friends. Seeing their treatment at the hands of those in power reconfirmed her radicalism and her
dedication to the victims of the world. She saw there was little justice for
those without power, and she experienced firsthand what the anarchist
analysis had previously taught her—that the world was corrupt and that
class bias killed her comrades. The experience rededicated her to the
ideal for which the two had stood. It also made her stronger. Rose had
lost much during the twenties: Kushnarev, her father, and Sacco and
Vanzetti. It seems that these trying eight years taught her to cope with
enormous adversity. Later she said she believed that "inner strength
comes from years of experience, that no matter how small the achievement, maybe in spite of adversities, one must go on."[36]

Years later, her nephew Jack Hochman, later an executive in the
ILGWU, would recall how important the Sacco and Vanzetti case was to
Rose. For his bar mitzvah, all his relatives gave Jack money or traditional
gifts. But Rose, he remembers, gave him a two-volume set of Upton
Sinclair's *Boston*, an account of the case.[37]

Rose was overwhelmed by the outcome, but she did not give up. It
was with great determination and fortitude that she faced the next challenges of her life. As usual, even with great loss and sadness, Rose found
the strength to go on with her life and to continue her political and labor
organizing work.

It was for Rose much as Upton Sinclair had written:

A hundred million workers shackled and blind, groping in a
poison fog manufactured by their masters, learned that two of their
fellows had been put to death for lifting the banner of freedom. . . .
That was a fact, the meaning of which could never be obscured: a
fact which shone like a pillar of fire in the workers night . . . to a
hundred million groping, and ten times as many in slumber. The
names of Sacco and Vanzetti would be eternal symbols of a dream
identical with civilization itself, of a human society in which wealth
belongs to the producers of wealth, and the rewards of labor are to
the laborers.[38]

4

Labor Organizing: The Early Years

Like a swimmer caught in the undertow.

The stock market crash of 1929 and the resulting Great Depression saw a massive increase in unemployment and economic deterioration. In 1930, three million workers were without jobs; by 1933, between fifteen million and seventeen million were jobless.[1] Wages dropped 45 percent, and by 1933, 75 percent of the population was living at or below subsistence level. Workers continually lost jobs, and, eventually, those most affected were women. By 1933, almost two million women were out of work. Unemployment among women was greater than among young men, increasing at a faster rate in many industries. Married women were particularly discriminated against, with most jobs being reserved for married or single men and single women, although eventually the percentage of married women in the work force grew.

As the crisis worsened, so did workplace conditions. Many of the work standards were abandoned, and sweatshops were reintroduced. Wages for all workers, particularly women, were incredibly low. Some women were not even able to make five dollars for a full week's work. Starving people were literally eating garbage from the streets. By 1932, 20 percent of the children in New York City suffered from malnutrition.[2] Rose remembered these times in her memoirs: "1929 brings the United States the black day of the Wall Street crash. The garment industry is hit as the nation tumbles into the worst depression it has ever known. . . . Banks close, manufacturers go bankrupt, thousands of dressmakers are close to starvation."[3]

In the garment industry, hard-earned gains were lost. Shops moved out of central cities, and jobs were difficult to come by. Once again workers who were lucky enough to have jobs worked from dawn to dusk, children worked long hours, wages were at bare subsistence level, and work at home was revived. For example, in the city sweatshops, some women earned two and a half cents for every apron they made, a total of twenty cents a day. One young woman got half a cent for each pair of pants she processed, making $2.78 a week.[4] Conditions in the garment industry were abysmal because work standards were abandoned and the sweatshops were revived.

Given the devastating conditions of the economy, men in the unions felt that jobs and benefits should be reserved for the "breadwinners," themselves. Previously won gains for women were lost during this time, and women were consigned to being cheap workers making marginal wages. Often these women supported whole families.[5] Unemployment and the fear of unemployment motivated women to seek jobs. Yet social pressure on women to stay home and tend the family continued. Women were often scapegoated as the cause of men's unemployment and were constantly pressured to leave the work force. Nonetheless, women workers remained a viable force, particularly within the domestic, clerical, and manufacturing areas.[6]

The depression had decimated the unions, beaten down the workers' spirit, and set off bitter competition for jobs.[7] Companies cut wages and their labor forces. Work was rationed. Some unions tried to stem this trend by striking to prevent further wage reductions, but generally the militancy was ineffective, given the severity of economic conditions.[8] The ILGWU, barely recovered from its internal strife, was demoralized and in debt. The membership was down from 105,000 in 1920 to 40,000 in 1933. Women fared quite poorly in the unions at this time. "They were recruited, sometimes reluctantly, as dues paying members, tolerated as shop-level leaders, and occasionally advanced to become business agents and local and international officers. But incentives and inducements designed to create a loyal and effective female membership were virtually nonexistent." In fact, the trade union movement mistrusted women and itself created friction, resentment, and defensiveness among them, reducing their value and undermining their ability to do good work.[9] Nonetheless, even though the union did not consider them important, the women remained loyal and dedicated members, fighting militantly alongside the men, especially during this period of hard economic times.

With the election of Franklin Delano Roosevelt and the major bills that he encouraged during his first one hundred days in office, significant measures were taken to turn the economy around. The most important act influencing conditions in labor was the National Industrial Recovery Act (NIRA) of 1933. The NIRA legalized trade association agreements on production and prices. Section 7(a) of the law recognized the right of labor to bargain collectively. The National Recovery Administration

(NRA) was established to enforce the NIRA. By 1934, the NRA codes covered 90 percent of all industrial workers.[10]

The New Deal years under the Roosevelt administration were a time of turmoil for the garment industry and for unions in general. The workers became more involved in union activities and engaged in battles on the picket lines and around the bargaining tables. Workers were now able to organize unions of their own choice, set up pay floors and ceilings, and demand that the government be concerned with the conditions of the American worker. During Franklin D. Roosevelt's first term in office, the International Ladies Garment Workers Union began a major organizational drive to restore its depleted ranks.

Involved throughout the 1920s in New York City labor activities, Rose became known to leaders in the union hierarchy because of her fierce anticommunist stand during the factional battles. In September 1933, Rose became a paid staff member when the ILGWU sent her to Los Angeles to organize dressmakers. The atmosphere in Los Angeles was virulently antiunion. In her first foray earlier that year as a volunteer, Rose had been discharged from a garment factory and blacklisted for union activity. Penniless, but resourceful, Rose had hitchhiked home; and five months later, she was sent back by plane as a paid worker to begin again in earnest.[11]

It was at this time that Rose began to address the question of how an anarchist could function as a trade unionist. The competing demands of anarchism and trade unionism often put her into conflict. Additionally, Rose found herself as the only paid woman organizer in a male-dominated union hierarchy. Given her position as a woman and an anarchist, she was often viewed as an outsider and different from other leaders within the union. As an anarchist, Rose was committed to decentralization and a large voice for the rank and file in decision making. As a woman, representing a largely female constituency, she was committed to making the voice of her colleagues heard by the men in the union decision-making bodies. She did so because, despite the fact that the locals were female dominated, women were excluded from positions of importance. As we will see, Rose's anarchism and commitment to women made her an outsider and were major issues that she confronted throughout her organizing career.

Rose was one of a growing number of militant women labor organizers who found their way to the ILGWU. These women, particularly Fannia Cohn, Pauline Newman, and Rose Schneiderman, worked in organizing the "unorganizable" shops. Rose was younger than the other three, but acted in the same tradition. Pauline Newman became the ILGWU's first woman organizer after the Uprising of the Twenty Thousand in 1909. Eventually she was employed with the Joint Board of Sanitary Control, which was a combined trade union and manufacturers unit designed to establish standards for maintaining sanitary conditions in the shops. Newman was a warm, open, and impulsive woman who had a successful long-term relationship with a woman, with whom she adopted a baby in 1923.[12]

Fannia Cohn, a national leader in workers' education, was the first woman to serve as a vice president of the ILGWU's General Executive Board (GEB) and did so for four terms, from 1916 to 1926. Throughout her life, she remained dedicated to labor education for the ILGWU, although she was mistreated by the union, which never allowed her to become its education director. It was Cohn who was instrumental in establishing Unity House and in fostering labor education programs for the ILGWU around the country. Cohn had chosen not to take sides during the battle between the Communists, socialists, and anarchists in the 1920s, which contributed to her defeat for a fifth term as vice president.[13] Additionally, she had many difficulties with the union because of the bias of male unionists against women leaders, the changing trends in workers' education, and her own rather difficult personality. In fact, she ran into many of the same problems that Pesotta would later encounter with the intransigence of the male-dominated hierarchy of the General Executive Board.[14]

Rose Schneiderman began her career in the ILGWU in 1903 organizing capmakers. By 1905, she had joined the Women's Trade Union League (WTUL), and later she became its New York president and the national vice president as well. She worked in the Uprising of Twenty Thousand in 1909, and was the first woman vice president of the United Cloth Hat and Capmakers Union. By the 1930s, Schneiderman was a close personal friend of Eleanor Roosevelt,[15] and Franklin D. Roosevelt chose her as the only woman to serve on the NRA's Labor Advisory Board.

Each of these organizers experienced ambivalence working within the ILGWU. On the one hand, they saw the discrimination against women—both in the union hierarchy and in the way women were treated in the shops. On the other hand, Rose and the others knew that without the union, conditions would be even worse. Sometimes these women, particularly Schneiderman, chose to work in all-women's organizations, such as the Women's Trade Union League. The WTUL was formed in 1903 as a coalition of working and wealthy women who saw themselves as feminists and trade unionists. As unionists, they sought to integrate women into the mainstream of twentieth-century labor; and as feminists, they sought to make the women's movement relevant to working women.[16] The league was an influential force in labor until the 1930s, and increasingly devoted itself to feminist causes, particularly women's suffrage. The league also worked for the eight-hour work day and for fire safety regulations. In its later years, it became a social welfare organization devoted to protective legislation, serving as a social center for young women. Periodically, Rose worked with the Women's Trade Union League on labor issues; however, in general she had little to do with feminists or women outside the labor movement. Her job kept her on the road, and she did not join any women's organizations until much later in her life, although she certainly identified with women's struggles.

For the most part, Rose chose to labor within the male-dominated ILGWU, while challenging positions taken by the male leaders. For this, as we shall see, she was viewed as a troublemaker and as someone with whom it was difficult to get along. Fannia Cohn and Pauline Newman, in contrast, tried to be more conforming, but were still placed in positions out of town and without any power.[17] All four—Pesotta, Schneiderman, Cohn, and Newman—challenged male privilege in the union, and each was handled accordingly by the men in power. Pesotta's main problems, however, were not to develop until she came into her own, much later in her career.

By 1933, when Rose began full-time organizing for the union, it had become clear that women—married as well as unmarried—were in the work force to stay.[18] The ILGWU committed money and resources to organizing them, and extended its efforts beyond the East Coast centers. The formation of the Congress of Industrial Organizations (CIO) in 1935 led to a substantial improvement for women workers.[19] The CIO was committed to organizing mass-production industries along industrial lines, regardless of skill, race, or sex. The ILGWU, part of the organizing effort to establish this new national committee of mass-production workers, was suspended from the American Federation of Labor (AFL) for aiding the new union. By the end of the 1930s, as many as eight hundred thousand women had been organized into unions, a 300 percent increase in ten years—double the 1920 figure. Although female participation increased in the rank and file, women were rarely found in the centers of decision making, and sex-based inequities continued. In fact, women rarely reached the high position that Pesotta was to hold. In a union such as the United Auto Workers, women like Dorothy Haener, Mildred Jeffrey, and Florence Peterson worked valiantly as union organizers. Nonetheless, they claimed to be in the right place at the right time, and none acknowledged a sense of ambition in reaching for leadership positions.[20] Women were not supposed to show any interest in upward mobility within the union; it was "unbecoming" to the role of women. In fact, even a woman

FIGURE 8

Rose Pesotta and David Dubinsky, Atlantic City, October 1935. "Strolling along with D.D. at A.F. of L. Convention."

Photo courtesy of Dorothy, Elias, and Edward Rotker.

as significant and public as Eleanor Roosevelt would deny that she ever wanted political power, or that she actually enjoyed the process.[21] It was socially unacceptable for women to be in, or aspire to, positions of power. Women were practically absent from the leadership of the unions, with the exception of the few mentioned, because they were still viewed as temporary workers; and unequal pay and separate seniority lists for women continued. "Despite the emergence of large female-dominated locals, women were excluded from position of any importance" according to Roger Waldinger. This was true for the era prior to Pesotta's own and was to continue through her tenure with the ILGWU.[22]

The following profile of Pesotta's labor organizing and years as a vice president in the ILGWU is based primarily upon my reading of Pesotta's personal letters, her book *Bread upon the Waters*, the papers of David Dubinsky, and feminist interpretations of her experience in the context of the growing historiography of women in labor. The most useful source for me has been Pesotta's own chronicle, which is partisan but accurately conveys her experience as a key participant in the events.

According to Pesotta, her first task in Los Angeles was to organize Mexican women workers for the union—a difficult undertaking on two counts. First, Los Angeles manufacturers were attempting to undermine all unionizing efforts; and second, according to Pesotta, Mexican women were notoriously difficult to organize because of cultural pressures on them to remain in the home. She said that in the tradition of "machismo," Mexican men believed women should work outside the home only when necessary to aid the family, not as career women and certainly not as unionists. Pesotta noted in her memoirs that it was general belief outside the Mexican community that Mexicans would "work for a pittance and could endure any sort of treatment."[23] In fact, recent scholarly research indicates that Mexican women were actually quite militant and showed excellent leadership qualities in other industries during that era. Vicki Ruiz has argued that in the cannery and packing industries in the 1930s and 1940s in California, Mexican and Chicana women showed a commitment to unionization and were able to form multicultural links with other ethnic groups in the same industry.[24] Recent work by Barbara Kingsolver on Mexican wives of mine workers in Arizona indicates the same militance.[25] In that strike in 1983 against Phelps Dodge Copper, Mexican women were on the line because they were loyal to the union and were desperate over their families' living conditions, and because the men were legally or physically barred from taking action.[26]

With her own stereotypes in mind, Rose went at her first task earnestly, contending that the dressmakers were simply normal human beings who needed to be organized. She bought spots on Spanish-speaking radio stations, published a newspaper in Spanish and English, and visited the homes of the workers with Mexican colleagues.[27]

Pesotta described visiting one Mexican home to find that behind the deceptively squalid exterior was a well-decorated and clean interior. She discovered homes with fancy radio sets, vacuum cleaners, refrigerators. In one home, she found a baby grand piano, being paid for by two parents, both working for lowly hourly wages, who wanted their daughter to learn the instrument. Pesotta was struck by the mother's devotion to the child's musical education; the woman even took work home to finance the payments. In another home, she saw a huge refrigerator in the living room, being used as a showpiece because the electricity had been turned off. The luxury had been bought on installment from "silver tongued salesmen."[28] Pesotta was struck by the manipulation of poor workers. This fit her anarchist analysis of the exploitation of workers under a capitalist economic system. These examples proved to her that poor workers were preyed upon by those trying to get rich "on the backs" of the poor and intensified her commitment to enlighten, educate, and aid the victims of this exploitation.

Pesotta was moderately successful in her Los Angeles efforts. She was able to mobilize cloakmakers and dressmakers, who eventually called for general strikes that influenced employers. At one point, according to Rose, the reemerging union, with herself as secretary, was able to shut down the entire Los Angeles dress industry in its efforts to gain its demands. She worked extensively with many colleagues to bring about changes in the industry. Her union joined forces with the Cloakmakers Union, the Waitress Union, the Central Labor Council, and the American Federation of Labor organizers to bring pressure to bear on factory owners. Rose met regularly with people from all fields to gain assistance in her work. Although she was not the only organizer for her union in Los Angeles, she was often the most visible.

During this time, Rose's style of organizing began to emerge. She was always busy, moving from picket lines to meetings. She would be involved in a strategy session and then run over to the commissary to cook for the strikers. She set up ration card systems, rented office space, spoke at meetings, and made reports to the international headquarters. She often spoke with reporters, emerging as a colorful character from these interviews. Her picture was often in the newspapers, appearing vibrant and sparkling. She gave quotable statements and was attractive enough to be photographed regularly. Although she was not alone in her work, she was the one often noted because of her style and flair. She was effective and gained attention.

Rose used "tactics of struggle that reflected the knowledge that moral outrage, not economic pressure, was their [her] trump card. She and other women repeatedly put themselves in positions where they forced the authorities to violate convention."[29] For example, Rose began to wear white gloves while demonstrating, insisting at all times that women should act like ladies and appealing to the chivalry of police and shop owners. These tactics had been used by earlier women unionists, but were repeated by Rose quite effectively during the entire period of organizing in the thirties. Certainly Rose was not the first to use colorful and unusual organizing strategies. Just a few years earlier, during a 1929 strike in Elizabethton, Tennessee, militant women had organized against the textile industry, using methods founded on the tradition of "disorderly women"—a term used for women who, in times of conflict and political upheaval, embody tensions considered to be half-conscious and only dimly understood. They, too, with irreverence and inventiveness, shattered stereotypes and, thereby, illustrated the complexity of working women's lives, just as Rose was doing through her own creative strategies.[30]

When the employers tried to stop the picketing with an injunction against the union, Rose and her co-workers mobilized thousands of striking workers to come out in force to picket. The numbers were so large that the police were "powerless against that mass of unionists."[31] Employers soon became mindful that an injunction would only increase support for the strikers, and that resource was not used again during the strike.

Rose believed in colorful organizing tactics that gained publicity and support. It was to become her style for the duration of her work. During this first strike, Rose rounded up three hundred children of the strikers on Halloween day. She had all the costumed children march around the garment center in two-by-two formation. The scene stopped traffic, drew countless reporters and photographers to the area, and antagonized the police, who had not been informed of the spontaneous demonstration. Subsequently, she made sure to work out agreements with the police in order to assure protection and aid for future demonstrations. Pesotta noted that according to Lieutenant Pfeiffer, an assistant in charge of guarding the strikers,

> The Red Squad was becoming a laughing stock because of our tactics. . . .
>
> For a change I used a pleading tone. "Please lay off. Let us alone. We have a couple of thousand girls and women on strike. If you'll let me take care of it, I'll see that they return safely to work."
>
> "All right, Rosie, I know you can do it."[32]

Although many strikers were arrested, Rose tried to ensure that there was no brutality. It seems ironic that Rose, an anarchist, would negotiate with the police. Nonetheless, she was realistic and wanted to guard against unnecessary violence. Later, when criticized for beginning to lose herself to the labor movement, she remarked:

> I still consider myself an active anarchist—organizing the most exploited, most backward people on earth. If anyone says I am deviating from anarchism I will tell him [*sic*] that this is my way to work for a new society.[33]

For her, negotiating with the police for the safety of others was not inconsistent with anarchist beliefs nor with her position as a woman organizer. She believed, foremost, in the sanctity of life and in promoting the well-being of others. She would meet and talk to the police to avoid bloodshed.

According to Alice Kessler Harris, Pesotta, like other women trade unionists, was trying to address "a nation committed to the rhetoric of chivalry, motherhood, and the ideal of the 'weaker sex,' [by demonstrating] the brutal treatment which daily violated ideas about womanhood—inside as well as outside—the workplace. Their actions called attention to the discrepancy between what society thought women ought to be and what working life made possible for them."[34] These women, including Pesotta, demonstrated differently than the men. They were not unequal, but "accepted and relied upon their special place as the moral basis of their demands for better workplace conditions."[35] For Rose, using children in demonstrations and negotiating with police were part of the moral suasion she found it useful to employ.

After just a month of striking in Los Angeles, the National Labor Relations Board ordered arbitration. The decision was not particularly favorable to the union, but nonetheless it was ratified. The decision said that working conditions would fall in the domain of the NIRA section 7(a), but it had no signed agreement under which the board's order could be enforced. Communist attacks on the union and a slow season for the industry further complicated the strike, which had allowed the employers to pick and choose whom they would rehire.

Even though there were setbacks in her work, particularly contending with the Communists in the industry, Pesotta was able to organize a local of dressmakers, the first of its kind in Los Angeles. "After [this] spectacular strike, the ILGWU penetrated the Los Angeles dress industry for the first time."[36] The strike was about employers not paying minimum wage, poor work conditions, and mass hirings of Mexican workers. Rose's work was exceedingly effective in establishing a foothold in Los Angeles for her union. She set up an office, helped organize an executive board, and helped the workers obtain a charter. Pesotta also established an education department for the workers based on the model of her New York local, thus beginning a pattern that was to continue throughout her years in the field. She believed that union organizing was more than dealing with just bread-and-butter issues. To her, organizing was a means of empowering workers in many spheres of their lives. Accordingly, she wanted workers to become knowledgeable in economics, social and political issues, public speaking, and writing. All of these subjects were taught on a regular basis after work hours in the union hall. Rose would often teach these classes herself or hire others to do so. Pesotta, like other women organizers, saw that education created good trade unionists.[37]

While based in Los Angeles, Pesotta made trips up to San Francisco in an attempt to organize Chinese garment workers in the sweatshops of Chinatown. Her description of the conditions under which the newly arrived immigrants worked are vivid and heartrending.[38] Workers were forced to work both day and night in poorly lit and crowded quarters. In fact, the workers actually slept on tables in the workroom, this being both their home and their workplace. Some of the shops were three stories underground, where light and fresh air never reached. Men, children, and women, sometimes four generations in one family, would take turns at the sewing machines.

Pesotta was appalled to discover that, except for the ILGWU, no union was willing to extend membership to the Chinese. That made it impossible for her to do any effective organizing. Rose found she could make no inroads in organizing in Chinatown. However, one can see from this undertaking, as well as from her work with Mexicans in Los Angeles, how Rose dealt with ethnic and cultural groups other than her own. She could form excellent working relations with people quite different from herself, even if her organizing efforts were not totally successful.

As in Los Angeles, Pesotta's San Francisco work included setting up educational and recreational programs for the ILGWU membership. She made sure that the workers were taught history, economics, and workers' problems, as she had been taught at the labor colleges. Rose was dedicated to education, knowing how study had lifted her out of workplace drudgery.

Pesotta also became involved in a general strike that rocked the shipping industry up and down the Pacific coast, offering ILGWU support for other unions and becoming widely known for her efforts. The general strike of 1934 began when San Francisco longshoremen went on strike to attain agreements with ship owners. When this failed, others, including teamsters, seamen, and licensed officers, joined the strike in sympathy. By May of that year, no ship was leaving any Pacific harbor. Hundreds marched regularly, and Pesotta was often at the picket line at the Embarcadero. By July, the strike had escalated to the point of violence. Two strikers were killed and hundreds were injured by the gas and gun fire of the uniformed forces.[39] This ignited the rising resentment of the city's workers; and for almost a week, San Francisco was totally shut down by a general strike held in support of the International Longshoremen's Association. No streetcars ran, all deliveries—except milk and bread—ceased, all stores, gas stations, and restaurants shut down. By the end of July, the strike by longshoremen had ended successfully. Of this event Rose remembered:

> We of the ILGWU talked with groups of the strikers, pledged our financial and moral support, urged them to call upon us for advice if needed, offered our headquarters to them for meetings, and promised that we would bring their strike to the attention of our International Convention in Chicago. Little did we dream that it would led to a general strike which would rock the whole Pacific slope.
>
> I spent a great deal of time now on the Embarcadero, historic waterfront. The scene there was remarkable. Hundreds of men, able-bodied and willing to work and asking only to be treated like human beings, were constantly shoved around by the police.[40]

Pesotta was in the middle of a significant event in the establishment of unionism on the West Coast. Furthermore, she finally saw her anarchist convictions put into action. Anarchists have long advocated direct action and general strikes as a means to achieving revolution. For the first time Pesotta was able to participate in an event that stopped a city from functioning. It was an exciting and invigorating experience for her. As a result of the West Coast activities, Rose became well known in labor circles.

When Pesotta reached the national convention of the ILGWU in Chicago in May of 1934, her reputation had preceded her. All of her endeavors on the West Coast drew the attention of both co-workers and those in the union hierarchy. Her East Coast friends were eager to nominate her to be the only woman among twenty-four vice presidents of the ILGWU's General Executive Board (GEB). Previously, there had been only two women vice presidents, Fannia Cohn and Molly Friedman, and Pesotta's colleagues believed that, with her record, Rose was the best candidate. Three-quarters of the union's members were women, but only one woman had served on the board at a time. For them, the time was right for another woman to take her place.

Pesotta was not eager for the nomination. She said she now wanted to return to a sewing machine in a New York dress shop. Up to this point, she was able to justify her position in the union because she was a lowly organizer. But should she be elected, she would be joining the bureaucracy, subject to greater control. How could she justify this position and be an anarchist too? Pesotta said she was afraid of giving up her freedom. She also knew how difficult it would be as one woman among the twenty-four vice presidents and felt that "the voice of a solitary woman on the General Executive Board would be a voice lost in the wilderness."[41] She felt she could serve just as well as a rank-and-file unionist. Nonetheless, even though she did not agree to be a candidate, she was nominated and elected by acclamation. She remembered this moment: "I felt hot and cold at the same time. It seemed as if I were being dragged down by some dread force—like a swimmer caught in an undertow. I wanted to cry out in protest, but my throat felt paralyzed."[42] In *Bread upon the Waters*, she writes:

> The greatest misfortune happened to me this morning. The convention delegates unanimously elected me to serve on the GEB for two years. Although there were several who aspired to that office, they were opposed, all favoring me. Someone else who wanted this honor would have been happy—I feel as if I had lost my independence. Cried the whole day.[43]

Pesotta never had ambition to hold executive authority. In accord with anarchist ideology, she wanted to keep from becoming co-opted and from stepping far beyond the rank and file. By accepting the task, Rose found herself often having to compromise her anarchist beliefs. It was a difficult position in which to be placed and one that would cause her a great deal of dismay. Because she left behind no actual evidence, one can only speculate as to why Rose allowed herself to be elected. Certainly she was ambivalent in making this decision; perhaps she chose not to let her friends down, as they were so proud and eager for her to do it; or on the other hand, it is possible that she was honored and pleased with the recognition that was being accorded her. Two other times she had come to a convention—as a member of the rank and file. Having no status, she had tried to speak to the delegation and had been treated disrespectfully. Now, here she was, a thirty-six-year-old organizer who had fame and notoriety. It is possible that her ego took over and she allowed herself to be swept away by the momentum. She may also have hoped to make a difference. Certainly, Pesotta enjoyed acknowledgment: She had stayed in the limelight in Los Angeles, and she chose to stay in it again in Chicago. On many levels, Pesotta seemed to enjoy the honor and appreciation for her achievements. She had worked hard and was rewarded for her efforts. She became a vice president and actually remained in that position for ten years.

5

LABOR ORGANIZING: THE CHALLENGING YEARS

A voice lost in the wilderness.

Upon assuming responsibility as a vice president, Pesotta began her long and varied association with David Dubinsky, the president of the ILGWU. Dubinsky was a "leprechaun" of a man, unpretentious and brash. He had been a garment worker himself and was at ease with his own people.[1] Dubinsky, referred to as "DD" by his colleagues, came from an activist background similar to Rose's. The two had much in common, although they often found themselves locked in battle. He, too, was fiercely anticommunist and a proponent of social reform. Unlike Pesotta, DD was authoritarian: "His leadership was characterized by a blend of democracy and Bonapartism, a reasonably firm adherence to rules and a straight domination from the top."[2] He was as quick to lose his temper as to indulge his generosity. When Pesotta first entered the GEB, he liked her work and vitality, and their collegial relationship blossomed. Later, as we shall see, she crossed him and was quick to fall from favor. But in 1934, Rose was new to the position, and Dubinsky took her under his wing.

On her first assignment as a vice president, Pesotta was sent to Puerto Rico. She saw herself doing missionary work for the union and, as usual, gave everything to the task. Pesotta was greeted enthusiastically by the women workers of Puerto Rico. They were pleased that the ILGWU had chosen to organize their fledgling industry, and Pesotta found the women charming and easy people with whom to work. She traveled the entire island, becoming familiar with the conditions and the issues facing her. She found single-room shacks built on stilts—there was no sanitation, and she observed garbage, slops, and rubbish in the mud below.[3] She witnessed cooking on small open hearths of stone, empty coconut shells serving as the cooking utensils. From her travels, she found that economic and social conditions left much to be desired. Even though the NRA had been in effect on the island, there was little recovery going on there.

Puerto Rico was a one-crop country, mainly producing sugar cane. The inhabitants of the island were starving, and the island could not produce enough food to feed its own populace.

Often, when Pesotta spoke in public, women in the predominantly female audience fainted of hunger. Pesotta began carrying extra food and drink in her lunchbox to feed these workers. Before the meetings, workers were asked if they had eaten. If not, they were fed before she began to speak.[4] Although she spent only a few months working in Puerto Rico, she made significant contacts, and the abhorrent conditions left an indelible impression on her. Again, as in Los Angeles, Pesotta showed her keen ability to work with people unlike herself. Even though she did not speak Spanish, she made important connections and reached large numbers of workers. She could communicate with governors, senators, officials in the NRA, as well as the lowliest worker in the most impoverished rural regions of Puerto Rico. Deeply moved by what she found there, Pesotta wrote and spoke about Puerto Rico for many years afterward and continued to remain in contact with the union there. Upon her return to the mainland, she attempted to influence officials in Washington to improve conditions on the island, but to no avail. Years later, in 1944, as conditions in Puerto Rico became more public, she continued by writing letters to the *New York Herald Tribune* and other major publications to bring further attention to the plight of Puerto Ricans.

In December of 1934, Pesotta was sent by Dubinsky to organize in Seattle, Washington. This time she was involved with yet other ethnic and cultural groups—Scandinavian immigrants, along with Irish, Icelanders, French-Canadians, Australians, and New Zealanders. Although the NRA was being implemented, workers were still exploited, and Rose had to overcome frontier attitudes and habits in order to reach these potential members. Seattle had been a stronghold of Industrial Workers of the World (IWW) organizing earlier, but by the time Rose arrived, it was a "ghost town" for unions. As usual, however, Pesotta was diligent in her efforts, and in a short time she had organized a local of dressmakers and set up her usual education department. She made sure there were dances and parties to entertain the workers, and slowly but surely ILGWU membership grew in Seattle.

Eventually, there were enough members for a limited strike against three shops to be called. Pesotta was again instrumental in setting up strike committees, commissaries, and picket lines. She found that, almost overnight, subservient workers were radically changed by the experience. She saw them emerging and finding themselves during the process of fighting their employers.[5]

While at a picket line in March of 1935, Pesotta saw a ripe tomato

FIGURE 9

Seattle, 1935 (Rose Pesotta, center).

Photo courtesy of Dorothy, Elias, and Edward Rotker.

land on the head of one of the shop owners. Rose was named as the
assailant and arrested. After being booked, she read the local papers and
learned that the authorities were trying to deport her for her activities.[6]
She was branded an "outside agitator." Because she was a naturalized
citizen, they were unable to complete their efforts; and Pesotta was
released without any charges, later speaking of the incident with relish
and pride. She enjoyed the notoriety and took obvious pleasure in out-
witting her antagonists. She gleefully called herself "#20399 of the
Rogues' Gallery."

In a vivid letter to Dubinsky in June of 1935, she described the
nuts-and-bolts activities she was undertaking.

> For ourselves I can report that we are doing nicely on the picket
> line from morning till time is up for the past 13 weeks. . . . Some
> wiseacre[s] say that the employers would have settled the strike
> long ago, but for that terrible woman. I challenged them if they are
> in earnest I shall leave on the midnight train after the agreement
> will be signed. . . . To close our campaign here we are holding a first
> annual ball, on June 21, to celebrate the chartering of the local and
> simply give the workers in the city something to think about. In
> connection with the ball I am also planning to publish a souvenir
> program with appropriate material and greetings from sympathetic
> and our own locals. It will leave a lasting impression upon these
> people here, I know, and incidentally will set a precedent our group
> to conduct such affairs annually.[7]

While she was working in Seattle, the U.S. Supreme Court declared
the NIRA unconstitutional, and within hours, shop owners were returning their workers to pre-NRA wages and hours. Without the backing of
the federal government, the unions had a more difficult time holding the
owners to agreements or even bringing them to negotiations. The repeal
was a major setback for labor. The strike that Pesotta was organizing
dragged on for three months, and the workers began losing hope of a
settlement. Consequently, Pesotta chose to leave Seattle, feeling that her
presence antagonized the shop owners. She hoped her absence would
allow the owners to save face and lead to a settlement. With this in mind,
and feeling overwhelmed and ill from her difficult task, Pesotta pleaded
with Dubinsky to relieve her. Ultimately, she convinced him to invite her
to the GEB quarterly meeting so that she could extricate herself
gracefully. He told her to expect that the strike would peter out with her
departure and to leave just one person on the payroll. When she left, the
workers drifted back to the shops. After a series of rousing achievements

in Seattle, Pesotta was finally faced with her first failure at organizing, and she chose to extricate herself rather than continue in the face of greater defeat. Two years later, the local she established actually began to thrive and even won collective bargaining agreements with needlecraft manufacturers.[8]

"Rose's continuing and impressive successes as a union organizer led the ILGWU to 'lend' her to striking auto workers [UAW] in Flint, Michigan, and to rubber workers [URW] in Akron during the massive industrial organizing drives of the late 1930's."[9] Pesotta was glad to get involved in both of these efforts, because for a while she had been serving as an emergency organizer, being sent from city to city and feeling very transient. By February 1936, Pesotta was in Akron helping Goodyear rubber workers. The strike was being led by the CIO and was her first experience in organizing workers outside of the garment industry. Although she was called in as a "woman organizer" to work with the strikers and their families, it was quite a coup for Rose, being the only woman organizer present.

The situation was a hot one, with thousands of militant strikers, angry bosses, and scores of police and state troopers called out to handle the crisis. It was Pesotta's job to work with the wives, daughters, and sisters of the strikers in order to raise their sagging morale. Even though she was assigned to the "woman's role," Rose made it a point to appear at picket lines and to deal with the strikers themselves. While touring the commissary and strike headquarters, Rose learned that her old friend from the Sacco and Vanzetti committee, Powers Hapgood, was there on a similar mission. Their fateful meeting would influence the next thirteen years of her life, during which she maintained a long and painful liaison with Hapgood (see chapter 7).

Pesotta often spoke at meetings of the strikers, lending them the support of her own union and leading them in union songs. She became the chair of the strike's entertainment committee and served as a source of encouragement and support during some of the more difficult moments. Pesotta toured the strike shanties and tents daily to converse with the strikers and to sing inspirational songs with them.[10] Rose had Fannia Cohn send ILGWU song booklets so that she and the strikers could relax and sing together while huddled next to bonfires, trying to keep warm.

Pesotta also reached the workers with the use of her movie camera. She was given a large amount of film with which to record action shots that could be used as educational and propaganda material pertaining to the strike. The strikers were eager to pose for her camera. Her established reputation was enhanced as she prowled the streets gathering useful footage for the union.

Pesotta was similarly involved in convincing the workers that the agreement worked out with Goodyear was an excellent one and should be ratified. She went from picket site to picket site explaining the agreement and urging ratification. Although there were efforts on the part of members of the Communist party to undermine the agreement, it was ratified, and Pesotta was part of the jubilant celebration. Because of her success, she was sent immediately to Detroit to work with the United Automobile Workers of America (UAW).[11] In the spring of 1936, Rose was aglow with the thrill of being effective in her work and deeply in love with Powers.

Conditions for auto workers had been quite difficult before the unionization efforts by the UAW. Wages had been cut below the cost of living, and working conditions were dangerous. A series of unorganized revolts by the workers between 1932 and 1934 had been quickly defeated, but small locals were established as a result of these strikes.[12] It did not take long before the AFL enlisted thousands of workers to join these locals, which they reorganized into federal unions.

When Pesotta entered the scene, she was immediately called to help with the sit-down strike at the Fisher Body Works in Flint in 1937. Rose went into the occupied buildings and spoke to the strikers concerning their efforts and demands. Again, she energized them with her songs and spirit. She later returned to run the strike headquarters, during which time the strikers were being arrested.[13] Pesotta played an important role in many of the negotiations, as well as providing a stock of winter clothing for the strikers.[14] Being sent by the CIO along with organizers from other locals to offer the support of their unions, Rose totally immersed herself in the effort. She worked alongside Adolph Germer, Leo Krzycki, and Powers Hapgood as the "four musketeers" who went everywhere together while supporting the strikers. It was exhilarating for her to be involved with these men, who were noted in their own unions as hard hitters. Rose was working with the "big boys" of the union movement.

The Flint strike was a particularly violent one, with a great deal of intimidation on the part of the owners and the police. Nevertheless, Pesotta continued to participate even in the face of physical danger. Although she never wrote of it, it was during this strike that thugs attacked and beat her, which caused a serious hearing impairment that forced Pesotta to wear a hearing aid and use a large microphone for the rest of her life. Rose's vanity and modesty kept her from writing of this in her later memoirs.[15]

Unionists occupied various plant buildings, and Pesotta found herself running, along with other supporters, from building to building, trying to aid the workers in any way possible. They brought in food,

FIGURE 10

Four musketeers—Akron sit-down, 1936.

Left to right,
seated: Leo Kryzcki, Vice President, Amalgamated Clothing Workers
Adolph Germer, Organizer for United Mine Workers
Standing: Rose Pesotta, Vice President, ILGWU
Powers Hapgood, Organizer for United Mine Workers

Photo courtesy of Fanya Peisoty Bimbat.

FIGURE 11

Rose Pesotta, November 10, 1937.

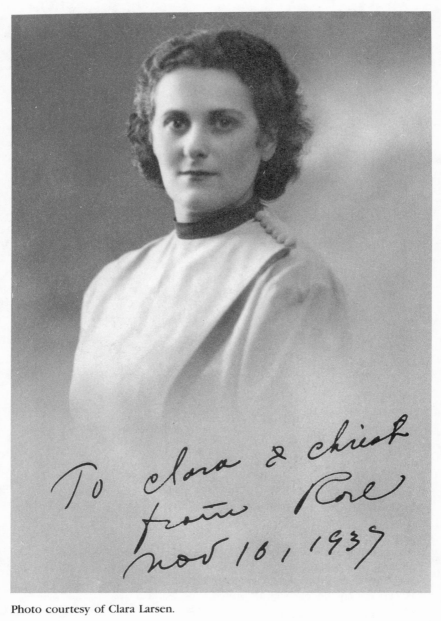

Photo courtesy of Clara Larsen.

clothing, supplies, and much-needed moral support. At times she worked with the Women's Emergency Brigade, a group of mothers, sisters, and daughters of the unionists, who did outstanding support work. Pesotta often entered the seized buildings to lend advice to the occupiers.

Eventually a warrant was issued for Rose's arrest. She was called "Miss Rose Partola" in the warrant and was listed with Roy Reuther and other activists. Pesotta was in good company in this situation, having obviously done enough effective work to call attention to herself. She seemed to revel in the excitement. Delighted when the strike was finally settled, Pesotta was among the CIO and UAW leaders who went to the occupied factory to lead the workers out. "When the main gate of No. 1 was thrown open, they came out singing, led by their band and with many carrying American flags. Tremendous cheers went up as they emerged." The atmosphere was like a Mardi Gras. The strike had been won after forty-four days of occupation. Pesotta was so moved by the event that tears of gladness streamed down her cheeks.[16]

The years 1936 and 1937 were busy ones for Pesotta as she also shuttled between Michigan and Montreal, having involved herself in strikes and organizing efforts in Montreal to reach ten thousand dress-makers between her stints in Michigan. In September of 1936, Pesotta organized bilingual radio broadcasts in Montreal to recruit for the ILGWU. Immediately, she ran into the ire of the Roman Catholic Church, which had helped the factory owners organize their own company unions or syndicates.[17] Again, she was labeled an "outside agitator," but she tried hard not to antagonize the church, in view of the enormous power it wielded. As an anarchist, Pesotta was an atheist ideologically opposed to organized religion. Nonetheless, she knew of the respect her strikers felt for the church and of the means the church would use on its own behalf. Pragmatic as she was, she called the workers' attention to the fact that other Catholic priests in the United States sided with the work-ers, not the owners, on issues of industrial conflict. She did not argue against the church, but instead used the teachings of the church for her own purposes.[18] Her tactics paid off, because eventually the strikers rallied behind her, and by early 1937 they had won.

Pesotta was practical and knew how to speak to the workers in their own language. She was willing to compromise her principles to reach attainable goals. In Montreal, her technique was conciliation, careful lan-guage, and demure behavior. It seemed to work, and she was willing to hold her own views in check in order to establish a union. In fact, in all her organizing she was always careful, rarely acting impulsively and with-out forethought. It was in her personal life, as we shall see, that she was far more spontaneous.

Again, in this campaign, Pesotta took the job as hall "chairman" of strike headquarters. This job generally entailed building up the spirits of the strikers and providing them with general information. Rose organized concerts, lectures, and picket lines in which the strikers were dressed in their Sunday-best clothing to make a positive impression on the daily shopping crowd. When the sit-down strike in Flint broke out, Pesotta rushed back to the United States. After the Flint victory, Rose returned to Canada to work with the Montreal dressmakers. When a general strike of the industry was finally called in April 1937, over five thousand women were striking one hundred shops. The city had never before witnessed a strike by women on such a large scale. It commanded a great deal of attention and antagonized the church even further. Priests called for her deportation from Canada, even going so far as attacking her from church pulpits.[19] But Pesotta had won the confidence of many French-Canadian women, some of whom spoke publicly and privately on her behalf.

On 1 May 1937, Pesotta was tipped off that she was about to be arrested. She handled the situation in her own inimitable way by finding a hiding place that would never occur to the male police establishment. Rose spent the day under a hair dryer at a beauty salon, ordering a facial, manicure, and as many services as possible so that she could continue hiding. Later in the day, she ate in a secluded restaurant, then continued her hiding at a movie. The warrant was not served, but Rose experienced a loneliness: "Weeks of cumulative fatigue and loneliness were having their effect. I felt like a castaway on a desert island, not knowing when rescuers would come."[20]

Shortly thereafter, her efforts were rewarded, however. The strike was settled victoriously. To celebrate, Rose decided to attend the ILGWU's national convention in Atlantic City. There she and the large Montreal delegation marched triumphantly to the platform with a brass band preceding them. They received a standing ovation from the assemblage. It was one of Pesotta's greatest moments.[21] The event was compared to the marching citizens of Marseilles during the French Revolution. Pesotta had finally participated in her own revolution.

After being reelected for yet another term as vice president, Pesotta was sent by Dubinsky to work on the Cleveland Knitting Mill strike during the spring and summer of 1937. Although she was only to have been there two weeks, the strike was particularly violent, and she was forced to remain for almost five months. Again she was arrested, this time on disorderly conduct charges. Pesotta was particularly proud of a photo taken during that arrest. In it, she is seen wearing white gloves: ever the lady, even in her militancy.[22] During this strike, Pesotta was slashed with a razor by company hired thugs, and the wound required several stitches to close. Rose remembered:

FIGURE 12

Montreal, 1937. Organizing staff "mapping out plan for general strike."

Left to right: Paul Furnier, Organizer Milinary International
Rose Pesotta, ILGWU Vice President
Bernard Shane, ILGWU General Organizer
Claude Jodoim, Organizer Montreal Dressmakers Union

Photo by Charlab. Courtesy of Dorothy, Elias, and Edward Rotker.

When I opened the phone booth door, four strange women
blocked my way. Dodging to escape a blow in the face, I felt a
stinging pain above my left eye, and pain, too, in my left knee. Warm
liquid streamed down over my face, blinding me, and I toppled
over.[23]

Undaunted, Pesotta was offered a pistol by one of the women strikers to
protect herself, but chose to remain weaponless, perhaps carrying out
her philosophical anarchism in its respect for all human life. She was
repeatedly arrested and one day decided to act deranged so the police
would leave her alone. She harangued them, talking quickly in a high-
pitched voice, and insulted the captain. In fact, her friend who had come
to bail her out feared for her mental state. However, the ruse worked, and
she was no longer harassed.[24]

By the end of 1937, Pesotta was exhausted by her repeated travels
and difficult work. She took a short vacation in Europe from December to
February 1938. While there, she made important political contacts with
Emma Goldman and her anarchist friends, all then deeply involved with
the Spanish civil war. Rose was invited by anarchists to Spain to see for
herself the work that was being done. Goldman had arranged for her to
receive the invitation and a visa. However, Pesotta was ordered back to
the United States by Dubinsky to engage in yet another labor effort.
Pesotta chose to return to the States, realizing too late that she had made
the wrong decision. She later wrote: "All too obediently, it seems to me
now, I responded to that summons."[25] Rose was still the dutiful daughter
in relation to Dubinsky and the union. She continued to do as she was
told and thus gained favor in the eyes of Dubinsky and the other vice
presidents on the GEB.

Upon returning to the United States, Pesotta spent two very difficult
years living and working in Boston. Rose had lived there off and on since
1916, and her sister Esther and family resided there. The ladies garment
industry in that city had been poorly organized, and she had to begin
with nothing. Boston was seen as a graveyard for organizers.[26] The treasury of the union was depleted, and the membership had dwindled. Rose
set up a more attractive union headquarters, recruited various crafts to
set up locals, and reestablished the education department. She tried to
revitalize the union by breathing her life and energy into it. Again Pesotta
was arrested, this time for distributing leaflets for the union. She challenged the arrest—later lost—and had to pay the small fine. Within two
years, Pesotta managed to get a contract developed. She again worked
with various ethnic groups, including Syrians, Irish, Italians, and Jews.
She even set up a sewing school to retrain workers for other jobs, and, as

usual, Rose threw parties, dances, style shows, and festivals. Her colleagues in these projects were Philip Kramer and her niece Dorothy Rubin, who served as an executive secretary. Pesotta felt successful in that the dressmakers' union was now a viable and healthy one. When Rose left Boston, the 24 December 1939 issue of the *Boston Globe* reported:

> Rose Pesotta, a comely miss whose figure and appearance belie her 43 years, known to labor leaders as an ardent worker in the needle trades vineyard and to police and some employers as a firecracker who knows her rights and stands for them, is being wined and dined by the members of the International Ladies Garment Workers Union during these last few days before she leaves to organize needle workers in Los Angeles.
>
> For two years Rose Pesotta has personified and symbolized the garment workers in Boston and although her transfer to Los Angeles is a promotion—a bigger job—both employers and employees will be sorry to see her go.[27]

With this type of recognition and fame, Rose was not pleased when in January 1940 her next assignment came through—a return to Los Angeles.

Pesotta's work in Boston was typical of the leadership style she had used successfully throughout the 1930s. In all of her work as a labor organizer, Rose always believed that her job was "to lay the groundwork, organize the unorganized, establish a union, and train the workers to take care of themselves." This was her "idea of union leadership."[28] Her style embodied her anarchist beliefs and was conveyed through her personality, which was egalitarian in dealing with workers. She was seen as a charismatic and natural leader. Years later Gus Tyler, ILGWU vice president, said of her:

> As a rank and filer, she was a natural leader because of her profound conviction, her inflammatory personality, her startling appearance, her gift of speech, and, above all, her innate love and sympathy for people. She was born to lead. She was fated to rise from the machine and to guide her fellow workers in the age old struggle for human dignity.[29]

As a leader, she maintained warm and cordial relationships with her coworkers and with the rank and file. Wherever she went, she was well liked and warmly received. She attracted many to the ILGWU because of her inspirational style. Often her followers went beyond mere affection, according her devotion and reverence. The *Boston Globe* article noted that six thousand Boston workers idolized her. As a successful organizer, she served as a role model for others, often putting herself on the line before them. Pesotta offered encouragement and support, while she provided education and empowered workers who had never before taken their work lives into their own hands so forcefully. In her work with staff and peers in the various locals, Pesotta was well liked and thought of highly; when she was left alone and in charge of activities she was at her very best. Without impediments or control by others, Pesotta shone.

Pesotta was often faced with adversity in her work. Nonetheless, she knew herself, her capabilities, and her capacity for endurance.[30] She felt that "inner strength came from years of experience, that no matter how small the achievements might be, in spite of the adversities, one had to go on." She took her strength from the belief that if a person "is dedicated to a cause so great as to embrace the welfare of humanity nothing is too degrading, nothing too trivial, nothing too lowly, whether one has to work with brain or brawn for the ultimate goal."[31]

Tyler noted:

> As a leader and officer she was an inveterate rank and filer. She was an officer of the union who distrusted officialdom. As a top official—indeed as a vice president—she feared that the higher one moved, the more likely was one to forget roots, origins, and purpose. Although a great believer in organization—indeed she was a superb organizer—nevertheless, she worried that too much organization could choke freedom of the spirit. . . .
>
> Rose Pesotta was in an eternal and internal conflict: born leader and innate rank and filer, she was one to whom workers turned as an authority, while she held fast to the anarchist distrust of all authority.
>
> Rose resolved the conflict between leader and rank and filer by being both—at different times and sometimes at the same time. Because she was both, there was none too high for her to assault and none too lowly for her to champion.[32]

One of Rose's greatest difficulties was with fellow anarchists, who saw her as a turncoat for having accepted a paid position in the union. An article in *Man* of January 1934, edited by Marcus Graham, said, "Whenever and wherever individual anarchists deviate from the cause and accept paid official jobs, they cease by such very acts to be part of the anarchist movement, which has at all times an uncompromising ideal to live for and to fight for."[33] In a letter to Hippolyte Havel in February of that year, Rose said she saw this as referring to herself and lamented how anarchists had reached the "state of Jesuits and Communists for ostracizing heretics or those who fail to comply with official ruling of the high tribunal."[34] She argued that anarchists had an important place in the unions as people who should disagree with officialdom and criticize their tactics if the criticism was warranted. Rose often did so, writing to Dubinsky whenever she felt he had done or said something inappropriate. To Havel, she said she felt that inasmuch as anarchists believed in the general strike as an organizing tactic, she should be among the masses when they were ready to rise. She said, "We must work within *these* [capitalistic trade unions] institutions to inject some of our own ideas. We must use these trade unions as a means to an end—the end being a free society."[35] She practiced what she preached by showing workers how to operate cooperatively, and often argued her radical politics without calling it "anarchism" per se. Rose had no sympathy for those who believed that they should live out on "some deserted farm and grow cabbages," arguing that instead anarchists should work and live "among the people, among the very downtrodden rabble for whom our ideal is the very thing." "Isn't it a fact," she wrote, "that anarchism is based on the human side of life and the workers are human?"

In this important letter on her anarchist philosophy, Rose goes on to say:

Living in capitalist society we understand that all anarchists have to compromise at one end or another. I have known some uncompromising anarchists who refused to be exploited by capitalists. Hence they lived on the labor of their brethren—other anarchists who knowing that by this method they will not abolish capitalism worked and supported their more idealistic, uncompromising comrades.

Peter Kropotkin said he would join the syndicalist movement to work among the masses if he were young. Not having such a movement in this century would he refuse to participate on the existing movement and abstain to work among the masses.

I do not expect the editor of *Man* nor any other man to hold brief to my activities in the labor movement. Nor do we (myself and comrade Anna Sosnovsky [Ed. note—also criticized in the article]) consider ourself out of the anarchist movement. We have come to the workers at their request to help them in their crisis and we have done as much as was physically possible for any human being to do in such time. It takes courage and conviction.

I feel if we would join him in his barking and acquire his brand of anarchism we would die of incest.

She concluded:

I still hold that anarchism is a human philosophy; we must have intercourse with human beings, we must actively participate in all social events. We must be among the people and teach them our ideal in practice, instead of fostering hatred and mistrust. We must be ready at any time to work and teach workers to use their initiative instead of following in blind obedience, if we consider the labor movements as a means to an end, we shall work within this labor movement to obtain our goal."[36]

It should be noted that Marcus Graham was notorious in his attacks on fellow anarchists. Indeed, he even attacked Emma Goldman upon publication of her autobiography in 1938. Goldman, too, saw him as a "moral censor and a judge of comrades."[37] Even with such attacks, Rose remained politically active in anarchist circles throughout her labor organizing days. Anarchist friends and activities were at the center of her political and personal life.

There has long been some question by comrades and some contemporary anarchists as to whether or not Rose should be called an anarchist, because of some of her positions. On many counts, Rose was willing to compromise; she was always pragmatic and resourceful in her behavior. Rose's conflict with anarchists in journals and through letters caused her much dismay, because to her—through her work—she was living her anarchism. She also maintained an active involvement in anarchist circles throughout her labor activities, keeping up a correspondence with her long-time friends Emma Goldman, Mollie Steimer, and other anarchists around the world. Pesotta knew that workers were more concerned with "bread-and-butter issues" than with theory. She often turned to David Dubinsky to use his pull on behalf of anarchist causes that might not otherwise be heard. In one instance, in 1935, she recruited his aid on behalf of Rudolf Rocker, an anarchist theoretician who was about to be deported from the United States.[38] Pesotta was practical and believed in forming alliances with those who might not meet with the satisfaction of her anarchist revolutionary comrades.

The more pragmatic and resourceful Pesotta became, the less ideological and revolutionary an anarchist she appeared. For example, the

NIRA was a product of government regulation of the conditions of work-ers. Anarchists are ideally opposed to any government, let alone govern-ment intervention. However, Rose knew how dreadful work conditions were and knew something had to be done. Even though she believed that government was the source of all evil, she decided to use the NIRA and work with it to ameliorate working conditions. She was realistic enough to know that revolution was not imminent and that one had to work on attainable and concrete goals, using any means necessary, including working with the government. At no time did she refuse to engage in any activities on the grounds that they were contrary to anarchist ideology. The more effective Pesotta became in her work, the less anarchistic she became in her actions. For this she has been called a "union bureaucrat" and accused of becoming part of the authoritarian union machine. Rose's ideals were still there, but she made the choice to be practical and down to earth based on her experience and real-life understanding of how the world operated. She had also developed an underlying pessimism regard-ing revolutionary change. Anarchism was her ideal, pragmatism was her strategy.

Because Pesotta was willing to compromise, there were times in her work when she did not mention that she was an anarchist and would not sell anarchist leaflets, fearful of antagonizing the workers.[39] She told the workers she was a "revolutionary," because she felt they were not ready to hear the truth.[40] Indeed, she was actually not really revolution-ary, in that she did not engage in violent or illegal activities. Nonetheless, she sensed that if they heard the word *anarchist,* they would disbelieve her ideas. She chose to reach them on issues that were close to their own situation and in words that were familiar and understandable to them. This was also cause for Pesotta to be chastised by other anarchists: Some felt that she did not spend enough time working for their movement. However, anarchism—its people and its ideas—was central to all of Rose's activities and was a life focus for her. She spent many years work-ing in anarchist groups, and the criticism pained her, often adding to her loneliness.

In addition to being in conflict with her political comrades, Pesotta also increasingly ran into difficulties with David Dubinsky and with the GEB in general. One, which may have looked trivial, was certainly based on the sexism of the union officials. In 1938, Rose was sanctioned for spending too much money on the Boston organizing drive. She was told that she was too lavish in her gift giving, which included buying exotic fruits from California and providing lunch for an entire basketball team.[41] After the latter incident, she was put on a per diem allowance, which curbed her spending. Pesotta engaged in what was a female brand of organizing. She believed in music, dancing, and parties as unifying tactics for reaching the workers. The men in power, DD and the finance officers, particularly, did not understand those approaches and instead saw her as extravagant and lavish. In fact, they were trivializing her efforts. Pesotta ran into trouble here, as one of the few female organizers who knew how to reach her workers' lives. It seems that Dubinsky and the others were not as committed to organizing women workers as she was. They were not willing to pay out the money to bring anyone into the union on other than "bread and butter" issues. At best, DD appears ambivalent, wanting the new women unionists, but not willing to pay for their participation. Dubinsky, in fact, was beginning to sabotage Pesotta's work.[42]

Later in 1941, Pesotta and DD had another financial run-in on her spending in Los Angeles. In that interaction, she wrote to him:

> If you repeat that I ought to be in jail for spending so much I will agree with you, for the work I have put into this joint, for the efforts to make the place habitable enough to attract new members, and keep those we have already organized, for all this your kind gratitude—I ought to be in jail instead of here. . . . My dear president, you of all people know how much you dumped into this city and the results you have made during the past seven years; you should be the last one to reprimand us now—*because you have a union now, not a racket.* . . . Is it any wonder I am so proud of my work? I have put into this field more than the ILGWU funds—I have put in my health and my very soul. Go ahead and send me to jail for it, nothing would please me more than being jailed for organizing these women.[43]

In 1939, Rose was outspoken in her criticism of Dubinsky for apparently allowing the *Journal American*, a Hearst newspaper, to print a story on himself and the ILGWU. Rose, as an anarchist, was openly dismayed that Dubinsky let a "yellow, violently anti-labor and reactionary paper" write about them. In her experience, "Hearst papers have attacked us, blamed the ILGWU and organizers for instigating strikes and causing people to lose their jobs." She felt that "printing your story is giving the dying Hearst papers a new lease on life."[44] In this letter, Rose's outspokenness is apparent. She acknowledged that she was being blunt and even added that in their union they had come to "mistake servility for service, sensationalism for fame, one man rule for statesmanship, genius for outstanding leadership." She went on to lambast Dubinsky by saying that the "head of the organization has become one man rule[;] and members, for fear of losing his favors, refrain from expressing honest opinions. We have developed cliques who keep within themselves and rule from above." It was at this point that Rose began to suggest that there be a limited tenure of office on the GEB so that new and dynamic forces could move to the forefront, thereby strengthening union morale. Pesotta let her anarchist voice be heard by Dubinsky and the GEB, this time by urging an anarchist idea of rotation of leadership. She recognized that the union had become bureaucratized and merely a reformist organization; this caused her great dismay. She wanted to see it change, and her colleagues vehemently resisted.

In this letter, Pesotta let all her dissatisfactions come to the surface. She mentioned that the ILGWU had recently entered electoral politics, including allowing paid organizers to work for a mayoral campaign in Boston. Such political activities are anathema to most anarchists.

But most of all, Pesotta began to voice her dismay with the position of women within the union. She cited the fact that women's names were cut out of *Justice*, the ILGWU's official publication, in order to save space. "Only a negligible few get mention," while countless others remain obscure. Rose gave as an example Fannia Cohn, who was "recognized on the outside for her contribution and unselfish efforts to the cause of workers education. She is a tragic figure among fellow workers. Were she a man it would be different." Pesotta was totally dismayed by the fact that "several top leaders are 'noodnicks' who get too much recognition. Even my reports in *Justice* (and I am a Vice President not just a plain member) were given under the name of a local manager. But I refused to ghost write so a number of good reports went to the waste basket instead of print."

Pesotta felt that as a woman vice president she was fulfilling her responsibilities to the rank and file by voicing her complaints to Dubinsky. She made it a point to urge that "no baby kissing, pretty girl photos, trophy for sports or banquets can give the membership more aid and comfort than feeling that elected leadership is honest, efficient, and sincerely rendering a service." And she hoped that her letter would be taken as a statement "with malice toward none, with hope that some good will come of it later."[45] Dubinsky's response to this missive was not recorded. However, we do know that one month later, Pesotta was transferred to Los Angeles, her own objections overruled, perhaps in retaliation for her diatribe. We also know that years later, Pesotta would write of Dubinsky in her autobiography and would try to portray him fairly. She noted that he was an "individual with strong feelings; sensitive and impulsive, he could alternately be ruthless or break into tears of humility."[46] She felt that he did not always understand situations as she did, because he was miles away, and she felt that she took liberties and made decisions that would sometimes run counter to her superior's instructions. Nonethe-

less, she found that "when there was a reckoning afterward, DD accepted
the situation like a sportsman."[47] On paper, Pesotta portrayed him in a
balanced style, but, according to her family and friends, she came to
vehemently dislike Dubinsky and found it quite difficult to deal with
him.[48] She came to view him as a sellout and a compromiser, eventually
losing respect for him. Publically she always maintained institutional
loyalty by not criticizing the union's top leader in public discourse.

In many ways, Pesotta's relationship with Dubinsky appears to have
been much like that with her father. Her writings indicate that, on the
one hand, she admired and needed both of them; on the other hand, she
was angered by their authority and power over her. Clearly he often
acted like the punitive father to her. Her respect was mixed with resentment and often played itself out in ambivalent behavior. At times, she was
the dutiful daughter and underling; at other moments, she was fiercely
independent and assertive, even when faced with their growing dismay
over her activities and attitudes. In the final act of her relationship with
Dubinsky, she would do as she did with her father. She left rather than
continue to be subservient and servile.

Rose's relationships with other men in the union and on the GEB
were strained. In 1933, Pesotta wrote, "Our late President Schlesinger
once told your humble servant to stop this kind of business and go home
and get married. I hate to hear that from an employer."[49] Despite this,
Rose was able to maintain very close working relationships with many of
the men she encountered during the course of her labor activities; further, as we shall note later, at times she became intimately involved with
some of them. At other points, Rose actually intimidated a number of
men with whom she worked. According to her sister Esther, Rose was
really sent to Los Angeles in 1940 because her old colleague Philip
Kramer had become jealous of her success in Boston and asked that she
be transferred.[50] This is questionable in that Kramer did write to Dubinsky asking that she be allowed to remain in Boston. Her best friend, Clara
Rothberg Larsen, remembered that a number of the organizers were
jealous of her because "she was educated" and they were not.[51] It is
certainly true that in the final organizing effort in which Rose was involved, in Los Angeles, conflict with Louis Levy would lead to her departure from the ILGWU: first, as an organizer; later, as a vice president.
Pesotta's relationships with men in general resembled those with her
father and Dubinsky. She would first be subservient and then, eventually,
gain her voice and the strength to become independent. She often ended
up leaving when the relationships became difficult, much as she had
done with her father. She would try to alter a situation, but when she saw
the futility, she would move on to another activity and location. This

accounts for a number of her quick moves during her organizing years, running away from bad relationships, trying to make a new start some- where else. Pesotta left Los Angeles the first time, as well as running off to Montreal, for just such reasons.

Rose's problems in the union were more than the product of her successes, education, and personality. She was also the victim of fac- tionalism. As an anarchist among increasingly conservative male vice presidents, she hardly stood a chance. As the male contingent became more reformist and centrist in orientation, Pesotta moved into a position of marginality. The factions that had been battling since the 1920s in the ILGWU were still at work, although less explosively; and Pesotta, always outspoken and forceful, confronted the issues whenever she deemed it imperative. For this she was seen as a troublemaker, one who would not keep quiet and had something to say about everything.

By the late 1930s, Pesotta was obviously having trouble on the General Executive Board. The minutes of the quarterly meetings rarely reflected Pesotta's attendance,[52] though she had carefully recorded her own presence. Even when she was listed as present, her comments were not always recorded, so that we have no way of knowing just what her exact input was. In 1937 when she was nominated for reelection, there was no seconding speech, as there had been for the previous nominees.[53] At the next meeting of the GEB, Pesotta's most significant input was to remind the board that the convention members had asked the GEB to participate in a commemoration for the fiftieth anniversary of the Hay- market event.[54] Little record appears that would document just how she operated at these meetings. It is obvious that she either said little or had minimal impact on what went on. We do know that later, in her resigna- tion letter, she referred to the "peanut politics" that were played within the GEB.[55] She felt that many of the leaders of the union were provincial, small, and petty, and she confided to friends that she was losing patience with the "old men" on the board.[56] The complexity of internal union politics was wreaking havoc with Pesotta's involvement on the GEB. She often stated that she wished the old men would resign so that new blood could take over. It was clear that she had little impact on what went on in the GEB and in influencing the other vice presidents.

Rose's personal problems with the GEB were not due solely to her personality or to factionalism. Sexism was perhaps the most crucial fac- tor in Pesotta's demise. Women in such positions either were seen as difficult or were forced to conform without power.[57] "Indeed they [unions] often insisted that women accede to the prevailing male meth- ods and goals and interpreted women's attempts to find new paths to loyalty and participation as subversive."[58] Pesotta was inevitably viewed

as subversive and unstable, because she dared challenge the powers that
be, alone and unsupported. As Alice Kessler Harris argues, the ILGWU
accepted women's activities until the women, building on their own
sense of priorities, began to demand democratic participation or insider
status. Women, having their own culture, based on gender, were not
easily assimilated into this male-dominated union. To women, issues besides bread and butter were crucial, and the men on the GEB failed to
grasp the importance of including these issues on the union's agenda.
Women needed a sense of belonging. Often they were excluded from the
higher-status positions of skilled workers like cutters and pattern makers.
As a victim of gender politics, Rose was on the losing end. Indeed, as a
woman representing women workers, she had become a "voice lost in
the wilderness," as she feared she would.

Pesotta's experience is not unlike that of women in other unions at
the time. In the UAW in 1937, women were lobbying for there being at
least one woman on the Executive Board and for being allowed to participate in the union as full-fledged members.[59] The UAW regarded women
as less than equal partners in the auto industry and had never systemat-
ically developed a program to organize women. In wages, job classifica-
tion, and seniority issues, as in the ILGWU, the UAW fostered male-
majority interests over those of the women.[60] Not surprisingly, although
the UAW hired very few female unionists as organizers, when women
were thus engaged they used a style similar to Pesotta's, including organizing all-women social activities where "women could assert themselves
without fear of male criticism or condescension."[61] This even included
holding a woman's style show, similar to what Pesotta did.[62] One woman
was able to reach heights similar to Pesotta's, within the UAW. Patricia
Wiseman, who had been at the General Motors plant in Flint, Michigan,
went on to become the sole woman on the union's bargaining committee
during the GM-UAW conference following the strike.[63] But for the most
part, it was not until the 1940s that women in the UAW were able "to
mount a serious challenge to sexual inequality in the auto industry."[64]

Pesotta's most difficult experience with the men in power came
when she was sent to Los Angeles, over her objections, by Dubinsky in
January 1940. Her Boston colleagues were not pleased, but she was told
that it would be a temporary assignment. Instead what occurred in Los
Angeles would demoralize Pesotta and lead her to give up her public
career entirely.

The labor situation in 1940 had changed dramatically as a result of
U.S. involvement in World War II. The economy began to boom, and
there were increasing demands for labor. First, the United States aided
the Allies and developed national defense programs, which led to an

industrial boom and national prosperity. As the demand for labor grew stronger, labor unions were determined to capture the new workers to their ranks. Labor energetically cooperated with government and industry in the growing war effort. However, the situation before World War II was not exceptionally good for women garment workers. Sometimes women were thrown out of work as materials were diverted to the defense buildup. Nonetheless, organizing among women garment workers continued.

Louis Levy, the Pacific Coast director of the ILGWU, had been hospitalized, and in January 1940, Pesotta was asked to serve as replacement until his recovery. Immediately, she engaged in one of the most colorful pickets she would ever establish. Because the image of the garment workers was deteriorating, Pesotta decided, early in her stay, to set up a picket at the Market Week and Style Show, a gala style show to be held at a posh hotel during Rose's first week in town. She arranged to have present twelve attractive union women, some dressed in white gowns and velvet coats, others wearing colorful full-length gowns and furs. They looked like "Park Avenue debutantes."[65] Dressed in their fancy attire, the women carried picket signs as they marched around in the street outside. They were protesting the unfair labor practices of the manufacturers who were exhibiting their wares at the fashion show. The scene was photographed, instantly gaining Pesotta favorable press coverage, which once again increased her credibility.

But Pesotta's problems in Los Angeles began promptly after the demonstration. Members of Levy's family, who were also members of the Communist party, attacked her for carrying out the demonstration without their approval. Later, she found that some people on the union payroll did nothing more than recruit members for the Communist party. She met resistance in trying to remove them. She also found that union meetings were run by a select group of people, who would not allow the noncommunists to participate equally.[66] As she scratched below the surface, she discovered countless problems with the local she had originally organized in 1933; Pesotta set out to clean house. She felt that recruitment of new members had been lacking, and tried to right that situation. "Retraining schools" to keep the workers educated on new techniques in the industry were also on her agenda. In the process, she alienated a number of people.

The plant that Pesotta chose to organize as a test case for the newly established sportswear industry was the Mode O'Day Company owned by the Malouf family. First she recruited members to a local that was established in the factory. She then published a weekly newsletter to keep the workers informed. The effort was so successful that when Dubi-

nsky was on the West Coast in the spring of 1941, he made it a point to
present the charter to the local officials himself.[67]

Pesotta also took measures to educate various appropriate workers
to positions of power within the union, which would allow them to take
over the operations of the local once she chose to leave. One such
worker was Susan Adams, descendant of the American presidential family,
who became one of Rose's staunchest supporters.

As Pesotta later saw it, problems with Levy and his wife developed
soon after her arrival in Los Angeles. Pesotta felt that Levy was "a hen-
pecked husband, he meekly submitted to the whims of his wife, a domi-
neering person who ruled that our union's business be conducted from
the Levy home, and who injected herself into affairs of which she had not
the slightest understanding."[68] The industry was divided so that Pesotta
was left in charge of sportswear, while other organizers were assigned to
the dressmakers' division. Pesotta felt that she had many political enemies in Los Angeles. She wrote to her friend Rae Brandstein on 9 August
1941 that she sometimes had to "do a man's job to prove to my colleagues [in L.A.] that a woman vice president has nine lives and so I
showed them."[69] As usual, she was acutely aware of the "difference" in
her position as the only woman vice president. She discovered that a
number of people whom she saw as "emissaries of the Soviet Union" were
actually trying to "bury her."[70] Although effective in gaining numbers for
the ILGWU, she began to feel ill and squeezed out of the scene.[71] Having
considered leaving because of the many hard days and sleepless nights
she spent, Pesotta felt she was not gaining any recognition for all her hard
work. She was alone, out in the wilderness, far from her support and
factional alliances.

In her struggle to overcome the "Communist establishment" in Los
Angeles, Rose, as usual, found allies in unusual quarters. This time she
made contacts with the movie industry and became a personal associate
of Melvyn Douglas and Helen Gahagan. She had both of them speak to
her workers and enlisted them in support of her union work. She also
worked with Edward G. Robinson and Douglas Fairbanks, Jr., as well as
extras and stunt crews on various film sets. Because Rose involved anyone she could who might aid her, she set out to meet these people and
engage them in conversation; she studied their lives, their work, and
their problems. It made her life more interesting and added insights from
worlds she had never before seen. Unfortunately, it did not stop the tide
that was building against her.

When Levy began to recover, he attempted to reassert himself in
the Mode O'Day situation. Without full knowledge of the situation, Pesotta alleged, Levy went to the owners of Mode O'Day to negotiate, thereby

undermining the work already done by the local officials. This dismayed the workers, who had not been informed of the meeting. Pesotta had to calm down the workers after Levy's alleged blunder. Eventually, Dubinsky wrote Malouf, the owner of Mode O'Day, to intervene on behalf of the Mode O'Day local.[72]

Mode O'Day had been a difficult shop to organize. It was virulently antiunion, but nonetheless was 99 percent unionized by the time the crisis between Levy and Pesotta arose. By March of 1942, antagonism between Levy and his Communist forces and Pesotta and her allies had reached gigantic proportions. Both sides were writing and calling Dubinsky to explain their versions. Levy alleged that Pesotta had organized hostility among the workers toward him. He felt that Pesotta was instigating trouble.[73] She appealed to Dubinsky to allow her full freedom to organize "one shop in one city" and to be fully responsible without interference from Levy. Forces on Pesotta's side sent letters to Dubinsky begging that she be given power in Mode O'Day, on the grounds that Levy made so many "blunders and tried to force his methods and personality into a situation he knew nothing about."[74]

Dubinsky tried to be impartial. At one point, he told Levy that "results will be obtained in my judgement not by issuing orders from the top but by consulting and advising with them [the workers] pertaining to shop matters and any dealings with employers."[75] In December 1941, he got to the point of telling Pesotta not to do anything until he could come to Los Angeles himself to assess the situation.[76] He was becoming quite distressed with the situation.

Dubinsky received information from various sources that indicated neither side was blameless. In February 1942, Clifford Gill, a male organizer hired by Pesotta, wrote to say that "Rose is a wonderful organizer but a poor executive."[77] She had, the letter continued, "followed the tactics of a jealous woman, who, if she cannot have a certain man, murders him so no one else can have him. Rose is determined to leave only the shreds of a union to Levy, no matter what she tells you. . . . She advised staff members to resign before Levy fired them. She told them 'only the stooges are staying.'"[78] In this letter, Gill turned against his mentor and might well have moved Dubinsky in making his later decision on this conflictual situation. Levy wrote to Dubinsky during the same month to "get her out of Los Angeles immediately before the [work] stoppage is called and irreparable damage is done."[79]

Pesotta's forces, including the entire executive board of the Mode O'Day local, wrote in February 1942 to Dubinsky to insist that he intervene so that Rose could stay in Los Angeles to participate in the local's negotiations with the Maloufs. They argued that Rose truly knew their situation in a way that Levy did not. They were afraid that their position would be weakened with Rose's departure.[80] They also passed a resolution outlining their objections to Levy for going over their heads to the boss, for demanding their confidential General Executive Board minutes, and for not understanding their situation. Levy responded by saying that he felt his thirty-seven years in labor meant that he did not need to study their most unique condition.[81]

It is not quite clear whether Pesotta chose to resign or did so at the suggestion of Dubinsky. On 10 March 1941, Pesotta wrote to Dubinsky saying, "Whatever is going on in the union has nothing to do with me, in accordance with your decision."[82] At a meeting between DD, Levy, and Pesotta in early February 1942, Levy had said there was no room for two vice presidents on the West Coast and wanted her removed.[83] It appears that Pesotta was asked to resign in order to avoid further conflict. On the other hand, she had written to many friends that it was time to move on. So it is possible that she, too, saw that the differences were irreconcilable. Pesotta later told others that she chose to resign, but that statement might have very well been made to save her pride and to protect the union's image. It remains unclear as to why DD chose Levy over Pesotta, except perhaps that Levy was the West Coast vice president and Pesotta had been brought in only to assist during his illness. It could also mean that Pesotta was increasingly being seen as difficult and a troublemaker. Whatever the reason, Dubinsky clearly chose to side with Levy on this battle.

There was a testimonial for Pesotta on 27 February 1942, at the Park Manor Ballroom, in which gifts and laudatory speeches were given. It appears that Levy was still somewhat bitter; one witness was noted as saying, "[That] was a lousy way for him to act at any testimonial."[84] His speech was insincere. He acted in a very grudging fashion and was entirely lacking in any appreciation for Rose's contribution to the union or the labor movement in Los Angeles. Pesotta handled the situation carefully, making no reference to the reasons for her departure, instead urging the assembly to become conscious of the racial intolerance rampant in the country at that time. She made it a point to note that she was leaving the union "in the hands of a loyal active leadership and membership."[85] However, in late March, Adams and a number of other local executive board members resigned because of Levy's tactics and the loss of Pesotta to Los Angeles.[86]

Rose left Los Angeles a short time later and traveled for a while with her niece Dorothy Rubin, Esther's youngest child. She remained quite bitter about the entire Los Angeles experience and, rather than accept another organizer's job, decided to return to the sewing machine at a dress factory in New York City—an extremely unusual thing for a vice president of the ILGWU to do. By June 1942, Pesotta had noted to her friend Sue Adams, "My presence in the factory is a thorn in the eye [*sic*] of our union. Official leadership has not asked for any explanation. Rank and file are buzzing. I cannot shout from the housetops that I was eased out of office against the wishes of the membership."[87] Pesotta said she was afraid that her removal would kill her, politically, for good. At the General Executive Board meeting in Atlantic City on 15 June, Pesotta delivered a very moving speech in which she clearly described her experience in Los Angeles and what finally drove her out. In it she said:

> It is common knowledge, and I assume that most of the members of the General Executive Board are aware of the fact that I have not been on the organizing staff of the ILGWU since our last GEB meeting, held in Chicago in February. In New York City, individuals close to the union know that I am back at the bench, and working in the same dress factory from which I took a leave of absence in the summer of 1933.
>
> Although a few of my colleagues on the board have asked me directly what made me return to the industry, none has been impelled to take this matter up officially. But many members of our union are asking questions about it, and so I feel that an explanation is now in order.
>
> I think I may say, without being accused of boasting, that through the last nine years I have made as large a contribution to the upbuilding of our union as was physically and intellectually possible for one person to make. I consider it a privilege to have worked in almost every section of this broad country, and to have worked in every graveyard of our past defeats. In some cases, I went twice into the same territory, a step that labor organizers almost never venture to take. I know that I have helped materially in enlarging our International with several new locals and several thousand additional organized workers.
>
> But as time passed I realized, to my dismay, that neither our president nor any of the men to whom I have been so useful in regaining lost membership and lost prestige, seemed to recognize the fact that I was competent not only to assume the full responsibility of organizing in difficult territory, but also of managing newly organized locals.

It is clear to me, from first-hand observation, that despite all
the growth and progress of our International, something vital is
missing, that essential something known as co-operation, which if it
existed among us would rebound vastly to the benefit of our International, both in members and in prestige. That some of our top
leaders remain as provincial, small and petty as they were when
they joined up. Peanut politics is still a blight on our organization,
hampering it sadly.

The recent Los Angeles incident is a case in point. When
President Dubinsky requested me in January 1940 to leave Boston
and go to Los Angeles, an emergency existed. Vice-President Levy
was ill, and Brother Wishnak could not cope with the situation
alone. Moreover, both of these men already had definite tasks before them. Levy was to manage the Cloak Joint Board and Wishnak
had been assigned to take charge of the Dressmakers' local. I was to
serve as the general organizer of whatever might turn up.

After some eighteen months of incessant labor, I succeeded in
organizing two new locals in Los Angeles and a third in Salt Lake
City—all three of them being made up of cotton dress and sports
wear workers. But the ink was scarcely dry on the agreement
signed with the sportswear group when I was informed that President Dubinsky was contemplating the sending of a manager from
New York for these locals. This manager was to be Moskowitz.
Whereupon I made this comment to Brother Levy: "If I am qualified
to organize these workers, negotiate for them, and sign a contract in
their behalf with the employers, I hold that I am fully qualified also
to manage their locals, with the understanding, of course, that you
as the Coast representative would always serve in the capacity of
consultant."

Subsequently I wrote President Dubinsky to the same effect.

That was the issue after our GEB meeting in Philadelphia last
October, when President Dubinsky, Vice-President Levy, and I met
at Unity following the sessions. There I learned, to my amazement,
that the Pacific Coast area, approximately 1300 miles long and 680
miles wide, including Utah (which I recently helped organize), was
too small to have two vice-presidents. I had to admit that this was a
new one on me, considering that in the New York Joint Board,
within a radius of only a few blocks, several vice-presidents work
together.

But this was not the point. That point was that I had to be eased out of the Pacific Coast area, at whatever cost to the organization. So I made it easy for those who desired this and agreed to leave that field.

As soon as the Los Angeles members heard that I was slated to be removed from this territory, they demanded to know who would take care of the business of their locals. Vice-President Levy told them that he was ready to take full charge.

That was the state of affairs when the GEB convened in Chicago in February last. President Dubinsky, Vice-President Levy, and I met the first evening and discussed the situation at length. What occurred then may seem trivial now to this board. In that conference we reached an understanding whereby Levy was to return to California and assume full charge there. Next day he departed, triumphant because he had won out over me. I expected President Dubinsky to make an explanation to the board and in fact I asked him to do so. But for some reason unknown to me that explanation was never made.

On arriving in Los Angeles, Vice-President Levy summoned the executive board members and officers of the newly formed locals and announced that I had resigned "for personal reasons." But when pressed to the wall, he shifted the responsibility, asserting that the president did not want me stationed in Los Angeles any more.

From Chicago I went to New York for a few days. While there I was called into President Dubinsky's office and he showed me resolutions of protest that he had received from groups of members in some of the Los Angeles locals. It was obvious that, after hearing the report submitted by Levy, these simple-hearted women, who had been in the organization only a few months, felt that if they appealed to their president, I would not be removed.

Soon after this I returned to Los Angeles, to settle some affairs which needed my attention, and to have my belongings shipped East. Ensuing weeks in the Los Angeles area were filled with turmoil. Open resentment was shown by many of our members against the policies in force under the new control.

I was asked whether I would consider remaining in charge of Mode O'Day local, and was told that "Levy wouldn't mind it now." To this I gave a categorical answer: "My first decision is final. If I am qualified to carry all the responsibility of organizing these workers, negotiating for them, and setting up officers for them, then I contend that I am fully qualified to hold authority as their full-fledged manager, not only of Mode O'Day local, but also of the other sportswear local, 266, until the industry in Los Angeles is completely unionized." (The latter local was still in the process of organization.) President Dubinsky telephoned to me, and I explained to him that after what had happened in Los Angeles, and because of the injustice done to me personally, I was determined, when I got back to New York, to go to work again in a shop.

A little later I left for Mexico to spend an enforced vacation.

On my return to New York, I learned that President Dubinsky was in Los Angeles trying to clear away mounting difficulties due to mismanagement. Not only was there trouble in the new locals, but also in the older locals of the Joint Board.

It is my firm belief that much of this could have been avoided if our president and Vice-President Levy had recognized the fact, that after nine years of service to our union, I was as competent as any of the men on our staff.

I feel a great concern for the workers in Los Angeles, whom I have helped to organize for the second time in these nine years. But I have the utmost confidence in their ability now to take care of themselves in any industrial struggle that they may have to face. They have stood the acid test of a major conflict. These workers—practically all women—are in the main Americans of old stock, whose forebears have been in this country for generations. many of them are former Dust-Bowlers, strong characters like Ma Joad and the other Okies now situated on the Pacific Coast. They have courage and native intelligence. They read our press, look upon it seriously, and know their rights under both the United States Constitution and the Constitution of the ILGWU.

I would like to make it plain here that I have keen admiration for President Dubinsky. He has many excellent qualities. He is militant. He has broad social vision. And he is alert to the significance of events that affect the lives of the masses of working people. But sometimes he makes decisions against his own better judgement. I can understand his sympathetic attitude and personal loyalty toward certain individuals. But I cannot condone actions which favor individuals yet which at times work to the disadvantage of the membership, causing irreparable damage to our union.

Weighing all the circumstances, it is clear to me that if I were to go on as an organizer for the ILGWU, I would have to continue doing the ground-work and pinch-hitting for others, some of whom I regard as dead wood and neither physically nor mentally able to carry on effectively the activities called for by our present standards. The Los Angeles situation is a classic example of this. Authoritative reports from that scene indicate that organization there has again been retarded by improper methods of management; that the spirit of co-operation is conspicuously lacking there; and that the present policy of espionage and misrepresentation of facts and the prevailing undertone of distrust, have again worked to the detriment of our organization.

So I have decided, for the present at least, to remain in the ranks of our 300,000 members, and earn a living as the rest of them do in the shop. Be assured that I shall always be an active and conscientious member of the International. Whenever it is evident that my services are especially needed, I shall be ready, as in the past, to give my time and energy for the good of the ILGWU.

In leaving the staff as a paid organizer, however, I have no intention of resigning from the General Executive Board. I intend to serve out my full term. And while I remain in New York, or wherever I may have occasion to go, I shall welcome opportunity to devote my spare hours to any of our union activities which might benefit from my experiences of the past nine fruitful years.[88]

In her diary kept during the June 1942 GEB meetings held in Atlantic City, she writes:

I have not a friend among them. I wanted to talk to DD tomorrow. how well we knew before that power can corrupt anybody.[89]

The next day she noted:

DD called on me to speak on the Coast situation. As I was talking I again lived through the humiliation and hardship of the last two years. Apparently the truth hurts, for all the vice presidents had more sympathy with Levy because they are all as sick as he is.[90]

And finally:

The meeting ended with a void in my heart. On the train I turned my chair to the window and read, not turning back to where my president and his entourage were sitting.[91]

Obviously Pesotta was devastated by the Los Angeles fiasco and felt unsupported and pained.

In her memoirs Pesotta tried to handle the situation delicately, with little reference to the internal squabble that took place in Los Angeles. Publicly, she announced that she had returned to the shop because she believed that all vice presidents should stay closely connected to the conditions under which the rank and file were working. Pesotta did not yet resign her position as vice president of the ILGWU and continued attending its meetings for another two years.

The next few years were trying ones for Rose. After being in the limelight for so long, it was hard for her to adjust to a "normal" lifestyle. She wrote sarcastically to Adams in June 1942, saying she was doing her "part for national defense by sewing lovely dancing frocks and wedding gowns for women to entertain our boys to keep up the morale of the army and navy."[92] Even though the economy was booming due to the war effort, she was periodically out of work because of the seasonal nature of her industry. She referred to her "seven fat years" being over.[93] Her correspondence reflected her unhappiness with being assassinated by her "friends" and her anger at Dubinsky and Levy. She remained active, writing letters to the *Herald Tribune* about conditions in Puerto Rico and attempting to join the government commission investigating them. She attended Women's Trade Union League conferences, worked on the summer labor colleges, spoke at local and AFL union meetings and at colleges for the ILGWU education department. She also took to washing her own hair, doing her own fingernails, making her own facials, and taking a sudsy bath twice a day. In fact, at times she noted that she was in good shape and had never felt better in all her recent years.[94] However, even upon her resignation, the anarchists continued to malign her. In August of 1942, Pesotta wrote an angry letter to her anarchist friends Fannie, Barch, Helen, Clara, and Sophia alleging that a whispering campaign was being carried on against her. She said: "I am not getting any money from the International. . . . There is a campaign about me—that I am lying. I left the GEB and went back to the sewing machine. . . . Tell my friends to keep my business out of their heads. I can very well take care of myself."[95] Even in her union alienation, Pesotta ran into trouble among the anarchists, feeling once again unsupported by them.

Periodically, Rose would lose jobs in the dress industry. Often the reason given was that she did not sew as well as the others. She sometimes ran into conflict with the bosses, particularly because of her previous years of agitational work. It appeared that Rose was searching for a purpose to her life now that her labor organizing work had ceased. Eventually, she hit upon the idea of writing her labor movement memoirs. In 1942, she began to work with John Nicholas Beffel, a socialist, editor, and friend from the Sacco and Vanzetti days, collaborating on her autobiography *Bread upon the Waters*.

During all these activities, Rose's growing frustration with the GEB was coming to a culmination. She had considered leaving the board in the past, but, finally, in June 1944, Rose attended the twenty-fifth convention of the ILGWU at the Hotel Statler in Boston and submitted her resignation. In her final statement, Rose asserted:

> It is my firm conviction that our International having grown to be the largest single labor organization with membership of 305,000—85% of whom are women and young girls, ought to reconsider its old established rule of having only a single woman on its high executive board. Some day I hope the membership will take this so called rule and throw it out the window. . . .
>
> . . . Some day the woman power of our International will have its say. Today I feel it is my duty to relinquish the only seat and allow another woman to take my place. In so doing I believe I am acting in the best tradition of our International's sense of loyalty and cooperation.[96]

But even as she was about to leave, DD had the last word, dismissing her feminist analysis by saying:

> I want to advise Delegate Pesotta and the delegates that I hope there will never come a time when the rules of our organization are thrown out the window. The rules of our organization may be changed, modified, corrected—but they will never be thrown out the window. And I don't believe that women, merely because they are women, or men because they are men, must be elected. Elect your officers on their merits. We are not going to judge them by whether they wear trousers or whether they wear skirts. We will examine them on their record, on their devotion, ability, and contributions they might make, but not on basis of sex.[97]

Beyond this official statement and then DD's dismissive and paternalistic statement, Rose left little record of any other reasons for leaving the GEB. Both her sister Esther and her friend Clara believe that she left because Dubinsky and the other vice presidents made "life miserable for her."[98] They both remember that Rose attempted to introduce a resolution urging all the "old" vice presidents to resign so that "new blood" could be moved in. After that resolution, the others attempted to push her out of the hierarchy. There is record that Rose once asked Dubinsky to let her be a "rank and file" member of the GEB. At the time he responded that "it would break decorum of the board and that others should do it too." Rather than allowing her to do so, she was called to Milwaukee instead.[99] There is no official record in the ILGWU archives of an actual proposal by Pesotta for a rotation of service for vice president, however.

Rose seemed somewhat abrasive to Dubinsky and the men on the GEB. She did not let issues drop and made it a point to be a gadfly among them. She is remembered as a "restless soul" by old-timers in the union.[100] She was seen as a "kicker" and a "firebrand," who always had something to criticize. Because of this, the bureaucracy was not very enthusiastic about her. In one interesting interaction, she wrote Sasha Zimmerman a snippy letter because he had included a photo of a recently hired Scottish woman in the ILGWU newspaper, while there was barely any work available for long-term union members. She said: "This time you were absolutely wrong. I consider it an April fool's joke on all the members of the union."[101] Pesotta was an outspoken and forceful woman. She would not give in to those she felt were wrong. She was powerful and, in fact, she did become, as she had prophesied, "a voice lost in the wilderness." She was the "voice of a solitary woman on the GEB," and even with all her force and power, she was overwhelmed by the opposition and the various factions. Pesotta had dared to speak out; she did not subject herself to their authority. She was an uppity woman who did not conform, and because of it she was labeled a "troublemaker."

Pesotta was a woman and an anarchist; ultimately, it was for these reasons that she was marginalized by the male bureaucrats who ran the union. Patriarchy, paternalism, and reformist politics were her downfall. She knew she had been victimized and scapegoated, but it would take the years of history to place Pesotta's marginalization into proper perspective. Some might say it was her personality, her style, or her education that threatened those in power. However, we now understand it as gender politics, including the subservient and powerless role of women in the male-dominated hierarchy that undermined her. Were she a man, none of the complaints about her would have been made. A man with her outspokenness and power would have been one of the boys. As a woman, she had dared to step out of her role, a behavior that was not to be tolerated.

Additionally, it was factional dispute and territorialism that led to her final defeat in Los Angeles. The Communists, her archenemies since the 1920s in New York, finally held sway over her when she ventured into their territory in California. Moreover, in view of the fact that Rose did not have a mass constituency of women who supported her as their spokesperson and also lacked organized feminist support and solidarity, the final nail was placed in her coffin of marginalization. Rose faced many adversities in her long association with the union, and it is no small wonder that she was able to be as effective as she was—for so long.

Pesotta retreated from the positions of power within the ILGWU, defeated, and eventually forgotten. It took many years of repeated effort and struggle before she would regain her sense of self-confidence. One could also argue that after the Los Angeles fiasco and her resignation from the GEB, Pesotta was never quite the same. She remained politically active, but she never again reached the fame and effectiveness that had been hers for eleven years as an organizer and vice president.

Nonetheless, Pesotta's fame and reputation lived on long after her resignation. In later books on this period, she has been singled out as "an invaluable fighter in the American economic revolution" and was noted for her achievement as a strike organizer and board member.[102] She is regularly noted in articles and books on the period, and later gained fame for the book she wrote chronicling her experiences as an organizer and vice president. Although she never attained such prominence again, her name has been long remembered by those who knew and worked with her, and, currently, feminist historians are discussing her role: her successes and failures in the union and the sexism that brought her down. Ann Schofield, for example, has noted that

> several decades before social historians acknowledged the need to study the interconnections between workplace and family, culture, and community, Rose gave us a clear sense of the relationship of family to labor militancy in her efforts to mobilize the wives of sit down strikers in Akron and Flint. She knew that workers could be organized effectively only if one had knowledge of and sympathy for their lives outside as well as within the shop.[103]

Of Pesotta, Pauline Newman, and Fannia Cohn, Alice Kessler Harris has said:

> Those who came before walked an uneasy tightrope—slipping first to one side and then to the other, tempted sometimes by the money and support of middle class women, at others by the militancy of a changing union leadership, alternately repelled by "ladies" and repeatedly hurt by their union's male leadership, women who tried to organize their sisters were in a precarious position. They were not feminist—they do not put the social and political rights of women before all else. They did draw strength and support from the solidarity of women inside unions and outside them. Their lives illustrate the critical importance of "female bonding" and of female friendship networks. . . . All were class conscious, insisting that the class struggle was preeminent. When their class consciousness and their identification as women conflicted, they bowed to tradition and threw their lot with the working class.[104]

During the course of her work as an organizer and vice president, Rose had to deal with a number of difficult themes and issues. The first was how to be an anarchist in the union hierarchy. There were competing demands between the two commitments, and often the union's needs won out. Rose decided to be practical in her behavior, while, at the same time, committed to the ideology. For this she received much criticism and felt alienated from her political comrades. She negotiated with police, dealt carefully with the Catholic church, implemented governmental law, and acted respectfully toward authority—hardly anarchism, but certainly effective organizing. She learned to accommodate and work with those in power in a way that was considered unacceptable to more revolutionary anarchists. However, hers was a philosophical anarchism, one that knew about inequality and revolution, but was also practical and pragmatic in dealing with day to day issues. Nonetheless, it was due to her anarchism, including her hatred of the Communists, her opposition to the growing centrism and bureaucratization of the union, and the increasing conservatism that she detected in the GEB that actually led to her resignation from the union hierarchy. In the end, it was her ideological anarchism that gave her the strength to walk away and the theory which helped her to explain it.

The second theme that Rose addressed was that of being a woman organizer and solitary woman vice president. Sometimes Rose used a somewhat traditional women's style to get what she wanted. She acted purposely wild at arrests and sat under a hair dryer to avoid arrest. She organized attractive seamstresses into wearing evening gowns on the picket lines and wore gloves to have her photo taken. Rose was hardly radical or nontraditional in her style, but it was unlike the style that male organizers used. She knew how to play up her feminine qualities and to use her womanliness while enjoying being a "disorderly woman." She also knew how to set goals, reach them, and demand that her needs be met. Rose engaged in organizing strategies that come out of the female experience. It was a style that is, as Kessler Harris has noted, based on women's culture. It involved developing women's spirit and encouraging the social needs of her constituents. She cared about dances, social hours, and education, and not just the traditional demands of wages and hours.[105]

Pesotta's style of leadership is worthy of mention. It is clear that Pesotta worked much better when she was fully in charge of a situation and allowed to make decisions for herself. She was far better as a general than she was as a lieutenant. In cities where she had full power and was only accountable to herself and her staff, she was successful and an artful boss. In situations in which she was second in command or in an otherwise subordinate position, Pesotta tended to be abrasive, cutting, and difficult. This led to problems with peers and bosses, who found her hard to work with and dictatorial. Certainly part of this dynamic was operative in Pesotta's final stand in Los Angeles and later with the GEB. Pesotta, in fact, was a gentle general, but a less than loyal and willing warrior. Clearly, there was a contradiction here between being an anarchist and being a general.

Nonetheless Rose found that, with all her creativity, strength, and resourcefulness, being the only woman on the GEB she could have little or no impact. She was far more successful in working with the rank and file than she was in dealing with the "old men" on the board. She was seen as out of line and a troublemaker for arguing, labeled "unruly" and "problematic." As Alice Kessler Harris has noted about Rose and women in positions like hers:

> The trade union movement offered women no access to the power structure and insisted that women in its ranks accept male assumptions about their role and place. It thus undermined whatever female leadership developed within the movement, leaving women like Rose Pesotta, who rebelled without support (labeled "unstable") and those like Cohn, Newman, and O'Connor, who conformed, without power.[106]

Rose was in an untenable situation. She was alone and isolated and as she said earlier of Fannia Cohn, "Were she a man, it would have been entirely different."[107]

It is quite clear that the ILGWU bureaucrats were not totally serious about reaching the unorganized women workers. At best, they could be seen as ambivalent. A union that supposedly represented many unskilled women workers had a leadership that was only representing a small strata of the upper echelons of the needle trades. They knew they needed the women. Women paid union dues and provided growing numbers to build the ILGWU ranks, but they were not heard in the boardroom. Their representative, Rose Pesotta, tried to make their voices heard, but women leaders were not listened to either. She was ridiculed, money was withheld, her ideas were maligned, her styles of organizing were trivialized. The men in power wanted the women's money and numbers to enhance their union. However, they did not want such potential members to be fully synthesized into the entire union system, nor would they listen to how they might be. Nor could they conceive of seeing women's issues, such as family, comraderie, even parties and food, as serious union matters. It was male power, privilege, and thinking that ruled, and Pesotta, alone, was unable to make a dent in this male-dominated system.

A third theme that emerges from Pesotta's labor organizing is that of working with various ethnic and cultural groups—unlike her own—and at forming good working relationships with all kinds of people: Mexicans, Scandinavians, ordinary workers, and many others. Pesotta saw herself as educating all types of workers toward a class consciousness. She tried to overcome ethnic and racial tensions to help workers realize their class similarities and the unity they could have as workers. Through her charismatic leadership, she evoked devotion and respect from those with whom she worked. Rose was quite effective as an organizer, embodying many qualities necessary for successful leadership. In later years, she was remembered by many for her ability to relate to anyone, regardless of race, class, ethnic origin, or religion. Rose was truly an egalitarian. Joan Jensen has argued that Rose was forced to operate under adverse conditions in organizing Hispanic and Asian women, with little support from her union. She points out that Rose was not sent to organize among "women of her own culture" (Jewish) and argues that these difficulties, combined with the increasingly conservative male hierarchy, are what led her to resign.[108] I disagree and feel, in fact, it was Rose's keen ability to work with all types of people that was her forte and gave her the will and strength to continue her work, even within the structure of a male-dominated bureaucratic organization. Pesotta left much evidence of her consciousness of race and ethnic issues and was supported in her efforts to reach such workers. In a letter to Dubinsky in 1933, she told of her efforts to encourage the

more class conscious workers . . . to entrench themselves in the organization. When I say class conscious, I say it advisedly, because we have race conscious workers and they have got a dose now that will last them a lifetime.[109]

Of Mexican workers in L.A., she said:

I contended that the Mexican dressmakers were normal human beings, who simply needed honest and intelligent guidance. . . . Give these an intensive training in elementary trade unionism, and it won't be long before they are up to the rest of the ILGWU organizing staff.[110]

Of American women in Seattle where she had a "hell of a job," they were

100% American white daughters of the sturdy pioneers. They are all members of bridge clubs, card clubs, lodges, etc. Class consciousness is as remote from their thoughts as any idea that smacks of radicalism.[111]

Dubinsky and the treasurer often sent her extra funds to reach workers of ethnic groups who had been previously untapped by the union. They saw it as important to attract minorities and other groups of unrepresented peoples. Pesotta, too, found this one of her more exciting challenges. It was, to her, one of the important missions in her work, educating and fighting for a workers' class consciousness, across all ethnic lines.

The ILGWU leadership knew it was important to reach such diverse workers; they were just not ready to hire organizers of these ethnic groups to enroll them. That awareness came much later.

A final theme is that of Pesotta's dealing with successes and dissatisfactions. Rose had a number of experiences that can only be viewed as achievements—most notably, her work in Montreal and in Boston, her early Los Angeles work, and the UAW strikes. She handled herself and these accomplishments well. They were significant enough to feed her ego and fuel her forward. Pesotta did well when she was in charge, had power, and could run the show, as in Montreal and Puerto Rico. She did far less well when she was second in command or when she had to work closely with her peers. Here she found it hard to take a backseat and could be abrasive with colleagues. She was less comfortable when dealing with people who disagreed with her or with adversity or failure. When things did not go her way, she was known to attack and pull out all stops to alter the course of events. For this she was seen as being egotistic, authoritarian, and difficult. When attack did not work, she would personalize the failure, see herself as wronged, withdraw, and eventually leave the situation, much as she did in Los Angeles and with the GEB. She would give these efforts all she had. But if failure was imminent, she left rather than struggle any further. In fact, this was not unlike what Alice Kessler Harris said of other women in the union who gave it everything they had and then simply ran away when there was "no dealing with the idiots."[112]

Pesotta was obviously not always an easy person with whom to deal. She was tough, strong, aggressive, and forceful, but under it all she was vulnerable and sensitive to criticism. Rose, most of all, was human, complete with human foibles. Although it looks as if Pesotta had no impact on the structure and functioning of the ILGWU bureaucracy, it certainly had a dramatic impact on her.

Pesotta's work with the union was her shining moment. For eleven years, she was a star: famous in labor circles and unique among women of her time. As a result of gender politics, factionalism, territoriality, and growing conservatism, Pesotta was removed from the public domain, taking a backseat in labor and anarchist circles. Pesotta became marginalized in the pages of history, the victim of male domination and factional wars. Although she often made forays into public, she never again regained the following or popularity she experienced earlier in her career. When Pesotta reached the age of forty-eight, her most active and prominent period had ended.

6

POLITICAL WORK

Plateless dinners and silent speeches.

It was anarchism—both its philosophy and the members of the movement—that most significantly influenced Rose's labor organizing and political activities. The ideology to which she was drawn early in her education remained an underlying theme of all her later accomplishments. It was her approach to the world. Rose adhered to the ideas of Kropotkin, who believed in the need for revolution and the development of communes and collectives as the basic unit of society. He also believed in people taking from society based on what they needed, not just based on what they earned. A more profound influence than even the ideas were the people in the movement. Rose became involved with the anarchists soon after arriving in the United States and participated in numerous anarchist activities, perceiving herself as an active and dedicated revolutionist.

All during Rose's labor organizing work, she remained active and involved with the anarchist circle. She worked with them politically, read their writings, and socialized with them extensively. Often, there was a tension between the two spheres of her life—her working hours were focused on union activities, while after-work hours found her engaged in anarchist undertakings. Occasionally they conflicted; at other times, they blended well. Most often, Rose thought of her two worlds as separate and wrote of them separately. She spoke little of anarchism to her union colleagues and, given the derision she received, chose not to speak openly of her union work with anarchists, except to her closest friends. It was as if Rose had one foot in each camp. The union members considered her a dedicated unionist, although a gadfly among them. To the anarchists, she was a dedicated anarchist, although a union bureaucrat among them. She was—to borrow the phrase from her mentor, Emma Goldman— "nowhere at home." Although Rose spent a lifetime trying to find a home for herself in the two camps, the tension was never reconciled, nor was the struggle ever fully resolved.

Rose's first major anarchist involvement was with *Road to Freedom* and the International Anarchist Group that met in New York City from 1924 to 1932. Rose participated in both groups, as well as in the anarchist conferences held at Stelton, New Jersey, every summer. Members of these various groups discussed the role that anarchists played in the labor movement and encouraged international anarchist events and activities. Rose is remembered as being "outstanding in her vivacity, her dedication to our ideas and her tireless activities. She was always present at all the meetings, demonstrations and mass rallies."[1]

Early in the publication of *Road to Freedom*, reports were made about anarchists' relationship to the unions, especially in the needle trades. On 4–5 July 1925, the anarchist conference at Stelton held a session on "our attitude toward the labor movement," in which a resolution was passed that because unions were important, anarchists should participate and "reaffirm their faith in the labor movement and insist on [their] right to propagate ideas among the workers, repudiate all dictatorship by the bureaucratic leadership or political parties."[2] Rose was present at that meeting and was at just that time becoming active in her local of the ILGWU.

In June 1926, after having been at the Brookwood Labor College for two years, Rose participated in, and wrote about, the Road to Freedom Camp organized by the International Group that was held at Croton-on-Hudson.[3] There, forty to one hundred people attended lectures by A. J. Muste, Harry Kelly, and Arthur Calhoun on sociology, economics, literature, cooperation, general strikes, social philosophy, and general tendencies in the anarchist and labor movements. In September of that year, Rose attended the second anarchist conference at Croton and remarked on the dwindling numbers within the anarchist movement. Because of disappointment with the Russian Revolution and the fact that United States workers really had no class consciousness, she doubted that militancy would arise within their ranks.[4] During that conference, Rose presented a report on the summer camp and was elected general secretary of *Road to Freedom*. At that camp, Pesotta was also elected to a resolution committee that led a discussion on what anarchists wanted the labor movement to be. In it she said, "The difference between European and American workers [is that] in Europe, they are proletariat, here [there are] shifting classes. The social forces are different here; the labor movement is now stagnant; our idea is to create a new society. We become lost when we take our grievances to the trade unions and bargain with the bosses. We lose our broader view. Anarchists should keep in mind daily that our contact with the worker should be educational."[5]

From 1 November 1926 until October 1929, Rose was listed on the *Road to Freedom* masthead as the general secretary of the publication. The masthead read: "Anarchy: a social theory which regards the union of order with the absence of all direct government of man, by man as the political ideal, absolute individual liberty."[6] It was during this time that the paper and Rose were integrally involved with Sacco and Vanzetti. Every issue urged general strikes, financial support, and direct action on behalf of the condemned two.

The third annual anarchist conference, 3–4 September 1927, was a most satisfying one for all participants. Members of the Rising Youth Group were present. Two sisters, Elizabeth and Sarah Goodman, militant youngsters starting their own newspaper, were at the conference "to stand on their own feet . . . but would hear suggestions from the older comrades."[7] Rose participated by leading a discussion on general propaganda and by urging that *Road to Freedom* include "constructive articles and the message of anarchism which should stand prominently in every issue."[8] Rose also helped *Road to Freedom* set up a benefit for 18 February 1928, which included a "plateless dinner and silent speeches."[9]

Rose's involvement with the anarchists continued to revolve around writing for the journal, setting up conferences and summer camps, and arranging and speaking at memorial meetings. In November of 1928, Pesotta began to share her secretarial responsibilities with another anarchist comrade. In February 1929, she organized a dinner for Hippolyte Havel, who was resigning as editor of *Road to Freedom*. That same month, she spoke at a memorial and propaganda meeting to commemorate the eighth anniversary of Peter Kropotkin's death.[10] Continuing to participate in many of the annual and semiannual conferences, she often led workshops and wrote articles for the magazine on the proceedings. Once she became a labor organizer, Rose reported to the gatherings on happenings within the labor movement and sought to discuss some of her issues and dilemmas. Initially, the anarchists were eager to participate in such debates and discussions.

But internal squabbles and hostility between individuals within *Road to Freedom* itself finally led Rose to resign from the secretaryship. She did so in September 1929 without offering any explanation, nor details about the controversy. These conflicts led to her comments in 1934 to Emma Goldman, which explained the situation somewhat.

But dear, our crowd became so bigoted and intolerant that, while working with them, I either have to side exactly with them, and you know their preconceived notion about activities, or else be ostracized. It came to a point several years ago while I was still in New York working with Van, Sadie et al. I did not resign from the group,

Emma, rather than do that I left of my own free volition for California without breaking up the work. But the result was that the group fell apart because people did not agree. They are still fighting around. When I came back from Puerto Rico, I wanted to remain in New York but, goodness, the backwardness and the diefness [sic] on the one side and the cock suredness and pugnacity on the other side was appalling. I threw up my hands in despair.[11]

Although Rose continued to write sporadically for the paper, by May 1932 *Road to Freedom* had ceased publication. Eventually, it died because the editors—first Havel and then Van Valkenburg—succumbed to alcoholism, and no one was willing to take over responsibility. Just before the demise of the group, a battle of such magnitude raged between its members that a gun was drawn during the argument. Unfortunately, the specific issues that led to this scene have been lost to history.[12]

Finally, *Road to Freedom* was transformed into a weekly paper, *Freedom*, which included a youth-movement section and also tried to appeal to a younger and more native-born population. Rose contributed money, but only wrote one article for the *Road to Freedom* successor. *Freedom*, like its predecessors, was not greatly successful in reaching large numbers of readers and appeared to continue in the immigrant tradition of American anarchism.[13]

In an article entitled "Merry Christmas," published in *Freedom* on 4 February 1933, Rose vividly described the affluent owners and the sad, demoralized workers at a Christmas lunch party in a factory. She cynically suggested that the owners dance, drink, and enjoy a Merry Christmas, while contemporary Christs languished in prison.[14] In later issues her name appeared periodically, associated with anarchist conferences. *Freedom* was published only from 1932 to 1934, subsequently evolving into yet another journal, *Common Sense*, which published from 1932 to 1946. Further outgrowths of these anarchist publications included *New Trends* from 1945 to 1946 and the short-lived *Challenge*, a magazine that Emma Goldman and Rose referred to in their correspondence for a short time.

Perhaps the single most important individual whom Rose was to meet and associate with through her contacts from her *Road to Freedom* work was Emma Goldman. "Emma was her teacher," and it was Emma who helped Rose to "believe in anarchism like a rabbi believes in God."[15] Although Rose first met Emma in 1919 at Ellis Island, while visiting Kushnarev, it was not until 1934 that their friendship blossomed. After her deportation, Goldman and her comrade Alexander Berkman spent two years in Russia working for the revolution by gathering material for a museum. In 1921, disenchanted with what they saw as the authoritarianism of the Bolsheviks and their uncompromising approach, Berkman and Goldman left Russia and lived in forced exile. Eventually, Goldman settled in St. Tropez, France, and commuted to London, where she married an older Welsh miner who offered her citizenship through this arrangement. The exile was a difficult one for Goldman, whose most productive years had been spent organizing and propagandizing in the United States. She attempted to lecture in England and on the Continent, but did not find as receptive an audience as she had in the United States. By 1934, a committee of civil libertarians was able to arrange a tour for Emma that allowed her to speak in the United States for a period of ninety days. Rose was not present for any of the U.S. lectures because her labor organizing work had taken her to Los Angeles, San Francisco, and Puerto Rico, while Emma had gone no further west than St. Louis. Nonetheless, Rose was able to catch up with her famed mentor in Montreal later that spring. The meeting must have been a meaningful one for both, because at that point they began a correspondence and friendship that would last until Goldman's death in 1940.

Letters between the two reflect a mentor/student relationship. Rose was most interested in helping Emma regain entry into the United States; as early as 1934, Emma asked Rose to use Dubinsky to help gain her a visa. She urged that Rose speak to Frances Perkins, secretary of labor, on her behalf. Rose diligently tried to convince labor leaders and government officials to intercede for Emma; however, her efforts—which continued up to Goldman's death—were futile. Goldman was never allowed back into the United States after her 1934 tour.

Rose often shared with Emma through letters the joys and struggles of her labor organizing activities. Once she described the "herculean task" of establishing a union in Seattle, seeming proud of her successes with "the women who for years slaved in the factories without seeing any light. Once they hear the message of unionism they want to hear more and more."[16] Emma, ever supportive, was "delighted to know you are having such tremendous success in organizing the girls." In fact, Emma began to identify with Rose:

It almost reads like in the early period of my battle in labor and the anarchist movement. In a way it is almost disheartening that things should go on the same after 45 years. But on the other hand it was good to see the greater solidarity and social awareness of the workers. There was nothing of the kind in my young days.[17]

In the same letter Emma referred to Rose as a "rebel and a fighter" and noted how glad she was that the movement had her. It was through these reassurances that Rose was encouraged to remain among the anarchists who had begun to question her union work.

As a mentor and teacher, Emma often gave Rose advice relevant to conflicting demands of the two movements. At one point Rose seriously considered giving up labor organizing for fear that, as a bureaucrat, she would compromise her values too much. Emma replied:

> [It would be] folly for you to give up your position. But after all one doesn't live by bread alone. However I would not for worlds want to influence you in any direction. The material issue does count. Each one has to decide for himself [sic] whether he [sic] is willing to launch out on the desperate road of material anxiety and insecurity.[18]

Despite her dedication to the movement, Emma was cautious in her advice, in view of her own grave financial problems. She had been unable to "earn a sou in Europe or Canada." She was appalled by the idea that she would be as poor in her old age and wrote Rose:

> Knowing what to expect I dare not suggest to you or any other comrade to cut himself lose from whatever material certainties he has and consecrate [sic] on our work which means starvation all the time besides danger.[19]

Emma's pragmatic advice differed from what Rose had received from other anarchists and seemed helpful; Rose decided to remain in her position. At times Rose attempted to identify with her role model, pointing out similarities in their situations. In one interaction Emma quickly put Rose in her place:

> There is a passage in your letter I cannot quite understand. I mean I don't know what might have called it forth. You write: "I have put up with exactly the same hardships that you had to put up with for so many years." Of course that is not quite the case, my dear. After all you are representing a powerful organization. Its backing not only means material security while you serve it, but also social and legal protection. I had nothing and no one when I began or even years after. I was dragged from pillar to post, more in police station houses then [sic] in my bed and in the face of the densest ignorance that existed in America forty years ago. . . .
>
> You will realize that your work, difficult as it no doubt is, is very much less so than the conditions under which we worked, we of the old generation.[20]

But even in her criticism, Emma was supportive of Rose, noting, "I am sure you must have a difficult time. That's why I appreciate your organizing efforts. Keep it up my dear. It is a thousand times more useful and I am sure more satisfactory than picking bugs off roses."[21]

This letter led to a poignant and revealing interchange concerning the doubts and dismay that they felt with regard to their political work. Rose apologized just one month later: "Far be it for me to compare my trials and tribulations with those you had to bear for 40 years."[22] But, she wondered, why was it that after forty years of propaganda and education, nothing had changed the attitude of the working class. She despondently noted: "Nothing matters to these complacent wage earners. They shower abuse, send to jail, kick and fight with me, just like they did years ago, regardless of the years of change, regardless of the powerful organization that is there to help them."[23] Rose, it appeared, had grave concerns regarding the ideology that underlay her work and was experiencing doubt regarding her involvement in the labor struggle:

Did not our dear comrades Peter Kropotkin and his associates over estimate the goodwill and cooperation of the poor and downtrodden? Wasn't it a little superficial to maintain that all the good qualities rest with wage earners and everything evil part of ruling class? For years I have worked among the working class. I have seen those susceptible to propaganda and those who have eyes and ears shut against us. I have had all opportunities to give these people education and enlightenment and still I find the road very, very hard.[24]

Emma's response included an economics lesson, as well as some encouragement to go on in the face of adversity. She reminded Rose that until 1929 there really had been no proletariat in the United States. The worker had no consciousness that "he" was a "special class" and was opposed to any idea that might make him "aware that his house was built on sand."[25] She also reminded Rose that American labor had never really wanted any fundamental social changes and had just tried to better work conditions and concentrate on bread and butter issues. It was the role of the anarchists to educate the workers, but, unfortunately, according to Emma, the international anarchist movement had devoted itself to immigrant groups and had failed to educate native-born American workers. Nonetheless, Emma believed that there was a "tremendous awakening in the States" and that "the very things I propagated and for which I have been driven from pillar to post have now entered the lives of millions as a matter of course." She noted that in every country which had had a revolution, the "intellectual and cultural advancement preceded the economic. So, too, is progress in America." Emma felt that there was really no need for despair, even though she might feel it sometimes because she could not be in the United States to participate. She considered that the "forge iron has never been hotter and redder than now."

And yet Emma, too, experienced despair and doubt. In an earlier letter, she noted:

> Our movement is in a bad state. The old ones died out or have become hoary with age. The young are in the communist ranks. There is unfortunately no one who could gather them up even if they were interested in our ideas. My only consolation is the certainty that the present trend to dictatorship is not for all times. Our ideas will have their day in the world court, though I may not live to see it. You are so much younger, you probably will.[26]

Rose obviously needed her relationship with Emma. She asked, "Come what may let's please keep up this correspondence. I need your counsel and advice. It is awfully hard to speak to our old-timers."[27] Besides discussing the labor and political conditions of the times, the two would often lament the "lack of talent, ability and determination" in the anarchist ranks.[28] They wondered if something was wrong with the movement, if perhaps they were too far advanced or lagging too far behind.[29] They discussed the bigotry and intolerance of their crowd, and both hoped for the time they could be enthusiastic about their movement again. Emma saw hope in Rose's youth and her involvement in the movement, urging that she remain a participant. It was during this time that Rose confided in Emma her dismay with the *Road to Freedom* crowd and their constant infighting that had resulted in Rose's resignation as general secretary. After that fiasco she had thrown up her hands in despair with the anarchists and gone into labor organizing with fervor.[30]

Emma wanted Rose to return, at least in part, to the active anarchist ranks. In 1935, she was delighted to hear that Rose was considering doing so. She commented:

> We certainly need a competent person like you. If at least we had able people, we might break through to the individual who still longs for a liberating ideal. But our material is so poor and odds so great. Our movement has no means for keeping those who devote all their time and activity above water.[31]

By 1936, Rose and Emma had formed such a close bond that Rose was asked to participate in the publication of Alexander Berkman's posthumous memoirs. In addition, she spoke at a memorial meeting in New

York for Berkman after he committed suicide on 28 June 1936. Berkman had been despondent about his deteriorating health and his homelessness. The anarchist comrades were shocked by his death and organized a memorial for 9 July that was held at Webster Hall on East Eleventh Street. Rose spoke, as did Harry Kelly, anarchist and founder of the Modern School. Also on the platform were Carlo Tresca, famed Italian anarchist orator; Harry Weinberger, Berkman and Goldman's U.S. attorney; and Abe Bluestein, then a young anarchist activist, writer, and propagandist. The meeting was sponsored by the Jewish Anarchist Federation, of which Rose was a part, and was attended by anarchists and friends of Berkman. Rose wrote that Berkman's death "left a void in my heart." Although she had not known him well, she felt close to him because he had corresponded with her with regard to the fate of her love, Kushnarev.[32]

In 1936, soon after Berkman's suicide, Goldman became deeply involved in the Spanish Civil War and the emergence of the Confederacion Nacional del Trabajo (CNT), an anarchist union influential in implementing anarchist principles in Spain. Spain had long been ready to use anarchist ideas, because of a history of anarchist propagandizing beginning in the 1860s with Pinelli, a follower of Bakunin. From 1936 on, Emma visited Spain a number of times, offering to serve as a nurse, canteen worker, childcare aide, disseminator of birth control information, and health educator. Unfortunately, comrades felt she would serve better as a propagandist abroad, and she reluctantly undertook this activity instead.[33]

Emma was thrilled by what she found in Spain. The revolutionists had set up agrarian and industrial collectives and ardently tried to introduce concepts of freedom and equality. Emma saw them as a "shining example to the rest of the world,"[34] offering an alternative to the Bolshevik model of revolution. Her correspondence with Rose at this time was filled with details concerning the progress of the Spanish comrades and the distorted accounts in the Western press. Emma was excited by the prospect of a lasting anarchist revolution in Spain and eagerly recruited her younger comrade to join the fight. She arranged for August Souchy, secretary of the anarcho-syndicalist committee, to obtain a "credential" for Rose, as well as an invitation for her to go to Spain as an organizer.[35]

At Emma's urging, Rose took a brief trip to Europe from December 1937 to February 1938, during which time she met with Emma and her friends Mollie Steimer and Senia Fleshine in Paris. Together they attended a syndicalist conference, where she met a few CNT representatives who urged her to visit their country. She applied for a visa and would have been granted one had she not written to Dubinsky, who urged that she return to the United States. Rose made a decision that she regretted the rest of her life. Following Dubinsky's instruction, she, in effect, chose labor over anarchism, while still trying to reconcile the two by soliciting financial aid for the Spanish revolutionists on returning home.

Rose's trip abroad brought her into close contact with Goldman, with whom she lived while visiting London. They attended political meetings, entertained comrades for dinner, and engaged in stimulating political discussions. For Rose these were heady times that gave her courage to go on with her work. But she was appalled by the conditions in which she found her famed role model living. The apartment, in a poor residential section, was unheated. Rose barely slept because the cold permeated her body from beneath the mattress and through the many layers of covering.[36] Emma had tried to add cheer to her apartment with photographs and paintings from friends and admirers around the world. Nonetheless, the squalid conditions so disturbed Rose that upon her return home, she worked doubly hard to obtain a U.S. visa for Emma. When this failed, she urged Emma to move to Canada so that she could at least live in "simple comfort."

While visiting, Rose found Emma busy aiding Spanish refugee children, visiting authorities on behalf of the Spaniards, conferring with heads of numerous civic organizations, publishing a newspaper, and lecturing. Emma had also organized a traveling photograph exhibit on the effects of the war on the Spanish people. Strongly feeling that the press was misrepresenting the struggle, she found photos of cooperative factories and farms to illustrate the collectivist nature of the Barcelona and Catalonia experiments.

Emma made numerous trips to Spain, where she was well loved. She visited factories, shops, and villages to evaluate the progress anarchism was making. When the fascist forces of Italy and Germany mobilized to aid Franco, Emma did her best to enlist public opinion for her comrades. Her work was to no avail; the fascist forces were eventually successful in obliterating the revolution that had taken hold and flourished for such a short period.

Because of a combination of forces—the mobilization of the fascists, the growth of Franco's military strength, the diminishing resources of the revolutionists, the undermining by the Soviets, and the dearth of Western support—the exceptional accomplishments of the revolution were lost. The fascists won in Spain. Emma was saddened by the death of this important revolution and conveyed her despair to Rose. Although she had not been pleased with all their decisions, particularly that of participating in the government and other compromises they made with the Communists, she was overwhelmed by the defeat of her comrades.

She had, she wrote Rose, struggled her entire life for a revolution that would work, and to see it fail was, to her, as if "you wanted a child all your life and at last, when you had almost given up hoping, it had been given to you—only to die soon after it was born."[37] By 1939 the great experiment was over.

Rose understood the devastation felt by Emma after the death of Berkman and the failure of the revolution. With this in mind, she renewed her efforts to bring Emma to the United States. Emma eventually decided to take up residence in Toronto, thereby trying to gain entry to the United States through the Canadian border; and Rose attempted to reach people in Washington on Emma's behalf. However, after the election of 1938, the political climate in the United States had changed to the point that even liberals in government came under scrutiny from the House Committee on Un-American Activities. It became impossible to mobilize any support for Emma. Emma continued to be hopeful and tried to enlist the continued aid of Harry Kelly, Roger Baldwin, Harry Weinberger, Carlo Tresca, and Rose. Nonetheless, all efforts were fruitless.

Their continued letters reflected Emma's growing despondency. She had suffered the death of her comrade Berkman in 1936, then came the failure of the Spanish Revolution, and now her continued inability to enter the United States. By 1939 Emma had moved to Canada, where she lived among friends and was financed by contributions made by supporters, including Rose. Shortly after arriving in 1939, she took up the cause of the threatened deportation of Arthur Bartolotti, an Italian alien who had been a militant antifascist. Rose sent additional funds to contribute to the committee established by Emma for his defense. Emma worked incredibly hard for this comrade, making public speeches in his behalf. Her health was failing, but she continued to work almost beyond her capacity, as if to struggle until the end. She immersed herself in cultural activities in Canada and remained active intellectually. During this period, Rose and Emma wrote each other only intermittently, primarily because of their busy schedules and Emma's failing health.

Rose visited Emma on the latter's birthday on 27 June 1939. During that party, which was attended by many comrades who wanted to pay tribute to their heroine, Rose took a motion picture of Emma. Later it was shown for Emma, who took great pleasure at seeing herself on film. Rose had her final visit with Emma on 29 September 1939, at a banquet held in Toronto to honor her fifty years in the labor and libertarian movement.

On 23 February 1940, Rose received a letter from Dorothy Rogers, Emma's friend and secretary. In it were details of Emma's stroke, which had taken place on 17 February. Emma had been laughing and talking with three friends when she drooped a little in her chair. At first they thought she had fainted, but eventually saw that it was more serious and called a doctor.[38]

Emma was hospitalized for a number of weeks and slowly improved. Many friends and colleagues, including Rose, contributed financial aid to cover her medical expenses. By March, a letter from Dorothy to Rose indicated that Emma's condition had improved to the point where she was able to say a few words, but not complete sentences. She appeared depressed, and even the news that Bartolotti had been saved from deportation did not significantly alter her mood.

Upon Emma's release from the hospital, a private nurse was hired for her. Rose became part of a major drive to raise funds for further medical expenses and to bring Goldman to the United States for her final months. Rose even prevailed on David Dubinsky and Fannia Cohen to become part of this group, which also included anarchists long associated with the cause.

By 1 April, Emma's condition had improved; she appeared stronger and the paralysis was slowly leaving her right side. However, Dorothy noted to Rose that, in all honesty, the clot on the brain had not dispersed as quickly as it should have. Emma also had insomnia and needed constant attention.[39] By 14 May, Dorothy was conveying the news that Emma's condition had deteriorated and that she had suffered a "slight hemorrhage." Her breathing was labored and she not functioning well. In fact, Emma's brother Morris and her niece Stella Ballantine had been summoned. By now, the doctor was saying that she would never leave the bed and that little time remained to her. Emma was not suffering any physical pain and was being kept comfortable in a semicomatose condition.[40] It was on the day this letter was mailed that Emma died.

Rose flew from Los Angeles to be at Emma's funeral, held at Waldheim Cemetery in Chicago.[41] Her recollections were vivid, and later she wrote and spoke of the moving experience of burying her friend. Ironically, Emma was allowed into the United States in her death as she had not been allowed in life. Emma's coffin had been covered by the SIA-FAI flag, symbol of the anarchist union in Spain. Floral arrangements were there from all over the country—from labor organizations and from friends. Many people passed the bier to pay homage. There were speeches and final tributes.

As Emma's coffin was carried from the hall, bystanders lined the street in silence. The sun came out after three days of gloom, and as the entourage approached the cemetery, chimes from the chapel rang out a requiem. Lines from the gravedigger scene from *Hamlet* were read, and "there," Rose wrote, "heaped with flowers in sunshine, with birds singing, we laid her to rest beside her Chicago comrades—asleep 50 years—her

spiritual fathers to whom she owed her birth into the anarchist movement and not far away from her friend and co-worker, Voltairine De-
Cleyre."⁴² Rose and Stella Ballantine, Emma's niece, chose two bouquets
and placed them on Voltairine's grave. Ben Reitman, Emma's greatest love,
took red roses and placed them in the arms of the statue commemorating
the Haymarket martyrs. Strangely enough, the day of her burial, 18 May,
was a day that Emma had usually commemorated with joy—it had been
the day that Berkman was released from prison after fourteen years of
incarceration.

Rose remembered this scene and spoke of it at a memorial meeting
held at Town Hall in New York on 31 May 1940. She shared the rostrum
with Norman Thomas, Rudolf Rocker, Dorothy Rogers, Roger Baldwin,
Harry Weinberger, Harry Kelly, and others.⁴³ In that speech, Rose gave a
moving and prophetic tribute to Emma Goldman:

> I was privileged to be one of her closest friends the last few years of
> [her] life. Her friendship will inspire me to endeavor to carry on, as
> much as I can, our work for labor, for freedom from oppression for
> all mankind and liberty for the individual: economic, social and
> cultural.
>
> Her indomitable, militant spirit and legend will grow with
> years, a mounting inspiration to all who knew her as one of the
> outstanding women leaders of our generation and a tradition those
> who follow will be happy and proud to revere.
>
> . . . Emma's passing left a void, not only in my heart but the
> hearts of many who shared her work and ideal. For she was one of
> the great women in history, because she was human, she was a
> living, inspiring, understanding friend, a leader to all of us.
>
> Hail and fairwell [sic], dearly beloved, may your great work go
> on and your dream for a free humanity come to pass.⁴⁴

Emma had obviously been an inspirational leader for Rose. She
embodied the social philosophy and ideology of anarchism, personifying
its principles and providing a role model for living one's life according to
anarchist ideas. By the time Rose encountered Emma, the elder had
become more pragmatic and less pure in her practice. This realism appealed to Rose. In Emma, Rose found the moral support that she had
never seemed to find before. This was one relationship from which she
did not run. She remained dedicated to helping her mentor and, through
her, was able to find the encouragement she needed to do her own
political work. Emma came into Rose's life at a crucial period. Their

relationship developed and continued during Rose's most active labor period and during the time she received the most criticism from other anarchists. Emma supported Rose and provided her the inspiration to go on. It is significant that Rose's final Los Angeles assignment came around the time of Emma's illness and death. Rose was to last but two more years as a labor organizer. Without her mentor's support, with all the criticism coming from her political comrades, with the continued undermining of her work by the Communists in Los Angeles, and with her problems with Dubinsky and the GEB, it seems inevitable that Rose would leave the ILGWU's hierarchy to return to the sewing machine. The tension between anarchism and labor organizing had become too great and, without the support and guidance of her mentor, her incentive to go on was lost.

Beyond her involvement with *Road to Freedom* and Emma Goldman, Rose also worked for a number of anarchist-based political causes, one of which was the Ferrero and Sallito deportation case.[45] Vincent Ferrero and Domenick Sallito, Italian immigrants who had entered the United States legally, had been in the country thirty and fifteen years, respectively. They were arrested on 11 April 1934 in Oakland, California, by immigration authorities. Ferrero's only crime was that he owned a restaurant and sublet space upstairs to an anarchist magazine, *Man*. Marcus Graham, the editor of *Man*, ironically was the anarchist who attacked Pesotta for being a sellout to the union. Sallito had once chaired a talk in San Francisco on the Reichstag fire in Germany—a fire that was blamed on the Communists by the Hitler regime. The talk was sponsored by members of the Communist and Socialist parties. Marcus Graham had also participated in this discussion. Immigration authorities had been hounding many subscribers to *Man*, whose names they had obtained through the postal authorities. The two were given a hearing at the Oakland immigration service because they had not followed to the letter some of the provisions of the immigration law. It was claimed that they advocated the overthrow of the United States government. They were notified of their deportation based on the provisions of anti-alien legislation, which had been used to deport Kushnarev, Goldman, and Alexander Berkman years earlier. Sallito's wife had recently died; he was raising his three-year-old daughter alone and had no relatives in the United States. Rose, along with others in the ILGWU and many anarchists, participated in their defense and attempted to have the decision overturned. A labor delegation had been sent to Assistant Labor Secretary McGrady in 1935 to argue on their behalf.

Rose was personally responsible for raising the two thousand dollars needed to bail out the two.[46] She heard of their need from an anarchist comrade and simply made a phone call to the Joint Board of the Dressmakers Union in New York, and the money was sent. Later, immigration authorities could not find any evidence that Sallito was an anarchist, so his thousand dollars was returned. Ferrero had been the editor of an Italian anarchist newspaper, *Emancipazione*, and so he could not be saved. He jumped his bail and disappeared, leaving the defense committee responsible, thus losing the thousand dollars they had pledged. The defense committee was never able to refund the money to the ILGWU.

The year 1934 found Rose involved in the fight to have Tom Mooney released from prison.[47] Mooney had been convicted, along with Warren Billings, of planting a bomb that killed ten persons at a war-preparedness march in San Francisco on 3 July 1916. In time, it was discovered that the trial had included perjured testimony and connivance on the part of the prosecution. The entire labor movement mobilized on behalf of the two. Seventeen years after that conviction, Rose was able to meet and form a friendship with Mooney. She continued to visit and support the defense committee while she was based on the West Coast and lent her union's support in obtaining their final release.

Rose was also a member of the League of Mutual Aid, founded in 1920 by Harry Kelly. This group provided money through loans without interest and was instrumental in finding jobs for the unemployed, giving guidance, sympathy, and help in financial emergency. It was inspired by Kropotkin's concept of mutual aid and had as its motto, "From each according to his ability, to each according to his need." Every member gave up to the maximum of two hundred dollars, with annual dues of five dollars. Each person could have her or his contribution returned on demand. Rose became a member early and remained involved throughout her life. She served as acting treasurer and became a vice president on the executive board just before her death.[48]

Rose often collected food, clothing, and money for needy comrades, both in the United States and abroad. At one point, her friend Valerio Isca made an appeal for aid to Italian activists. Valerio writes:

A few days later she called me to her house and delivered to me a small mountain of clothes that our comrades had brought there. Later she made an appeal, in the columns of the *Freie Arbeiter Stimme* for clothes for needy Italian comrades. This enabled me to send about a hundred packages of clothing to Italy. . . . She was a good, beautiful and strong personality in the movement.[49]

In addition to all the anarchist work, Rose belonged to numerous other civic organizations. She was a vice president of the New York

chapter of the League of Industrial Democracy and a member of the
Workers' Defense League, the Women's Trade Union League, the Jewish
Labor Committee, the American Red Cross, the Workmen's Circle, and
the ILGWU's education department. Rose obviously found it important to
keep herself occupied with political work, which was not always anarchist in orientation.

It seems that although Rose began her labor organizing work as an
anarchist, as she aged and became more cynical, her dedication to anarchism diminished. Her political beliefs appeared to become less radical
over time. As a young woman, Rose believed that revolution was imminent and necessary. She had a private idealism but a public pragmatism.
However, after the deportation of her friends and loved one, what she
saw as the failure of the Russian Revolution, the death of her father, the
execution of Sacco and Vanzetti, the failure of the Spanish experiment,
and the growing bureaucratization and conservatism of the labor movement, Rose lost her revolutionary zeal. She had been hit hard by failure,
loss, and resistance to change. As a result, her views altered, and she
became increasingly conservative and mainstream in her attitudes. Although at most one could say was that she became a liberal democrat,
this was a far cry from the knapsack toting would-be revolutionist of her
youth. Rose became less radical as a result of many outside factors that
destroyed her hope for revolutionary changes. For example, in 1936 she
wrote:

> We believe political action is the bane to the working class. History
> shows workers in political parties collapse like a house of cards—
> an example is Germany and Austria. While the Spanish labor move-
> ment is based on its own strength and the economic power of the
> workers has withstood.
>
> Many in labor are attracted to the glamor and charm of Roose-
> velt who has made liberal gestures to labor—remember he is first
> and foremost a devoted Democrat and is sponsoring the creation of
> a war machine toward an imperialist war.
>
> The labor party is also no good—it functions under a capital-
> ist system and must play by its rules. It would be compelled to cut
> budgets (unemployment and social insurance) during crises.
>
> I do not approve of attempts to divert attention to political
> action.[50]

However, by 1943 her mementos include an article she wrote entitled "Our Women Will Not Fail," in which she urges women to buy war
bonds to bring the world holocaust to a speedy end.[51] During the war,

she describes being a Red Cross union liaison officer, in which capacity she organized blood donor campaigns, first aid classes, water safety, home nursing, nutrition programs, and a canteen. And by 1964, Pesotta actually attended the Democratic National Convention in Atlantic City with a senior citizens forum.[52]

Perhaps one of the most significant alterations in political ideology was Rose's stand on World War II. Before 1940, Rose had been vehemently anti-interventionist. She believed, based on anarchist doctrine, that intervention in a world war would actually best serve the interests of the rich in protecting their property and served to their economic advantage. Most anarchists were fiercely against participation in the war, viewing themselves as internationalists instead. In 1936, Rose had joined the American League Against War and Fascism, and in 1939, she gave a speech covering the major anti-interventionist arguments. She spoke to a youth group of the catastrophe and hardship that occurs when a country is at war, citing what happened in World War I. She was fiery and inspiring and obviously believed what she was saying.[53] On 10 November 1939, she spoke at Carnegie Hall for the New York Committee to Keep America Out of War Congress. Unfortunately, that speech has been lost. In August 1940, she was lamenting that the labor movement was endorsing Roosevelt's interventionist platform. She was distraught that her union had endorsed Roosevelt, whom she felt was a warmonger.[54] She was appalled that she had to stand up and address a dressmakers meeting to explain why the ILGWU had voted in favor of Roosevelt, even though she had voted in the negative at the July 1940 ILGWU executive board meeting. Her war views were quite consistent with those of other radicals during that time who were hearing more about Hitler's activities and moving more toward an interventionist stance.

By the fall of 1940, Rose was actively supporting Roosevelt's campaign, and by November of that year, she had even received a letter from Eleanor Roosevelt thanking her for participating in Roosevelt's reelection.[55] She had participated for the first time in national electoral politics. Rose also volunteered for the American Red Cross Ambulance Corps while in California, and she wrote to her friends after leaving California that by now she was fully participating in the war effort. Previously, she had been urged by her friend Al Desser to change her antiwar stance and had refused vehemently, but by June of 1941, she wrote to her friend America Thatcher that "willy nilly I am now involved in this holocaust."[56] She was sick at heart and felt helpless in the face of global war. She began to think her only alternative was to involve herself in the war preparations. By 1942 Rose was saying that "wars have gone on for centuries and will continue as long as humanity exists."[57]

Rose's switch was based on a number of factors. First, there had been a reversal in attitude on the part of many anarchists when details began to emerge on Hitler's activities. Rudolf Rocker had toured the United States around the time of Rose's change. He convinced many anarchists that "Hitler had to be stopped at all costs."[58] Some anarchists contributed to the war effort, even serving in the armed forces. Second, and more importantly, there were also personal reasons for the change. Rose's family lived in one of the war-torn regions of Russia that was attacked by Hitler on 22 June 1941 in Operation Barbosa. Two siblings and their families were in the war front, where the most disastrous fighting occurred.[59] For a very long time, their fate was unknown, in spite of the fact that Rose tried every possible means to find and help them. She began to feel that United States intervention was necessary to change the power balance of the countries at war. It was one day after the invasion when she wrote to her friends that she was being forced into the war mentality. Later, she was to discover that her sister Miriam, along with her husband and daughter, had been killed by the Nazis on 16 October 1941 in Odessa. Her brother David and his two sons and wife were also murdered a short time later by invading troops. Fortunately, the other family members—Hannah, Luba, Abraham, and Fanya—had avoided the holocaust by running from Odessa when they heard of the invasion. David and Miriam believed that the Germans would not kill the Russian Jews, because they had not done so during their 1919 venture into the Ukraine.[60]

Rose's attitude was also influenced by the death of her niece's husband. Dorothy Rubin had married George Snyder shortly before he was shipped overseas. Taken as a prisoner of war, he was killed by the Germans late in 1942, after Pesotta's L.A. experience. They had been married a mere six months. Obviously, the combined political and personal forces were so great that Rose was compelled to alter her ideological position. Ever the pragmatist, she took the evidence to heart, swallowed her pride, and chose the practical approach—this time by throwing herself fully into war support work. The final reason for the switch was the pressure exerted by her colleagues in the ILGWU. Rose was one of the few who held an anti-interventionist stance for as long as she did. She had been out of step with her colleagues. With this combination of political and personal pressures, it was inevitable that her attitude would have to evolve.

Another position that Rose altered over the years, as noted above, was that of nonparticipation in political parties and campaigns. In 1936 she had said, "Political action is the bane to the working class. History shows that workers in political parties collapse like a house of cards." She felt that even labor parties were of no value, because they functioned under the capitalist system and played by the latter's rules. Later, however, Rose participated in the campaign to reelect Roosevelt, and many years later, just before her death, actually joined the Liberal party for a very short time and attended the Democratic convention as a senior citizen observer.

Initially, Rose's anarchism was the philosophy that underlay her political work as well as her labor activities. She was adamant in her beliefs and always identified with progressive and anarchist causes. As a labor organizer, she believed in the freedom of the individual and the rights of the worker to a decent life. As we have seen, in her labor activities she treated each of the individuals and various groups of people she encountered with respect and with the expectation that they could be educated and mobilized for political action. She was nonauthoritarian and participatory in her style of organizing with workers, although an authoritarian and general-like in her dealings with peers. Her anarchist ideology clearly informed her organizing, helping her to create environments for workers in which they could take power in their own lives. Rose took seriously what she had read, studied, and learned from her anarchist comrades

But as we have also seen, Rose's anarchism was a realistic one, one that she was willing to compromise in the face of defeats and contrary evidence. Although she may not have been pure in her theory or in her practice, neither was she a violent revolutionist. She was a radical thinker, a participant in radical activities, and basically a humanist at heart. She knew what the ideal was and should be, but she had also lived and worked in the pain of the real world. She was down to earth in her approach to problems. If one theory did not work, she would try something else. She said a number of times that she had been inspired by her famed role model to go on in the face of adversity, as well as to put up with the imperfections in people and situations. As we have seen, she became much less of an anarchist—or even a radical—as she aged. Life had given her a series of hard blows, and, as a result, she was willing to change her views. The anarchists had been difficult to get along with, revolutionary activity had failed in her eyes in Russia and in Spain, and radicalism was dead within the union. Additionally, her father had died at the hands of antirevolutionary forces, her lover Kushnarev and her friend Emma Goldman had been deported by antiradical forces, her friends Sacco and Vanzetti had been executed for their ideals. Anarchism was all but dead in the United States. It was inevitable that she was would adjust her perspectives based on her life experiences. Because of her pragmatism and willingness to alter positions, she was criticized by many, but nonetheless she always held onto her own adopted credo, "The world is my country, to do good is my religion." Sometimes she failed, but she was always reaching, trying to harmonize her lifestyle with her ideals.

7

PERSONAL LIFE: HOME, FRIENDS, AND FAMILY

The inside agitator.

Anarchist women, with whom Rose chose to associate for most of her life, had long tried to transcend conventional moral dictates. They were at the cutting edge of social change. On a very personal level, they questioned what the majority deemed acceptable behavior. These women often denied the concept of female subordination and attacked conventional marriage as obsolete. They urged economic and psychological independence from men, believing that personal autonomy was an essential component of sexual equality.[1] Anarchist men were not quite as open in their ideas about female anarchist behavior. The traditional anarchist "patriarchs" Proudhon and Kropotkin adhered to more conventional attitudes. Proudhon felt that the family was the fundamental social unit and that women would always have domestic functions. Kropotkin expected women to do political work. Both created conventional families and believed that there were certain "natural" behavior patterns for each sex.[2]

Anarchism did not have a clearly delineated theoretical position on women, but at the heart of anarchist theory was the idea that every individual possessed the right to complete liberty. One should be limited by moral obligation only to the extent that one did not encroach on the freedom of others. "As a result, though anarchism was by no means an expressly feminist ideology, it had the capacity to become so."[3] With this in mind, anarchist women called into question the role of the nuclear family and sexual relationships in general. Some anarchist women wanted women to be self-supporting and to engage in "sexual varietism," nonexclusive sexual relationships, or what we, today, would call "nonmonogamy." Some wanted to alter the structure of the nuclear family, with communal childrearing and large cooperative houses. Others believed that lovers should not live together. Generally, anarchist men were

not as open to these changes as were anarchist women. Thus, within the anarchist community, one was likely to see many different family and relationship formations. A few of Rose's friends were married and had traditional families; some lived together without marriage. Others engaged in "serial monogamy," while still others had many lovers at the same time. A number of Rose's friends sent their children to the Modern School at Stelton and tried to rear them communally, whereas others sent their offspring to public schools and appeared to lead "normal" family lives.[4]

Rose herself had a number of different types of relationships. At times her position on marriage is somewhat unclear. In her memoirs she noted that she had married twice. However, there appears to be documentation for only one legal marriage, which occurred later in her life. In any event, Rose did live with a number of men and had quite a few additional love affairs. One might presume that Rose was rather "unlucky in love."[5] In her first real relationship, with Theodore Kushnarev, she lost. Soon after their romance began to blossom, the young man was deported to Russia, eventually fell in love with another, and shortly thereafter died.

Her second documented affair was with Israel Kasvan, with whom she lived for a few years during the late 1920s. Rose saw Kushnarev as her first husband and called Kasvan her second. Rose and Kasvan lived in a common-law marriage, as did many of their anarchist friends at that time. In fact, while they were together, it appears that he was involved with another woman. But Rose felt that her parting from Kasvan was, in part, caused by ideological differences, not jealousy. Kasvan was a Zionist and eventually became a Communist zealot, while she remained dedicated to anarchism. However, they remained good friends and, in fact, agreed on almost everything, except their respective movements.[6]

Rather than say she was unlucky, we can note that Rose actually believed in "free unions" in which partners could choose to be or not be together. She believed that people should not be constrained by the conventional dictates of marriage. With this in mind, Rose fell in love with married men a number of times throughout her life. Once she placed herself in exile in Los Angeles so as to avoid the difficulties of an affair with an unnamed man:

> I am hopelessly in love with A. I ran away to L.A. to escape one hopeless affair and to find another hopeless case. I have spent two days crying. I will tell him not to visit me anymore. We had our fling, now it is not what it used to be. Why this torture. I shall never forgive myself for having written to him when I arrived—it would have been much better not to have done it.[7]

In 1934 she received an anonymous letter accusing her of an affair with another married man, perhaps Paul Berg, an organizer in L.A. Her response indicates her belief in freedom within relationships. She felt that a woman should not chain down a partner and argued that if one of her partners had an affair, it was none of her business. Rose felt that if a woman had a suspicion, she should confront the other woman and have a heart to heart talk with her, rather than "meddle" and make anonymous threats. She said, "If I love a man who doesn't care for my love anymore, I would never try to chain him." She goes on: "We live in a civilized world where people read and discuss things openly. It behooves any intelligent person that even similar questions brought out in your letter could be discussed intelligently and without hard feelings."[8]

While at the Brookwood Labor College in the 1920s, Rose had an affair with Horst Borenz, a German who had come to the United States to study. This relationship ended when he returned home, but they maintained contact during the 1930s. They lost touch during World War II, but he reemerged after the war. Rose did research on him to see what his affiliations were during the war. Finding that he had not actively colluded with the Nazis, she willingly met with him when he returned to the United States for a visit. He had become an administrator in the coal mines and had grown old and portly. During this visit, he had told her that no "German in their right mind dare oppose the Hitler regime."[9]

Even though she espoused freedom, Rose's relationships appear to have been difficult and painful. Her diaries of the 1930s indicate she was often hopelessly in love. When rejected, she spent days and nights alone, crying.[10] Although none of the lovers are named specifically, the theme remains the same. She would fall in love with someone, they would spend a blissful time together, and then the man would leave her, either to return to his wife or for another woman. In 1931 and 1932, she was hopelessly in love with A., to whom she gave herself "willingly, lovingly, passionately. My whole being was his." In November 1931 she wrote:

Lying in bed this a.m. trying to decide my fate. Why am I a loser in everything. . . .
> where are my friends
> who are my comrades
> where are the admirers.

How many times I have to walk alone after spending an evening entertaining others. How many days am I spending either at home or outside alone with no one even to call up to find out whether I am dead or alive?

My lover! Where is he? . . . How much love do I get and when? Is he really loving or simply performing an unpleasant duty? After seeing him, I feel removed. I must end it.[11]

In Seattle by December 1934, and slightly so in Puerto Rico, Rose began to experience periods of loneliness and self-doubt about her life and work. Both her autobiography and her diaries reflect the growing isolation Rose felt on the road.[12] Her loneliness was lifelong, but became acute when she was visiting new areas without friends and family to call on. Her diary often reflected her image of herself as a loser, and a 1931 entry notes: "Everyone will imagine that a person like myself is always happy, always cheerful, has scores of friends and admirers. What more does a person need. Nobody knows how many cheerless, sleepless nights I have spent crying in my loneliness. I wish I had someone to confide in—to be all alone in this world—goodness will it ever stop?"[13] And just a few days later, she lamented, "Now I can understand how a person feels in solitary confinement. To spend a whole day alone brooding is equal to prison life. Now everywhere life goes on. I sit at the window watching the snow clogged empty street."[14]

Rose was not without admirers. It is obvious that many men who heard her speak became infatuated with her. In 1937, she received love letters from a man who wanted to see her regularly and wanted to show her his feelings. He wanted to be with her more than anyone else in the world.[15] Thomas Smith was an Irish steelworker in Cleveland and worked for the CIO. His letters reflect his infatuation, calling her an "inside agitator," even suggesting that he move to New York to be with her. Rose handled him carefully, but with little encouragement. She urged him to become involved with others, especially Irish women. That little romance ended quickly.

Other admirers wrote letters that clearly indicated their respect and enamorment.[16] Ralph Fol heard her speak to a youth group against the United States' involvement in World War II. He found Rose to be an inspiring speaker, describing her as "eloquent and grandiloquent" and intended to dedicate a book to her, originating from gems of thought that she shared in speeches and writings. Another admirer—and possible lover—Paul Berg, called her the "most beautiful woman in the world" and was afraid that she was in his mind too much for his own good.[17] Berg was an officer in the dressmakers union in Los Angeles, and it was about him that the anonymous letter was written. Rose and he were involved during her first visit to Los Angeles, and they remained friends for years after their romantic period had ended.

Perhaps the most significant and certainly the most well-documented relationship that Rose experienced was with Powers Hapgood. Hapgood was the son of William and Eleanor Hapgood of the well-known, politically active Hapgood family, all of whom engaged in liberal and progressive causes. According to biographer Michael Marcaccio, they participated in the "social and intellectual ferment of their time."[18] Hutchins Hapgood, Powers's uncle, had long been active with radicals and anarchists, including Emma Goldman, and Powers's father, William, owned and operated a producers' cooperative canning firm.

Rose met Powers while working on the Sacco and Vanzetti defense. Powers Hapgood, born on 28 December 1899, was a Harvard University graduate, then a miners' organizer. He had met and married Mary Donovan, Socialist party candidate for vice president and national secretary of the Sacco and Vanzetti defense in 1928. They had two children and lived in Massachusetts and later Indianapolis, Indiana, where they farmed the Hapgood family estate. Hapgood was a noted labor organizer. Beginning with the United Mine Workers of America in 1921, he went on to organize for the Amalgamated Clothing Workers, the Textile Workers of Kentucky, the Socialist party in Massachusetts, and the Southern Tenant Farmers Union in Arkansas. In the 1930s, he went to work for the CIO, organizing rubberworkers, auto workers, steel workers, shoe workers, marine and shipbuilding workers, and farm equipment workers. Later, he became a regional director for the CIO in New England and Indiana. In addition, he authored a book on coal miners and wrote for the *New Republic* and the *Nation*. It was in his capacity as a CIO organizer that he was sent to Akron and reencountered Rose, whom he had not seen since a Sacco and Vanzetti memorial meeting.

By February 1936, Rose and Powers were spending enormous amounts of time together because of their activities in Akron and Flint. By April, Hapgood wrote to Rose that he was "hopelessly in love with two women at the same time, my wife and Rose." He continued, "I can't help loving you for your generosity, courage, and beauty that make you one of the loveliest women I have ever met."[19] Although most of Rose's responses to the hundreds of love letters written by Hapgood have been lost, perhaps destroyed over the years, it appears that she, too, was deeply in love. Their relationship blossomed; in June, he accompanied her to New York, where he met her mother and her dear friend Rae Brandstein.[20] At the beginning of their relationship, they frequently exchanged letters, many of which describe the details of their respective labor work. Others reflect Rose's growing pain at "his disloyalty to his family and being 'unfaithful.'"[21] She was disturbed enough to consider ending the sexual nature of their relationship. Hapgood was honest with his wife about his affair; he was also honest with Rose. He stated that even though she was brave, loyal, and beautiful, he would in no way end or jeopardize his marriage and family to be with Rose.[22]

Rose even corresponded with Mary and visited their farm to meet the children. She went so far as to describe in writing to Mary how the "inevitable happened" and shared her guilt and love for Mary and the children. In September 1936, in what is an unusual letter from a mistress to a distressed wife, she wrote:

> During the first week of the rubber workers strike in February I received a telegram from my general office to proceed at once to Akron. . . .

> I found Powers in bed sick with a heavy cold. He looked so pathetic in the untidy hotel room, with the rest of the union organizers paying very little attention to a sick man that the former professional nurse arouse [sic] in me. I administered some aid and comfort, much to the amusement of the rest of our colleagues. To me this incident was closed as soon as the sick man was able to again resume his activities. . . .

> When I returned I found a letter from Powers. It actually broke my heart, for I never meant to do anything wrong by chumming with him, as I know how fond he is of his family, so much so that I began to feel as if I knew you all. I promptly answered his letter with the hope this thing will smooth out. After that we kept up a friendly correspondence. . . .

> The president instructed me to stop on my way also in Ohio and Chicago. Hence I again met Powers at a steel workers meeting. He told me of his feelings and I then advised him to forget this foolishness and devote himself to his family. . . .

> I had to speak at the Bryn Mawr Summer School and there I learned Powers was sick at a Germantown hospital. We all went to see him there and I spent exactly 5 minutes at his bedside. He looked so sad and ill it broke my heart.

> Thus I began to have a feeling of more than friendship. When realized that, the first thought uppermost in my mind [was] to leave NY as quickly as possible

> When President Dubinsky returned I told him I was ready to leave for Montreal (for over a year they were after me and I consistently refused to go there—my president must have thought I was crazy now): I chose Montreal—a cool place and far away from

mischief. I wrote Powers that I was leaving Monday. He came to New York on Saturday and what transpired between us he may have related to you himself.

President D. assigned me to attend as the ILGWU representative to the Rubber Workers Convention which was held last week in Akron. Again I met the CIO reps and Powers was one of them. This time [I] could not resist the persistent affections and the inevitable happened.

Mary, I have a mingled feeling of love and guilt before you and your lovely children. It hurt me to the core to realize that I did not keep my resolution to keep away as far as it is only humanly possible from the person I began to love more than a friend. I made an honest attempt—and left NY after I realized that it was phisically [*sic*] impossible for me to live in such close proximity, but the meeting in Akron was the climax—I was completely lost. I feel ashamed that I failed you and above all I failed myself, for I was foolish enough to admit that I was in love with him.

For the present I cannot see my way clear. Shall try to bury myself in our work (now I need a violent strike or something to keep my thoughts away from myself) but I hardly know anyone here and it will take me weeks before we get going.

I do not know why I am writing you this, only to let you know how stupid we women are, neither age nor experience is an assurance that we will not commit something foolish that is supposed to be inherent only among the the younger generation. My only hope is that you will understand me[23]

Clearly Pesotta had much guilt and was trying to assuage herself and make amends to Donovan. She also spoke up, in keeping with previous statements about jealousy between women and the need for open communication. This is certainly an unusual and brave way to handle an affair as "the other woman." Unfortunately Donovan's response to this letter is nowhere to be found. However in 1941, Donovan wrote to Pesotta that "marriage is an unfortunate experience" and that she "would never do it again.[24]

Clearly Hapgood had much responsibility here in pressing Rose into an affair. But he would not give Rose up and insisted that Mary not restrict his behavior. He wrote Rose that "restrictions and inaccessibility will only increase my desire and make you all the more unhappy." He even went so far as to insist that Mary should know such things are inevitable, and "the more easily she takes it, the easier it will be to hold you."[25] He was in the position of having two women adore him. He was not about to relinquish this power.

The pain was so great for Rose that she tried to end the relationship a number of times. She attempted to be stoic and to hide her pain. But the situation was complicated and unrewarding, and in a letter to Powers she lamented,

> Life has been rather cruel to me. Every inch of space I have had to fight for, if I want to win. Because I had to fight, it was necessary to equip myself with stamina and courage. Each time I had to fight it out if I wanted a bit of enjoyment—because of that each minute I enjoyed, because I knew that it will not repeat I relished every second.
>
> My brief experience within the last few weeks were of the nature I knew would not culminate in permanent happiness. But the brief moments were an idyll.[26]

Hapgood, however, refused to let Rose out of the relationship and at the height of their affair wrote:

> I have never known how selfish I am. I always thought I was generous because I did not go after wealth, good jobs, or esteem of the mob because I was willing to submerge my own interests to that of the masses. Until now I never wanted anything enough to be selfish. If I were generous darling, I would let you forget and sever our relationship now. Instead of breaking everything off, if you won't consent to be lovers, can't we at least be pals? Won't you at least hold out hope that if you come back to New York you will let me know, and that if at the end of six months I still feel 'ceaseless longing and ceaseless ache' we can meet somewhere.[27]

Even when they tried to end their relationship at a later point, they kept coming back to each other. They hoped to evolve a relationship much like that of Emma Goldman and Alexander Berkman, who had started out as lovers but ended up devoted comrades and lifelong friends. At other times, they went back to the sexual, which caused all three— Mary, Hapgood, and Rose—enormous distress. Mary was quite jealous and could not handle the situation,[28] and Rose felt badly about being a "home wrecker," wanting to find a way to help him patch up his marriage.[29] Hapgood finally felt guilty because of the pain he was causing both of them. He rationalized his guilt to Rose:

FIGURE 13

Rose Pesotta and Powers Hapgood, New York, December 1937.

Photo courtesy of Dorothy, Elias, and Edward Rotker.

Our relationship deepens and we miss each other. We are growing closer and the more I know you, the more I love you and want to come to you and stay. But I have my children and I can't forget what a comrade Mary has been, participating in labor struggles, sharing jails with me, keeping house and having a baby on miners wages. I wish she wasn't so jealous.[30]

Rose and Powers continued their relationship throughout their labor organizing careers. They continued to write, to visit periodically, to provide advice and support for each other's political undertakings. In the course of things, Mary became accepting of the friendship when Rose and Powers finally cut down their assignations. He wrote that Mary "feels a lot different about a certain friendship of mine than she used to and she hopes I will see my friend soon."[31] Having ended the physical nature of their relationship, Rose visited him during his 1937 incarceration in Maine during a CIO strike, and they wrote to each other often while he was imprisoned. She even called him on the phone while he was incarcerated.[32] After her visit, he wrote: "I wished we could have taken a long walk and had a real talk. As it was, just to see you looking so well and as lovely as ever helped me a lot. I will never forget what a wonderful comrade you have always been and will always be."[33] In July 1937, Powers wrote to Rose:

> I am a man very, very much in love. I have admired you as a class conscious fighter. [I feel] comradeship, friendship and love for all your beautiful qualities. I will always long for you as a lover even though you were to prohibit any closer relationship. We are more than lovers, sweetheart. We are comrades in the anti-capitalist struggle. We are friends and pals forever.[34]

For a while they found a way to continue their relationship by not being honest with Mary, as when Hapgood wrote:

> My visit home was quiet and peaceful. No questions were asked and Mary is quite happy. I don't think she will ever ask again because she knows I can't forget such a beautiful companionship as I have had with you. It's better for three people to be modestly happy than for one to be constantly nervous and sleepless, another to miss a companionship that must mean something to her, and a third to be worried.[35]

Powers Hapgood had a problem with alcohol and may have even been an alcoholic, which was to become a major factor in his relationship with Rose. During the honeymoon period, he had been able to curb his consumption. However, with the tension between the three and the continued strain from work, Hapgood again overindulged. Bitter scenes ensued in which he and Pesotta would battle about his drinking. After one such scene, he drank too much and did not phone Rose later because he was too ashamed. Instead, according to Rose, he chose oblivion.[36] A number of times he was hospitalized because of his problem, and Rose came to his aid, providing support and counsel. It was at these times—when he felt guilty—that he tried to let her go. At other times, under the influence of alcohol, he treated her unkindly, and she withdrew once again.

Hapgood was sometimes so immobilized that he was unable to work, as when he could not speak in Madison Square Garden in 1938, spending the evening, instead, collapsed on a park bench.[37] Eventually, Pesotta realized that she was "giving him up to a bottle of scotch."[38] She tried to convince him to "go on the wagon" and was encouraged when he moved, with his wife and children, to the family home in Indianapolis. There, she hoped, he might recuperate and regain some of his strength and self-esteem. Hapgood knew that his problem took its toll on Rose and feared that it would diminish her love for him. This fear surfaced when, in July 1938, Rose urged:

> Please go to a sanitarium. It must be cured as any other illness. My good friend and comrade Van Valkenburgh died while drunk. He never regained consciousness. I hope that no other friend will end his days the way he did. If you want to retain your position in the labor movement and your name in the revolutionary movement you must get cured. If you don't it will be impossible for me to see you again.[39]

By August, Hapgood had lost his driver's license and had refused to go into treatment. Accordingly, Pesotta withdrew once again. Her numerous letters diminished markedly to one a month and became more businesslike, discussing Emma Goldman and labor issues. They saw each other even less when he retired to the farm to tend his gardens and animals. During 1939, although they saw each other infrequently, he continued to long for her, and she continued to entreat him to get help.

But again by 1940, the two were warm to each other and visited regularly. By the fifth year of their relationship, they had settled into a pattern of visiting, sending letters and flowers, making loving phone calls, and sharing warm and playful times together. Periodically Hapgood would overindulge in alcohol again, and Pesotta would force herself to withdraw rather than show the deep hurt and dismay that she felt concerning his behavior.[40] In 1941, while Rose was working in Los Angeles, he spent two months on the West Coast. The two spent a good deal of time together and appear to have had a good time; they were able to negotiate a contract pertaining to his drinking, to which he adhered. But soon after this visit, Hapgood lamented:

> Oh darling I am so unhappy about it all. I love you so much that it keeps me always on edge when I feel I bore you, as I did on the auto trip . . . when you read to yourself all afternoon of a day when we were soon to depart. It is so different from the one who clasped my

hand in front of the whole world in Niagara Falls. I feel you really care; at other times, I feel you have lost interest.[41]

After his departure from California, Pesotta saw him in Chicago when she attended the GEB meeting. In February 1942, just before she left the L.A. situation, Pesotta records: "Powers and I went to see 'How Green was my Valley' and danced all night at the LA conga."[42] Soon thereafter he again slipped back into alcohol, and their relationship floundered yet another time. From mid 1942 to 1945, Rose saw Powers very infrequently. Their visits diminished to one a year, and their letters were distant, mainly discussing political and labor matters. Pesotta had become rather maternal toward Hapgood, showing a continued interest in his activities, but in a detached and aloof manner. She removed herself psychologically from the situation rather than be hurt once more. Hapgood did assist Pesotta in some of her research for *Bread upon the Waters* and in reviewing it for labor publications, but their intense involvement diminished. For a while, it seemed possible for them to become colleagues and comrades rather than lovers, but then their correspondence abruptly ceased. From 1945 to 1949, no letters appear, and contact ended entirely.

Then on 4 February 1949, Powers Hapgood died in an automobile accident in Indianapolis. Pesotta believed that he died because of the alcohol, although he also had a heart condition.[43] The news of his death came to her over the radio, and she "felt a void in her heart," seeing it as an irreparable loss of a friend who had meant so very much to her. "He was a likeable fellow that one could not help loving. He is gone forever from our lives. No longer will we discuss his deeds, his faults and his virtues."[44] According to Pesotta, Hapgood appeared to her to have "died of a broken heart," and she was deeply grieved at his loss. She may have even felt some guilt over his drinking, fearing that some of it was because of her and the difficulty of their relationship. Upon receiving a telegram inviting her to his funeral, Rose attended and gave a eulogy at the simple ceremony.[45] In it, she extolled his simple handshake, the humorous twinkle in his eye, his anecdotes, and his zest for life. Remembering Hapgood, Pesotta called him "an idealist, a crusader for human rights, a seasoned agitator, and a champion debater who was equally at home in drawing rooms and with strikers. He could debate in court or with a local police officer or a provincial judge. . . . He was always on the picket line or demonstrations. Jailed, he feared nothing. . . . He was devoid of pettiness and had no enemies." Tearfully, Rose noted that he died as he lived, at a wheel, driving into the dark unknown alone.[46] He was just forty-nine years old when he died.

Hapgood had been an immensely important friend and colleague for Pesotta, having participated with her in important events in her labor work, and having given her support and encouragement during difficult moments. Most importantly, he had been deeply in love with her for many, many years. Although the relationship did not come to a happy ending, it did provide Rose with an education in working through difficult relationships and in evolving love into friendship, as well as finally providing her with at least one long-term and loving relationship. The Hapgood affair was important in teaching Pesotta how to be in such a relationship and how to struggle together, as one, through adversity. In fact, it was her longest and, apparently, most dedicated love affair. Through it, she tried living her anarchism on a very personal level. Here, too, she found that the real and the ideal were difficult to reconcile. Despite her belief in nonmonogamy and free unions, Rose reacted as one might expect; she felt guilty and enmeshed in a difficult situation. Rather than live her ideals, she evolved the relationship into a more conventional friendship between a married man and a single woman. Rose found in her personal life, as in her political one, that the theories are fine in print but difficult to implement in reality. There were actual consequences for her behavior, and these were not easily dismissed. Rose had tried to live an unconventional life outside the confines of a marriage. But there had been no models for this, and ultimately it was doomed. Rose experienced the great highs and debilitating lows of a deeply loving relationship through her involvement with Hapgood. But once again, as with Kushnarev and her father, Pesotta lost the man she loved. Because she refused to live the conventional life of a married woman of her day, it was necessary for her to walk on alone—once again.

Pesotta's unfortunate history in relationships also warrants a psychodynamic interpretation. Pesotta was a woman who was tough, strong, and independent. She also tended to choose men who were similarly tough and strong. This led to bad matches, because neither Pesotta nor her partners seemed able to bend their wills or compromise with each other. Rose was a sometimes difficult woman, one who wanted her way and could be abrasive and snippy when crossed. Such a disposition, when matched with equally powerful types, led to failed relationships. Pesotta did not know how, nor did she want, to be a traditional wife. Marriage, as Carolyn Heilbrun has noted, is a "bargain, like buying a house or entering a profession. One chooses it knowing that, by that very decision, one is abnegating other possibilities."[47] She adds that a sign of a good marriage is one in which everything is debatable and challenged, never made into law or policy.[48] Rose was never able to find a man willing to enter such a bargain with her. She made poor choices in men, a few times even with married men, which led to a lifelong quest for intimacy and connection that was never satisfied. One must also wonder if there was not an element of fear of closeness and sharing that caused this pattern. Often she left the area and ended relationships because they were not satisfying, rather than stay on and work to change them. Whatever the cause, the fact remains that Pesotta had no long-term satisfying partnership. In fact, Pesotta's organizing activities and successes in her work became a substitute, albeit a poor substitute to her, for a loving lifelong relationship.

Rose's only legal documented marriage was with Albert Martin. Martin, whose real name apparently was Frank Lopez, was an alien from Spain; it is unclear whether he was a legal or illegal alien. Lopez introduced Rose to the Sacco and Vanzetti Defense Committee and served as secretary of that group for a short time. Rose maintained contact with him after the deaths of Sacco and Vanzetti. Later, Lopez was either deported or escaped deportation by leaving the country for a while.[49] According to an anarchist comrade, Lopez had actually been placed on board a ship in the New York harbor; however, a Spanish seaman assisted him in jumping ship, and Lopez swam to shore, thus escaping the planned deportation. It is unclear just what activity led up to his intended deportation from the United States. After arriving back in Manhattan, Lopez joined his lover, Mary Berkowitz, and they disappeared together for a number of years. Years later, after Mary died, he returned to New York, having assumed the name Albert Martin. Soon thereafter, he sought out Rose and begged her to marry him. In 1953, the two were married and, by that spring, had bought a brownstone together on Park Place in Brooklyn, which they proceeded to remodel and turn into a two-family home.[50] Rose chose to retain her name; she said: "Call me Rose Pesotta— I have lived with this name so long, I will never part with it."[51]

It appears that the marriage with Martin was also an unhappy episode in Rose's life.[52] Martin, a carpenter by trade, was a loner. Often, he would sit in the corner at social events, appearing distant and aloof in contrast to Rose, the extrovert. There appeared to be many tensions between the two. According to family members, Rose wanted to maintain her active political and social life, and this caused friction with Martin, who was far more solitary and withdrawn. At one point, she wanted to go to a convention in Cleveland, and he wanted her to stay home and "dedicate [her] life to me." They argued and Rose insisted, after years of independence (by now she was fifty-seven), that "you can't keep me in these four walls." Allegedly, he then slapped her, which caused a black eye. Rose ran from the home to friends in New Jersey and soon thereafter sued him for divorce. For a while, he stayed in the house in Brooklyn; when he finally left, he gave her a bill for the hours he had worked on

FIGURE 14

Albert Martin, Rose Pesotta, and Clara Larsen (early 1950s).

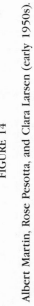

Photo courtesy of Clara Larsen.

remodeling the house.[53] They battled over financial matters for a while and, ultimately, after just two years of marriage, parted ways. Yet another, and this time final, love affair concluded in pain. Rose was an independent woman who could not be subjected to another person's will and authority. In fact, she was a woman far ahead of her time in rejecting the constrictions of marriage. Once again, as in so many earlier difficult involvements with men, including her father and Dubinsky, Rose chose to remove herself from the confinements and restrictions of what was expected of women. Rose continued, as she had first done in 1913, to "find a way out" as a single woman. It was lonely, but it was the only way she could maintain her independence, and, as I have noted, it may well have been rooted in her lack of desire to compromise, which a stable marriage requires.

Throughout all Rose's relationships, she saw herself as a "loser" and an abandoned woman.[54] Her journals reflected days and nights of crying alone, mourning her plight. She recorded evenings of entertaining others and then going home alone. She spoke of many New Year's Eves, meeting yet another year all alone. Rose saw herself as "alone in this world" and wondered if it would ever stop.[55] In fact, except for brief periods, the answer to her sorrowful question was that she would always be alone. In her love relationships, it appeared that Rose was never able to find satisfaction. Instead, it was with her friends and family that Rose was able to form the kind of closeness and union that she was seeking with a man. Given her unconventional lifestyle, it was the solace and community of others that provided her the intimacy she so sorely wanted and needed.

Rose's friendships, in effect, became her family. Even those she befriended soon after immigrating to the United States remained lifetime comrades and confidants. Having come from a warm and close-knit community in the Ukraine, Rose tried to create a similarly nourishing environment in her new home through a network of friendships. Rose's social relationships were also an important part of her anarchism. Much personal energy was expended in maintaining connections to other anarchists and in building a close network of support. Many letters were sent to her while she was on the road, and she visited often with fellow anarchists and labor organizers as she traveled around the country.

Alice Kessler Harris has said that Pesotta, "unlike Newman and Cohn, sought solace in men and depriving herself of close women friends exacerbated her loneliness. Tormented by the gossip of her female colleagues, she struggled with her self-image."[56] This actually is not the case. The fact is that Pesotta chose to have close friendships with women who were in the anarchist circle, rather than among other labor organizing women. Most of her friends were dress shop seamstresses and comrades from her anarchist activities.

Rose actually had a number of close female friends, and among her closest were Anna Sosnovsky, Rae Brandstein, and Clara Rothberg Larsen. She had met Sosnovsky and Brandstein while studying at the labor colleges in the 1930s, and had worked with Anna on *Road to Freedom* and the anarchist summer camps.[57] Anna died in 1949, the same year as Hapgood—a particularly difficult year for Pesotta, because of the loss of two such intimate colleagues. That she always lost the people with whom she was the closest became a constant lament in Rose's life. When Rose spoke at Anna's memorial in Chicago, she remembered, "Anna, you will always be alive, as I have seen you last, in your home, on the picket lines, in committee sessions, at school where we spent the happiest years of our youth, in the movement where we endeavored to build a new society. The memory of you will live with me, as a visionary, an idealist, and as an anarchist."[58]

Rae Brandstein and Rose carried on a very active correspondence while Rose was on the road for the ILGWU. They shared an apartment in New York for a while, and Rose introduced Rae to Hapgood, who would often visit her when he was in New York City. Rose and Powers often tried to help Rae find work because of her chronic unemployment problem. Carolyn Heilbrun has described friendships between women as "societies of consolation," places in which women would nurture and console each other as they waited in fear of what "life would force them to endure."[59] Rose and her friends supported each other in this way.

Clara Rothberg Larsen met Rose soon after the two came to the United States, and they remained lifelong friends. They picketed together, participated in labor organizing and anarchist activities, and even shared apartments and clothing. In fact, after Clara's marriage to Christ Larsen, Rose and Christ went on a trip together because Clara was too busy with shop organizing to take the honeymoon with her new husband. Many years later, when Christ died, it was Rose who picked up his ashes at the crematorium. She and Clara then buried the ashes under the flowers in the garden of the ILGWU's housing project, within sight of Clara and Rose's apartments.[60] Their friendship was deep and close, and Clara remembers that Rose "cared for me like a baby." As Carolyn Heilbrun has said of friendships, "If we look beyond the public face of those few notable women in the past, we may find an untold story of friendship between women, sustaining but secret."[61] This friendship was clearly one.

Because friendships were extremely important to Rose, she discerned that they "do not grow like weeds in a garden."[62] Of friendship, she said: "Friends must be cultivated and appreciated; otherwise, people are to remain alone and friendless. . . . do not use friends against each other, call them derogatory names, and throw intimate friends about."[63]

In keeping with the need to cultivate friendships, Rose was always generous with her friends, spending her organizer's salary on those she loved.
She often sent gifts from her various travels and entertained friends in
her home. She loved to throw lavish parties for her colleagues, where she
was able to show off her culinary talents. She loved having small, intimate
dinner parties, as well as big gatherings. Rose was quite a "social but-
terfly," and everyone who knew her remembers her fabulous parties and
lovely social events. Being an excellent cook, Rose used every opportunity to have friends over with whom to share her home and food.

Rose also went out of her way to help her friends. She was particularly involved with Mollie Steimer and Jack Abrams, two anarchist
friends who had been arrested for distributing leaflets against United
States intervention in the Russian Revolution and, in 1921, deported.[64]

Rose met Steimer when the two were working for anarchist groups
just before World War I. They met again when Rose visited Europe in
1937 and began an active correspondence that continued until Rose's
death. The two traveled around Paris together and attended the Syndicalist (anarchist unions) convention with Emma Goldman during the 1937
visit. When Rose returned home, Mollie enlisted her aid in refugee assistance work for the Spanish comrades. Steimer's husband, Senya Fleshine,
was a photographer, and Rose helped him set up an international photographic exhibition in 1938.[65]

Steimer and Fleshine had endured ill health, privation, and government persecution through a good part of their lives. After deportation,
Mollie had lived in Russia, where she met Fleshine. They were imprisoned, tortured, and deported from there in 1923. During the twenties, they had lived in France and Germany. When Hitler came to power,
they fled to France from Germany. In 1940 Germany occupied France,
and Steimer was sent to a concentration camp; Fleshine was not incarcerated. After months in the camp, Mollie escaped to an unoccupied part of
France.[66] Meanwhile, Fleshine had been in contact with Rose, who tried
to get visas for the two to return to the United States. When that failed,
she raised money so that Mollie and Senia could immigrate to Mexico.
Rose negotiated with Jack Abrams, who had previously gone to live in
Mexico, so that a home would be ready for the two refugees when they
arrived.[67] Just before their relocation, Rose wrote of her hopes to Jack
Abrams:

> Someday we will have a grand reunion this side of the border with
> you, Mary [Abrams], Molly, Senya, Emma, and all the others in our
> midst. In the meantime, we have to equip ourselves with patience
> and answer the SOS calls of our martyred comrades.[68]

Finally, by May 1941, Mollie and Senya made it to safety from Lisbon, Portugal, to Mexico. Eventually, with the help of Rose and other U.S. colleagues, enough money was raised so that Fleshine could work in a photographic studio, SEMO, which gained popularity. Fleshine's work was even recognized by the famous Mexican artist Diego Rivera, who became a friend of theirs. Upon reaching safety, Mollie wrote to Rose:

> I embrace you all for all that you have done in our behalf. Not a day passes we should not think in deepest terms of gratitude towards all of you who got us away from the hell which is present-day France.[69]

In April 1942, after leaving the GEB of the ILGWU, Rose visited the Fleshines in Mexico. It was a heartwarming reunion, since Rose had been working for years to bring her comrades to a safe haven. She was heartfelt in her joy at seeing them alive and well.

From then on, Mollie and Rose gave each other much support and affection. Rose often came through with money, visits, and gifts. Mollie often wrote about how proud she was of Rose, most notably when Rose resigned from the GEB. She said Rose was not like "most functionaries who once they had a leading position never could go back working in the shop. . . . You proved to us there are exceptions, that you remained and always will be your old self."[70] The two also offered each other solace as more and more of their political allies died, and Mollie encouraged Rose in her book-writing efforts.

In 1952 Jack Abrams became ill with cancer. Rose used her leverage in the labor movement to obtain a visa so that he could return to the United States for medical treatment.[71] Rose journeyed to Philadelphia to visit him and enlisted the aid of the Jewish Labor Committee to handle the legal matters on the case. When his cancer was in remission, Rose arranged finances so that he and his wife, Mary, could return to Mexico. She also contributed regularly to a fund established for Jack and Mary, which allowed the two to be more solvent while living in Mexico. In 1953, when Jack died, she became a regular contributor for Mary's upkeep.

Rose obviously took her friendships and family responsibilities very seriously. In 1928 her mother, Masya, emigrated from Russia. It had been difficult for her to obtain permission from the Communist government to emigrate. Eventually, they let her leave in order to be reunited with her children. Unfortunately, she had to leave her other children in Russia, although she had hoped to send for them later—after she was settled. Rose supported her financially, and she and Esther shared caring for Masya. Masya maintained a home in New York and also lived periodically

FIGURE 15

Mexico City, 1942.

Left to right: Mary Abrams, Jack Abrams, Rose Pesotta, Senya Fleshine,
Mollie Steimer.

Photo courtesy of Dorothy, Elias, and Edward Rotker.

with her eldest daughter, Esther, in Boston. She lived to age ninety-eight,
outliving Rose by three years.

Rose saw herself as a devoted daughter and family member. But
there were also many problems between mother and daughter. In her
diaries, Rose recorded incidents in which she felt forced out of her home
by her mother. They argued a great deal, and her mother appeared
somewhat dismayed at some of Rose's behavior.[72] According to family
members, Masya and Rose were equally hard people with whom to live,
which very often led to inevitable mother-daughter skirmishes. Unfortunately, little has been written on Rose's relationship with her mother.

Family members indicate that their struggle was lifelong, and yet we know that Rose did choose to dedicate *Bread upon the Waters* to her mother, as well as to her father. In that dedication, she indicated an appreciation for her mother's infinite loyalty and patience. Certainly we know that Rose was not an easy woman with whom to get along; she was egocentric, impatient, and liked things to go her own way. Undoubtedly, Masya encountered these traits and battles ensued. Additionally, Masya maintained orthodox Jewish practices after coming to the United States, while Rose had been thoroughly assimilated and Americanized. In fact, she barely spoke with an accent. Rose was also a totally "modern woman" in her work associations and her personal relationships, and one can only imagine that this lifestyle must have been somewhat troubling to the Old-World mother. Nonetheless, the two remained devoted and loyal to each other, even in the face of inevitable conflict and tension. As much as Rose chose to separate herself from her mother, so, too, she was bonded and deeply committed to her.

In addition, Rose felt responsible for the siblings she left behind in Europe. When her mother immigrated, she tried to arrange for them to come as well. The Communists would not allow them to leave. During World War II, Rose tried to find them, and once they were located, she sent money and assistance through international relief agencies to ease their poor economic situation. She sent money so that two sisters could move to the United States, and in 1950, although they did not immigrate, Luba and Fanya finally came for a three-month visit. Rose's sister Fanya remembers her fondly, and although the 1950 visit turned out to be the first and last, they managed to form a close and loving bond through correspondence. Rose also provided financially for other family members who stayed behind in Russia, and, in fact, left her estate to them upon her death. She also had a favorite nephew, Jack Hochman, whom she wanted very much to adopt.[73] She did take him under her wing, helping him gain a position in the ILGWU, and he went on to become the manager-secretary of Local 66 in New York City.

Rose was also very involved with Dorothy Rubin Rotker, her sister Esther's daughter. When Rose organized in Boston and Los Angeles, she found positions there for Dorothy, and after her organizing days were over, she traveled extensively with her niece, in Rose's elegant 1930 Pierce Arrow automobile. Together they met Diego Rivera and his wife, Frida Kahlo, and enjoyed Rivera as a tour guide in Mexico for one month of their two-month visit. In fact, Rose purchased a Rivera painting. Rose also provided a home for Dorothy, her second husband, Elias, and son, Eddie, when Elias returned from World War II; they lived with her from 1946 until they bought a home in 1949 in Levittown. According to

Dorothy, Rose's apartment on Twenty-fifth Street in New York City was
kept extremely neat and clean, and the family remembers her as a dicta-
tor who insisted that things be done just her way. Although she was hard
to live with—"Who could live with Rose Pesotta?"—Rose gave up her
bedroom and slept in her living room for four years so that the Rotkers
could have a home.[74]

Periodically, throughout her life, Pesotta entertained the idea of
adopting children. Although she left no record of her thinking about
having a family, she often treated nieces and nephews as her adopted kin,
particularly Hochman and Rubin. It seems that Pesotta longed for a family, but eventually settled for treating her friends and extended family as
her closest supports.

It is clear from Rose's personal relationships that she loved sincerely
and deeply. She was devoted as a friend, lover, family member. She cared
for others and gave of herself fully. As a woman known to be somewhat
difficult to get along with in deep personal relationships, she nonetheless
gathered a large following of friends, admirers, and lovers. Her exuberance and charismatic style endeared her to many, family and colleagues
alike. Even those who had problems with Rose appreciated her strength
and granted that she was charming and personable.

Obviously, Rose tried to live a lifestyle somewhat unusual for wom-
en of her times. Rose did not conform to the traditional definition of what
a woman of her generation was supposed to do, refusing to form conventional associations with men and clearly devoting herself to her friendship, work, and political undertakings as much as to her love life. It was in
her work that she found more long-lasting satisfaction. As a professional
woman who did not place a traditional home and family first in her life,
she tried to live a free life unencumbered by familial responsibilities, but
found it lonely and alienating. There were times when her life was full
and exciting, but she ran into difficulties in affairs, finding that it was nice
to be free, but harder to live out that freedom. Rose worked hard on
maintaining relationships while still trying to define herself beyond the
confines of who she was in relationship to men. While caring deeply
about her relationships, Rose, first and foremost, saw herself as a working
woman and professional organizer. Rose was not alone in choosing such a
lifestyle. Other professional women affiliated with her union, including
Fannia Cohn, Rose Schneiderman, and Pauline Newman, also chose to
live independently. Additionally, although women in other unions certainly lived as Rose had chosen to live,[75] Rose was unusual in the public
nature of her life as compared to most women of the rank and file; she
evoked a great deal of publicity and gathered many followers and admirers. Hers was a flamboyant style, and she was most unique in being able

to just pick up and leave a community, even to the point of hitchhiking away, if she so desired. Rose was able to maintain a sense of personal autonomy while still cultivating her home, friends, and family. Although she clearly rejected being a wife, mother, and lover who subordinated herself to others, she did live out the roles of dutiful daughter, sister, aunt, and friend. It was from these sources that Rose was able to gain the confidence and love from which she could grow and reach toward an ever-evolving definition of herself.

8

FROM ORGANIZER TO AUTHOR
TO RANK AND FILE

An outward atheist but a closet Jew.

In September 1942, Rose returned to the sewing machine as an operator for the firm of Freedman and Bucholtz on Broadway in New York City. She made ladies' garments and earned as much as a hundred dollars a week, working overtime.[1] Working with the seasons, according to the demand within the industry, her work life kept her busy and tired. She started early and stayed until after six every night, even working Saturdays to bring in extra money. Returning to the machine was a highly unusual choice for a labor leader to make, causing a stir among union officials and within the rank and file. Nevertheless, Rose seemed content with her decision.

In the evenings, Rose began working on her labor autobiography. Using a portable typewriter, Rose sat at her kitchen table, churning out the manuscript of *Bread upon the Waters*. She worked closely with a collaborator, John Nicholas Beffel, a writer and socialist activist whom she had met while working on the Sacco and Vanzetti case. Rose turned out page after page, which Beffel would edit. Often they sat for many hours discussing what should be included in the book, along with the style and format best suited for its presentation. Beffel suggested how to handle various literary difficulties as they arose, contacted people from Rose's labor background to fill in gaps of information, and did extensive research on the incidents and situations Rose described. Often they took long walks to process the day's work and plan for further sections.

It appears that they were romantically involved for a short time.[2] However, their major involvement was the collaboration on Rose's book. Rose eventually introduced John to Lisa Luchovsky, her friend Anna Sosnovsky's youngest sister; John and Lisa began a deep relationship that

lasted for seventeen years.[3] Luchovsky remembers Rose and John working together, with Rose sitting beside him telling the incidents of her life
as he typed and interpreted the story.

Rose tried a number of publishers, including Farrar and Rhinehart,
as well as hiring an agent to market her manuscript. Finally, after many
rejections, *Bread upon the Waters* was published in 1944 by Dodd, Mead
and Company. It was Rose's intent to tell the "inside" story of the labor
movement, one written by a woman and an active participant. In fact, her
goal was to tell the human side of the American labor struggle. She was
incredibly proud of herself and the work she had done on the book,
writing enthusiastically to her friends that she was "thrilled the book will
soon be ready. It is a good book and I sometimes pinch myself to feel I am
not dreaming."[4] The book itself is not so much an autobiography as a
labor history, in that it is a first-person narrative on the day-to-day activities of a labor organizer. In it Pesotta describes the nuts-and-bolts activities in which one must engage to reach workers. She vividly portrays
important historical events from the inside, as one who participated in the
incidents and who had an influence on their outcome. It is filled with
revealing detail and thorough descriptions of her ten years of labor activity.

The day that the book appeared, Rose held a book-signing party
right in the Freedman and Bucholtz factory. The *New York Post* reported
the event, in which "dill pickles, corned beef and tongue sandwiches, lily
cups of whiskey and cream soda" were served to the sewing machine
operators who converged to congratulate Rose.[5] Rose wore a candy-
striped seersucker housedress and went back to the sewing machine
after the event. The next week, the event was reported in the ILGWU
official newspaper, *Justice*. They called the event a "literary tea (with
celery tonic)" and noted that the book had clicked, becoming one of the
season's runners.[6]

The reviews were favorable, with the *New York Herald Tribune*
calling it a "human and colorful book, rich in people, incidents, action,
struggle, fun and pathos."[7] The *Boston Globe* said, "This Russian born
seamstress's book can be enjoyed as a personal adventure or read as a
chronicle of a great sector of the labor front."[8] The *Jewish Daily Forward*
reviewer said that the book should be made a textbook and saw that Rose
obviously loved her work and the people with whom she worked. He
noted that Rose lived among the workers and made them understand that
she was one of them by not keeping above them nor snubbing them. He
felt that she came to them, not as a leader, but as a friend. He also
commented on her taking on the hardest task, the most dangerous, as the
first on the picket lines, the first arrested and beaten. The reviewer was
impressed by how she could win the respect, admiration, and love of her
soldiers.[9]

FIGURE 16

New York City, 1944. Rose Pesotta's co-workers stage a party in the dress shop where they work, celebrating the publication of her book. Will Steinman's Shop, 525 7th Avenue, New York, New York.

The book was even given a full-page review in the 15 December 1944 issue of the *Hatworker*, in which Rose was called "warm hearted, imaginative, and full of that compassion that is not the do gooders charity but the sensitive persons reaction to injustice and misery of fellow men [*sic*]."[10] The reviewer wrote that Rose had a flair for drama and an eye for detail that are the marks of a born storyteller.

However, Rose also received much negative feedback on her book from people within the labor movement. Mark Starr, the education director for the ILGWU, refused to endorse the publication of the book and would not recommend it to the many local education directors around the country. He even refused to send it to the ILGWU libraries. Starr, believing that Rose's handling of the Los Angeles problems with Levy was inappropriate, wrote to her that it was a "family quarrel," and that it was a mistake to put the story in the book for consumption by the general public.[11] He said:

> Please put yourself in the position of the Los Angeles office. What would you have said if the Educational Department sent to the library of a joint board, of which you were the manager, an attack made without any attempt to permit any reply? When one is in an organization, there are certain things which cannot be done.[12]

Rose was irate at the official ILGWU reaction and at the affront she once again received at their hands. Not only had she been eased out of office, but now they would not let her tell her own story to her constituency! Her return letter to Starr asked, "Since when is criticizing a lazy, good for nothing, shameless work dodger who has sponged on our union for a long time a family quarrel?"[13] Rose defended herself by pointing out that her book also included a candid criticism of John L. Lewis and other labor figures. She also noted that she had quit her job as an organizer so that she could engage in free speech. She found it strange that she was expected to "trade freedom of expression for an easy job. I gave up the comforts of a weekly 'fat' salary, preferring a job in a factory so that I might speak my mind as I chose."[14] Rose also defended her right to tell the Los Angeles story, especially in view of the harm that had been done on the Pacific Coast. In fact, Pesotta did not go into many of the humiliating details of her L.A. story in her book. She insisted it was not a family quarrel and urged that the ILGWU education department send free copies of her book to the ILGWU libraries. However, the officials continued to refuse to endorse the book.

Nonetheless, *Bread upon the Waters* was a success. By February 1945, the first one thousand copies had sold out, and the book went into its second printing, with Rose becoming quite a celebrity. Rose was proud and happy again. She had finally had her say and gotten her revenge at Levy and "the old men on the GEB." During this time, invitations came to speak at colleges and to the American Association of University Women. She opened a labor library for the International Brotherhood of Sleeping Car Porters, having been invited by A. Philip Randolph; addressed the Women's Trade Union League's annual conference in 1945; and appeared on radio programs, as well as being listed in *Who's Who in American Labor*. She received letters of thanks for complimentary copies of her book from Eleanor Roosevelt and Frances Perkins. There is also evidence that Eleanor Roosevelt invited her to visit at Valkill, Eleanor's cottage at Hyde Park, which Pesotta found to be "a wonderful place to rest and contemplate. FDR is a very human and broadminded person."[15]

Kudos were coming in from many fronts, and Rose was particularly pleased at finally being vindicated.

> Am I happy? Just guess. With all the stones hurled at me these last several years, with our two stinkers from L.A. strolling like Pavas at the convention, they won out over me, with the little big shot [Dubinsky] having stricken me off his list, with all their flunkies shunning me—a has been—with the officials of my union crossing off my name from their list, this came like a bombshell. Now everybody "has known it all along."[16]

Dubinsky appeared to like the book, but according to Pesotta, "His bulge eyes nearly popped out when he heard it was going into a second printing."[17] Rose's comments were unforgiving of her union critics; indeed, she seemed to revel in her moment of revenge. For a short time Rose was able to regain the self-confidence and shining moments she had once known; however, in these scathing comments, she also manifests those qualities that were problematic in her personality. These were not qualities that she often displayed for public viewing, but ones seen by friends, family, bosses, and colleagues with whom she clashed. Rose liked things to go her way, and when they did not, she retaliated. With her short temper, she insisted that others see her viewpoint. When they did not— or when she felt betrayed— Rose could resort to manipulation or harassment to meet her ends. She was known to be snippy, with a biting tongue. Here her experience with the union and Dubinsky had embittered her, and she would have her revenge.

Rose's revenge was sweetened when there was some interest expressed by the movie industry in making the book into a feature-length film. She asked a director at Warner Brothers for advice after having been contacted by an agent who wanted exclusive rights to market it as a film. If a movie were to be made, Pesotta, ever seeking control of matters, wanted a hand in all aspects of the production, including choosing a director, casting, and technical consultation.[18] Unfortunately, although the story department editor at Warner's felt there were movie possibilities, the film was never made, and Rose lost her chance at greater fame.[19]

Because of its popularity, *Bread upon the Waters* was translated into Japanese and went into its third printing in the summer of 1945. By 1952, it had been translated into Spanish and German and had become required reading in many U.S. labor classes. Pesotta's fame spread, and she was invited to join the Pen and Brush Club, a group of professional writers and artists that included Clare Booth Luce and Mrs. Irving Berlin.[20] She was asked to serve on the General Executive Board of the National Religion and Labor Foundation and addressed the Socialist party in Philadelphia at a labor forum in May 1945.

As her reputation grew, Rose was offered a job by the Anti-Defamation League (ADL) of the B'nai B'rith in August 1945. The league was founded to be a watchdog and to stem the tide of anti-Semitism. Later it added interracial and interreligious awareness and propaganda to its agenda. Rose's job was to visit the labor unions, labor schools, and fraternal groups to educate them concerning the nature of prejudice and discrimination.[21] Pesotta attended labor conventions, educational conferences, mass general meetings, and conclaves of working people, where she spoke out against bigotry and the segregation of "Negroes, Japanese, and other minority groups." She pointed out what happened to Jews in Nazi Germany and urged that the workers engage in mutual aid and cooperation. She wrote articles, spoke publicly, and distributed leaflets and other informational material wherever she went.[22] Rose traveled again for this job; this time her journeys took her to the Midwest, including her old stomping grounds of Cleveland, Akron, Cincinnati, Chicago, and Detroit, even returning to Los Angeles and working on the issue there. Rose made use of her contacts with old colleagues from her ILGWU work in reaching people in labor. For example, she arranged luncheons featuring Frances Perkins as speaker where the topic focused on prejudice and interracial issues. She also arranged talks through her old rubber worker contacts so that all types of workers would be aware of racial tensions rampant in the labor movement. This job seemed perfect for Pesotta, given her long-standing interest and writing in the area of discrimination and ethnic and racial conflict.

In 1946, Rose was invited to Norway to participate in a summer school for the Workers Education Association. It was twenty years after her own education at the labor colleges, but now she was to return as a teacher. Held in Oslo during the month of July, the program was an international one; labor leaders from Great Britain, Denmark, Sweden, Finland, and Norway attended. Rose paid for most of the trip herself, with a little aid from the American Friends' Service Committee. Having been invited to Norway by Haakon Lie, the secretary of the Norwegian Labor party, who served as her guide, she traveled in style, taking a berth on the *SS Stavangerfjord* out of New York.[23]

Pesotta's speech to the fifty people at the institute was well received. She stressed the U.S. labor situation and interested them in the intercultural and interracial material she had carried for the ADL. Through her social contacts, Rose was also invited to Sweden and Poland. Always the traveler and eager to see postwar conditions, Rose took advantage of the invitations and later reported on her travels fully. She was particularly concerned with the plight of Jews after the war and was astonished to find that out of fifteen hundred Jews in Norway before World War II, only seven hundred remained.

Before World War II and the Holocaust, Rose had never been particularly concerned with her Jewish heritage, nor did she actively identify as a Jew. She had been cynical about the family observance of the holidays and tended toward atheism in her religious beliefs. Her family felt she was "outwardly an atheist, but actually a closet Jew."[24] It was during and after the war, and especially after this trip to Europe, that Pesotta became actively concerned with her Jewishness. The trip shocked her, especially after seeing what seven years of Nazi occupation had done to Poland. She called attention to the bombed-out terrain; fields lying fallow, the land filled with pathos and desolation. In Warsaw, there were "canyons of destruction and death" and rubble where there once had been a railroad station. The stench of the city was unbearable, because the sewage system had been wiped out. In an orphanage she found children twelve to fourteen years old looking like United States children of seven or eight, undernourished, tubercular, and crippled. Some of the children had rickety legs and protruding bellies from the poor diet, and their heads were shaven; some even had eyes missing. Many showed no happiness, staring into space, their shrunken faces making them look like old men and women.[25] Indeed, Rose was shattered by what she saw and could not ignore the plight of the Jewish survivors. Her identity with Jewish communal life was rekindled by these devastating sights. Had she not left Russia in 1913, this fate could have well been hers, and she saw that these victims were her people and felt compelled to do something for them. It appears that she now substituted Jewish ideology for the anarchism that had for so long been her religion. Although hers was not the orthodox religious Judaism of her childhood, she began to identify with cultural aspects of the community. She began to practice her Jewishness while still remaining an anarchist politically.

While in Poland, she was asked to speak to a gathering of Jews at the Polish Bund headquarters. Her father had been a Bundist, and this talk was significant to her. The audience was, for the most part, members of newly formed cooperatives of bakers, carpenters, and tailors. These cooperatives had also set up boarding homes for returning citizens. Pesotta spoke to over four hundred repatriates who were emaciated and dressed in rags. They all felt that the United States owed Poland a debt because of the inferno through which they had lived. Rose was moved to tears after this talk, as she had been again and again during this painful journey. Her vivid memory of these four hundred survivors, all dedicated to democratic principles and living in such squalor, inspired Rose to work to alleviate their situation. Never had Rose experienced such destitution, even in her most horrific labor organizing efforts. This misery was beyond anything she could comprehend.

While in Poland, Rose also discovered that much of the aid intended to reach the victims was instead diverted to the black market. Seeing people begging for bread and dying of starvation—even though millions of dollars had been contributed to the relief efforts—outraged her; and she began immediate efforts to change the situation.

Perhaps Rose's most wrenching experience was visiting the Maidanek concentration camp near Lublin. Her memory of it was vivid and gripping. She described miles of barracks with the odor of death pervading the area. The museum she visited was one and a half miles from the death camp, and the smell was akin to that of a funeral parlor. On the walls were photos of the victims and the implements of torture, with skulls and skeletons of the victims arranged on the shelves. Ashes were in piles; and in the piles, she saw bones and teeth. The Nazis had mixed the ashes with manure for compost and fertilizer. Upon seeing eight hundred thousand pairs of shoes, all in neat order—row upon row—Rose picked up a baby's shoe from the pile to keep as a reminder. With painful empathy she toured a building filled with men's clothing and another with piles of women's shorn hair, as well as visiting the "bathhouse," where naked victims were led to a room containing a dozen ceiling showers. The victims were bathed and then crowded into a second room to the point of suffocation. The doors were hermetically sealed; zyclone crystals were dropped in and the steam turned on. Within fifteen minutes, everyone was dead. The other prisoners carried away the bodies to a spot where they were piled up like wood on iron rails, then covered by kerosene or gasoline and set on fire. Scenes of these crimes so scarred

Rose that she was to talk and write of it for years to come. She could not believe the horror, destruction, and misery that had existed here just two years earlier.

Pesotta found it hard to convey the depth of despair that the war had wrought. She saw famine and disease everywhere and knew that Jews experienced Europe as a vast cemetery for their fathers, mothers, and children. She was so moved by what she saw that she felt compelled to mobilize the friendly countries to find jobs for the refugees immediately. Her genuine concern was clearly evidenced upon her return to Norway, after visiting Poland, when she personally made sure that several hundred refugees were sent to Norway for work. When she returned home, she energetically launched a concerted effort to raise money for the displaced persons she had met in Poland. She began lecturing around the country on what she had seen and sought out lecture agents to help her arrange speaking engagements so that she could mobilize support.[26]

After returning to the United States, Pesotta decided to resign her position with the ADL. One can only speculate as to why she left this position. Perhaps she was tired of yet another bureaucracy. Perhaps its workings did not fit her ideology. Pesotta left no mention of why she stayed such a short time with this organization. By November 1946, Rose had returned to the sewing machine yet another time, all the while working hard on refugee relief.

Soon after returning home, Rose also undertook the writing of two more book-length manuscripts. She hired an author's representative, Carl Leonard, to market her book *Family Album*, which was set in Derazhnya. The story was based on her own life, but featured a fictionalized character, Sarah Narodny, the name coming from the underground group of which she had been a part as a youth. The manuscript reached over two hundred pages and was written and rewritten many times. Although many publishers were contacted, none were interested. One publisher, Ray, felt that the book was deficient in style and in characterization. Another manuscript she submitted to them, as yet untitled but focusing on foreign affairs, was critiqued by readers as being sketchy, matter of fact, wanting in style, and lacking in color.[27] Eventually, after many failures, Rose gave up hope for the publishing of either book.

But Rose continued to write during her evening and weekend hours. Fragments of other novels, *From My Left Hand Pocket* and *The Unconquerables*, are found among her papers, although neither was ever completed. In 1950, Rose began to write *Days of Our Lives*, a real-life account of her experiences in Russia during her childhood. Much of the material was taken from the previous two unfinished novels. It, too, was written with the help of Beffel. Rose sought numerous publishers for this book. Eventually, by 1957, Rose turned to Aldino Felicani of the Sacco and Vanzetti defense group, who owned a publishing company, Excelsior, in Boston. He published it for her, but the book never gained the popularity of *Bread upon the Waters*. The cold fact was that the book was not widely reviewed, and Rose had to handle distribution and publicity for it herself. Unfortunately, it never sold beyond its first printing. Once again Rose was faced with failure and disappointment.

In January 1949, Rose took a leave of absence from her job as a dressmaker at the Will Stenman Company, where she had been employed after leaving the ADL. She accepted a job with the American Trade Union Council for the Histadrut as their Midwest regional director. The Histadrut was the labor branch of the Zionist movement, and it was Rose's task to enlist financial support in the United States for the Israeli labor movement. Pesotta had decided to take this position because, after leaving the ADL, she had settled into a tedious lifestyle in New York; she became bored and dissatisfied, even with herself.[28] She was hopeful that getting back on the road would enable her to motivate empathy and financial aid for the Jewish state through the auspices of the United States labor movement. Early on she had decided that a Jewish homeland was the best hope for refugee resettlement, and her goal was to help Israel become self-supporting. Again she threw herself into her work, traveling by night and visiting labor leaders by day, hoping to get them onto a newly formed committee or to donate money to her organization. She believed that the Histadrut was the backbone of Israel in that it focused on industry and farm workers. Tirelessly, she contacted old friends, including Walter Reuther and James Hoffa, and spoke at CIO conventions, local ILGWU meetings, and various trade conventions, including that of the laundry workers.[29]

This work for the state of Israel is certainly a far cry from the antistatist opinion held by anarchists. But once again Pesotta was being practical and was evolving her ideological position. She was now substituting a labor Zionism for her previous beliefs in anarchism and the labor movement. Once again it was pragmatism that won out. There was great appeal in the concrete actions of helping to build a Jewish state. "Zionism could absorb various motivations in its broad appeal of helping DPs, dealing with guilt about the lost 6 million or in identifying the need for Jewish survival in the world." "By 1948, 711,000 Jews were involved in Zionist organizations and contributed more than 90 million dollars for the state of Israel."[30]

In this new position, Rose saw herself as an educator and fundraiser, by showing American labor what Israel was doing innovatively. She believed that Israel was engaging in mutual aid by their system of cooperatives, and that it was almost as exciting as what she had seen of the Spanish experiment ten years earlier.[31] She had not let her anarchist idealism disappear entirely; and for her, Israel became the hope for a revolutionary new society that did not happen through her anarchism or the labor movement. Zionism rekindled her dream for a just society. Rose tried to answer difficult questions, including those dealing with the Arab situation, as well as to interpret the latest news out of the country. However, her fund-raising efforts were not notably successful. Dismayed, but unwilling to abandon her objective, Rose resigned as regional manager in order to focus her energies on just one city, Chicago. There she found herself hamstrung by an executive committee that wanted to know everything she was doing. Rose, ever the free agent and unwilling to be controlled, disliked having to account to anyone in authority. Not too much later, the Histadrut gave up on its labor appeals and turned over the entire operation to a larger and better organized fund-raising organization, the United Jewish Appeal.[32] By March 1950, Rose decided to resign from the Histadrut altogether, having stayed at this job for only fourteen months. She was not able to find work that could give her the kind of purpose union organizing had provided.

But Rose was resourceful and, true to her greatest pleasure, she decided to travel yet another time. During April and May 1950, Rose traveled to Israel and then spent two weeks in Paris visiting anarchist comrades. In Israel, Rose went to cities, villages, cooperatives, reception centers for immigrants, nursing homes, workshops, union offices, factories, and the Israeli Parliament.[33] She visited most of the major cities and some small villages in an attempt to get a feel for the country and the people. She was quite impressed with what she saw, believing in all sincerity that Israel was "on the right road." Even though the people were facing adverse conditions, they had not lost their sense of humor. The Israelis were trying to live in complete democracy and to actively criticize the government when they found problems, according to Rose. Inspired by an overwhelming admiration for the courage of the Israelis, Pesotta returned home with an eagerness to help them by enlisting financial aid from the United States—from both the citizens and the government, much as she had done after her 1946 trip to Poland.

After this journey, Rose once again made her way back to the sewing machine. She remained a dressmaker for the next fifteen years, making good wages and supporting herself, contributing to her mother's upkeep, and sending money to her family in Russia. Rose contributed a great deal to worthy political causes, chiefly using the ILGWU as a conduit for her charity; in fact, most of the profits from *Bread upon the Waters* and her union pension were distributed in this way. She continued to be a member of the Joint Board of Dressmakers in New York City, ever the loyal union member; and as far as being a seamstress was concerned, she boasted of her pleasure in a U.S. Labor Department questionnaire.[34]

After her final trip abroad, Rose settled into a quiet lifestyle. Her hearing problem became more acute, and she progressively needed larger and more complicated hearing aids. She took an apartment in New York and visited friends and family on a much more regular basis, continuing her lavish entertaining and party giving. With the completion of her job with the Histadrut and her trip, Rose returned to the rank and file, this time for good. Nonetheless, in this later stage of life, she had found a new direction and focus for her energies. As she aged and became more attentive to the sensitive position of Jews during the Holocaust, she felt an inner compulsion to help yet another underdog, the survivors. Her long-dormant sense of Jewishness came to the surface, and she once again dedicated herself to "doing good as my [her] creed." Jews, Israel, anti-Semitism, and prejudice were the new issues with which she chose to deal.

At this point as she labored in the work force, Rose was counted among the 29 percent of workers who were women.[35] No longer was she the exceptional woman; millions of others were now part of the change in attitudes and values regarding working women. In the fifties, women who might once have quit their jobs when they married were now staying on. Women who had children returned to the work force after a leave for childbirth. By 1950, a third of all women worked, and half of them were working full time.[36] The new climate also encouraged "wage earning women to raise again the question of equal pay" and also led to new educational opportunities for women in the work force.[37] Many of the issues that Rose had been struggling for were now becoming facts of life in the field of labor. In 1954, the White House established a Conference of Womanpower and included women union members. "Government policy began to encourage women to move into the labor market and women began to accept their status as permanent wage workers with a right to a job."[38] Issues about women in the work force that had been raised by just a few daring women in the twenties, or ideas actually tried by pathsetters—like Rose—in the thirties, were now being actively pursued by a large number of American women. There were still inequalities for women, but the work of rectifying them was to be left to the next generation. Pesotta had done her job and had done it well. It was now time for her to retire to her home, the tranquility of the shop, and to move on to other issues. Her struggle for the worker was completed, and it was her time to work less and to rest.

9

Epilogue

The gentle general.

Rose was quite philosophical as she approached old age. By the time she was in her sixties, she saw herself as improving with age, much like a fine old wine.[1] She tried to do as much as she could in accordance with her abilities, which were slowly becoming limited; and she felt that "time, the great teacher [had] taught her many lessons." But, fundamentally, Rose remained her old self, with her "old pet notions and ideas."[2]

Activities focusing on politics, writing, union involvement, and opposition to the Communists continued to claim her interest. Even in later life, she remained a dedicated activist and public person, although certainly with diminished energy and endurance. Rose continued to work in the shop regularly, which is how she supported herself. She kept herself informed of union matters and maintained contact periodically with David Dubinsky. After returning to the sewing machine, she felt it was her duty to inform him about life at the front lines. Once in awhile, she would send him a missive describing Communist activities in the shops and once urged him to issue a proclamation banning Communist organizing.[3] She insisted that he "call a conference of all New York managers and lay down a policy, as a guide for future action. Have the shop chairman informed ahead of time to beware of false issues; give us, the people in the trade, an opportunity to offset this sinister movement that is fast beginning to make itself felt in our everyday life."[4]

Rose's anticommunism continued and flowered once again during the McCarthy era. She was greatly disturbed by the inroads Communists were making in gathering members and also remained bitter about the conflict within the ILGWU in the twenties, which she felt had destroyed the union. She remembered what had happened in Spain, remained deeply angry and hurt by the Los Angeles fiasco, and was distraught over the inability of her siblings to immigrate because of the Communist regime in Russia. She now gathered more information about the Soviet Union and the rise of Stalin to fuel her critique. As the anticommunist attitudes in the United States became institutionalized, Rose joined the ranks more vigorously. She was also greatly disturbed by the growing anti-Semitism and anti-Israel attitudes of the USSR. In 1952 she wrote to the editor of the *New York Times*, stating that she had

> known communists since they first set up shop in the Russian colo-
> ny in New York and later in the labor movement. They are all alike,
> speak balderdash, repeat the same slogans, adopt the same pro-
> grams and use the same brutal methods against opponents. They
> are drilled military fashion to rule or ruin. They were decent, but
> party discipline demanded civility—they were trained to serve one
> power—the Soviet Union.
>   They never express their own opinion—they are afraid to.
> Nothing exists except the current line decreed by the party leader.
> Today [they] gave an order, the next day [they are] the enemy of the
> state, maybe executed or banished. Ex-communists publicly profess
> repentance, join church or reactionary organizations. I despise
> breast beating ex-communists—[they] are a suspect quality. They
> spied, betrayed, licked boots and did dirty jobs. I have no use for
> them, but they make converts of countless innocents—who be-
> come enmeshed in a web of lies and treason.[5]

The *New York Times* chose not to publish her virulently anticom-munist tirade, but she continued to write in the evenings and on week-ends and had articles published in other political newspapers and jour-nals. Starting in 1935, Rose periodically contributed short articles to *Freie Arbiter Stimme* (*FAS*, The Free Voice of Labor). Her first article had been a congratulatory piece on *FAS*'s thirty-fifth anniversary. In it, she identified with the paper as standing alone against enemies and friends, as she had so many times herself.[6] She had maintained friends at the paper, served on the executive board, and now in her later life contrib-uted articles. She also wrote for another Yiddish paper, the *Forwartz* (Forward), on life in the shop. One such piece, "Unzer Tani Kald in Shop," appeared on 6 July 1953, describing the garment industry from a wom-an's perspective. It was well received by the readers, who urged that she write more from that vantage point.[7] Once again Rose had reached her old colleagues, this time using the written word as her medium for change.

It was during this later period that Rose wrote *Days of Our Lives*, excerpts of which were published in *Commentary*.[8] She spent an enormous amount of time writing, editing, having the book published, and then marketing it herself. She also bought the copyright of her first book, *Bread upon the Waters*, so that she might reissue it herself, although this never actually happened.

Even though she had at times moved away theoretically from the anarchists, she continued to be involved with various anarchist groups, friends, and causes. The movement had all but died out by this time; many of the old-timers had passed on, and a new generation had yet to emerge, but this group still served as her circle and support group. She was a guest speaker at anarchist gatherings (including the twenty-fifth anniversary of the Alexander Berkman Refugee Fund)[9] and a contributor to anarchist causes (including a school named in honor of Carlo Tresca in Italy).[10] Additionally, she continued on the executive committee of the League of Mutual Aid, spoke at memorial meetings for Sacco and Vanzetti, and was a charter member of the Libertarian Book Club—an anarchist discussion group—which initially published books of interest to anarchists. She steadfastly maintained her involvement with refugees, aiding Bulgarians and Spanish displaced persons.

Rose was one of the few old-timers remaining in the movement. In ten days, Rose and her comrades had lost three close friends and felt the pain of "outliving those we love."[11] Seeing her friends die, Rose felt that she, too, was slowly dying. Her will and verve were slowly diminishing, although she tried to hold true to her ideals and values.

Besides working with the anarchists, Rose became involved with the Jewish Labor Committee (JLC), Women's Division. The JLC was formed in 1934 by Jewish workers to rescue "all those threatened to lose their freedom under any totalitarian rule."[12] It set up children's rehabilitation homes and nurseries in Poland, Italy, Belgium, and Scandinavia. The women's division adopted orphans, collected food and toys to send abroad, and worked to fight racial discrimination. Pesotta joined this progressive organization in the 1950s; by the 1960s, she was the national vice chair for the women's division. In this capacity, she chaired luncheons, one of which included Michael Harrington as the speaker, discussing his book *The Other America*.[13] She was also in charge of a bazaar that raised over six thousand dollars for homeless war orphans stranded in Europe after World War II.[14] This same group also actively supported the Selma and Montgomery, Alabama, civil rights marches and educated on anti-Semitism in the Soviet Union. With seemingly unending vitality, Rose continued to chair meetings and organize luncheons through the early 1960s; and in 1964 she also became a member at large of the national JLC.[15]

On 15 January 1961, a testimonial luncheon sponsored by the Jew-

FIGURE 17

Rose Pesotta, early 1960s, New York City. "Aging like a fine old wine."

Photo courtesy of Dorothy, Elias, and Edward Rotker.

ish Labor Committee, Women's Division, was held at the Atran House at 25 East Seventy-eighth Street in New York City, honoring Rose and her work in labor and with the committee. Over one hundred people attended to pay tribute to Pesotta's tireless activities. Rose spoke at this event, summarizing her years of struggle. She expressed gratitude for the praise that was heaped on her and pointed out that she now knew her capabilities and capacity for endurance.

I do not fear self knowledge—it always serves as a good antidote for self pity, self assertion and arrogance. My inner strength comes from years of experience that no matter how small the achievements may be, in spite of adversities, one must go on.

Citing her anarchist heritage, Pesotta continued:

Emma Goldman taught me courage to go on in spite of discouragements. Alexander Berkman [taught me] humility, and others taught me how to face up to situations when times are tough.

When a person is dedicated to a cause so great as to embrace the welfare of humanity, nothing is too degrading, nothing too trivial, nothing too lowly, whether one has to work with brain or brawn, for the ultimate goal. I will settle for nothing less for all humanity.

What would I do if I could live my life over: I have no regrets of my chosen path of the past because I have my vision before me.

The world is my country, to do good my religion.[16]

In this, her last public speech, Pesotta summed up her philosophy on life and gave an explanation of how she learned to cope with all the trials and traumas that she had experienced. Even in her later years, Rose maintained her dedication and commitment to social change and to the welfare of humankind. Even in the twilight of her life, she continued to go on, facing life's challenges, and chose to go on alone, as she had for most of her life.

Rose maintained an active pace throughout the early 1960s. In 1963, she moved into the recently completed ILGWU Penn South cooperative housing, near many of her old colleagues, including Clara Larsen and Valerio Isca. She joined a co-op credit union, supermarket, and pharmacy, always trying to live her anarchistic cooperative beliefs. While continuing to visit her aged mother, who maintained a home in Boston, she also sent money to her family in Russia. She even attended demonstrations and political events. In 1963, Rose, now sixty-six years old, attended the famed Civil Rights March on Washington, traveling by train with her Dressmakers Local 22 of the ILGWU. Before going, she wrote to

a friend how "neither Emma nor Sophia ever dreamed of such a movement . . . what will come out of this march on Washington the future will
tell."[17]

Rose was also invited to attend commemorative events under the
ILGWU auspices. On 19 October 1962, she participated in the twenty-
fifth anniversary of the founding of the Montreal Dressmaker Union,
which she had helped to establish. She wrote a short article for the
memorial booklet and had her picture included as well.[18] In 1964, she
was invited by David Dubinsky to be an honored guest at a luncheon and
public meeting to commemorate the fiftieth anniversary of the ILGWU
Health Center in New York City.[19]

It was important to Pesotta that she not be forgotten. Her inactive
union years were not only the most lonely, but left a void that was never
to be filled again. Having lost the excitement and élan that had come
from participating in the dramatic struggle, she developed a sadness with
the world and, according to a colleague in the labor movement, seemed
to have experienced a loss of faith.[20] This faith was never to be regained.
According to her nephew, Jack Hochman: "Rose had dared to rock the
boat . . . life had passed her by."[21] But she went on with fortitude, pained
and unhappy.

By August 1965, Rose was hospitalized with what she described as
"a couple of cracked ribs and then pleurisy which required hospital
care."[22] She took sick leave from the shop and stayed close to her bed and
couch to rest. It appears that by this time, Rose had been diagnosed as
having cancer of the spleen, which might actually have appeared as many
as eight years earlier.[23] She had concealed the malignancies from friends
and family alike, not wanting to frighten them with her illness. In the fall
of 1965, she was again hospitalized at Beth Israel Hospital in New York.
Soon after release, Rose moved to Miami, Florida, where she took a small
apartment near her nephew Milton Rubin, Esther's son, who looked in on
her regularly and managed her business affairs. Her family in New York
knew very little about her condition, and the few friends who did know
were greatly disturbed that she had left New York.[24] Rose lied by saying
that she was going to recuperate in the sunshine. Instead, she chose to go
off to die, relatively alone. By December 1965, Rose was hospitalized at
Mount Sinai Hospital in Miami, where she soon lost consciousness.[25] Her
nephew Milton visited often and was there when, on Monday, 6 December, Rose died. She met her end without her many friends, with little
family, with no lovers, and minimal support. Ever the valiant fighter, she
had lost this final battle. Her life ended as it had been lived, very much
alone.

On Thursday, 9 December, a funeral service was held at the Gramercy Park Chapel at 152 Second Avenue in New York. Four hundred people attended; the overflow crowd was left standing in the street; the famed Norman Thomas, her friend, could not even enter the building. Israel Breslaw, the manager of Dressmakers Local 25, presided. The eulogies were glowing.

Bernard Shane, the ILGWU vice president and Montreal manager, flew from a meeting in California to be there. He remembered Rose's effectiveness and the faith she imbued in others, particularly in dealing with the Cardinal's pastoral letter in Montreal. According to him, it was Rose's energy that led the workers to win the strike. Sol Lipnack of the Workmen's Circle Branch 122 remembered her leading picket lines despite gangster and police brutality, while Harry Rappaport, who was the League of Mutual Aid Chair, said that "Rose was rich in ideas and inspiration. Always on the front of battle lines, she was ever ready to serve." Ahrne Thorne, editor of the *FAS*, spoke, remembering Rose's participation in the numerous anarchist and civic organizations. Even in death Pesotta's identification as an anarchist remained.[26]

Perhaps the most moving tribute to Rose was a eulogy given by Gus Tyler (ILGWU assistant president), substituting for David Dubinsky, who was at an AFL-CIO convention in San Francisco. Tyler obviously knew Rose well, and tears fell from the eyes of the assemblage as he spoke:

As a rank and filer she was a natural leader, because of her profound conviction, her inflammatory personality, her startling appearance, her gift of speech, and above all her innate love and sympathy for people. She was born to lead. She was fated to rise from the machine and to guide her fellow workers in the age old struggle for human dignity.

Rose Pesotta lived in the great tradition of the woman warrior. This was the tradition of a Mother Jones coming out of the minds of an earlier America. It is the tradition of a little girl from the French countryside putting on armor to liberate her people. But, Rose was never so much a warrior as to forget that she was a woman. In her memoirs she writes of her Ukrainian village that Derazhnya, like Kentucky, was famous for its beautiful women. She was a beautiful woman, physically and in spirit. A truly *gentle general*.

As a leader and officer, she was an inveterate rank and filer. She was an officer of the union who distrusted officialdom. As a top official—indeed as a Vice President—she feared that the higher one moved the more likely was one to forget roots, origins and purpose. Although a great believer in organization—indeed she was superb organizer—she nevertheless worried that too much organization could choke freedom of the spirit.

Indeed she said so very frankly. Here is what she said in her memoirs about herself when she was nominated for a Vice Presidency: "I had no ambition to hold executive authority. Valuing my own freedom [how typical of Rose Pesotta!], I wanted to avoid getting into harness and to keep from being enmeshed in inner circle politics. I felt I could serve the cause of my fellow unionists just as effectively as a rank and file member."

Rose Pesotta was in an eternal and internal conflict: born leader and innate rank and filer, she was one to whom workers turned as an authority, while she held fast to the anarchist distrust of all authority.

Rose resolved the conflict between leader and rank and filer by being both—at different times and some times at the same time. Because she was both, there was none too high for her to assail and none too lowly for her to champion.

Inevitably, she reminds one of Morris Sigman who came out of the same mold: a man of deep convictions equally proud to be President or presser. Rose was equally ready to run a sewing machine or run the world.

Our union claims her as our own, and we do so with pride. She claimed the ILGWU as her own and did so with pride. But, her world was not bounded by the trade or the jurisdiction. She went wherever she was needed—to organize auto workers or rubber workers, to carry the message in Canada, California, Seattle or Puerto Rico. She was the incarnation of the spirit of the militant and idealistic woman worker.

The Wobblies had a popular song that ran:

> The Rebel girl
> She is a precious pearl
> She is the pride of the working class

Rose Pesotta was the Rebel Girl.

It is hard for us to imagine her not being with us: she was so everlastingly alive—she brimmed over with the zest for life; she was like a torch that ignited whatever she touched. She aroused the apathetic; she shamed the cynic; she spurred the jaded; she lived to give life. She called one of her books "Bread upon the Waters." She cast bread upon the waters to come back a thousand fold to give bread, the bread of life, to everyone who met her.

Rose Pesotta had a philosophy. It is contained in four brief lines that appear as an introduction to her book entitled "The Days Of Our Lives." It was a poem that she chose written by Leonid Andyev, and it reads:

> Swift as the waves
> Are the days of my life
> Each day shortens our path to the grave
> Fill the cup my brother, let's drink to our health
> For who knows what lies ahead.

It is that voice that still echoes with us this morning. One can still imagine Rose Pesotta saying "Farewell my comrades, fill the cup so I may drink to your health."[27]

After the funeral, the procession took Rose's body to Mt. Moriah, a Workmen's Circle cemetery in New Jersey, where a small service was held. Her grave is there today, far from friends, family, comrades, and lovers. It is visited occasionally by Clara Larsen and by Rose's nephew Jack Hochman.

Rose Pesotta, indeed the *gentle general* lies alone—almost forgotten.

As one considers the legacy of Rose Pesotta, there are a number of themes that emerge as highlights of a life of activism and controversy. Rose's life offers insights for those who choose to find the lessons in her experiences. I have immersed myself in Rose's life for a number of years, trying to assimilate and understand its many facets. In that discovery, Rose's portrait emerges as one with many images arranged into a complicated scrapbook. I sit here now, among the five hundred photographs I have gathered, with the framed portrait of Emma Goldman, done by Senya Fleshine, scowling over my head. It was the photo that graced the entrance to Rose's home for over thirty years. Behind me on the shelf is the carved penholder that Vanzetti gave to Rose before his execution. I am surrounded by Pesotta, trying to understand so that I may make some sense and assure that Rose will not be forgotten—will not be lost to history.

Rose Pesotta was obviously aware of her own historical importance, because she saved all her letters, writings, and materials collected over sixty years. It was as if she knew that "someday these will come in handy to someone," as indeed they have. We are now able to use those documents to piece together an account of the life of a person struggling alone as an anarchist, a labor activist, and a woman. Life may have passed her by in her later years, but her life is significant to a new generation of feminists and labor activists who can draw an understanding from her experiences. In addition, Pesotta's life helps us comprehend the experiences of women in the historical period immediately preceding our own so that we can see that things actually change very little with the passage of time.

Rose was a complicated woman, one who was both charismatic and exciting, yet authoritarian and vindictive. To sum her up in a few words is practically impossible. And yet a number of things, what she was and did, were most unique and significant; it is upon these aspects of her life that I chose to focus.

Pesotta lived her fight with male domination her entire life; it began with her father and only ended in death. It was because of this that she was a feminist, an anarchist, a labor agitator, and a damned hard fighter. For this reason, it is best to read Rose's life in the social context of gender roles and sexism. Rose was a victim and a product of a patriarchal social structure and context. All that she did, all that happened to her, can best be understood by keeping this overriding social order in mind. She wanted cultural, sexual, and psychological freedom in the form of social revolution, struggling in her personal life to achieve this freedom and in her working life to achieve economic revolution. In fact, it may be argued that Pesotta was a feminist. She did not make a dichotomy between class and gender. She was a feminist because she struggled for equality for women workers. As Nina Asher alleged in her biography on Dorothy Bellanca, a contemporary of Pesotta's who worked for the Amalgamated Clothing Workers, "she and her trade union sisters did not submerge their gender perspective when they chose to join with their working-class brothers in a male-defined trade union."[28] According to Asher, some women limited their feminism to a trade union constituency and advocated specific women's issues within a working-class organization, just as Pesotta did in the ILGWU.

As one of the few women who made it into the bastions of male power in the labor movement during the twenties, thirties, and early forties, Rose takes an important place in history. From that vantage point, she is able to speak about the nature of patriarchy and the place of women within the labor movement during that era. Within this male-dominated hierarchy, Rose tried to introduce her own brand of female or women's culture. This culture was different from the male organizer and vice presidents' methods and made her quite unique among them. Being a woman meant more to Rose than just being the token female in the group, she opted to show the organizers and vice presidents how women might do things if given a chance at the helm. For example, Rose's version of women's culture included rather unusual organizing tactics and strategies. As Alice Kessler Harris has said, "While trade union leaders insisted on what the ILGWU male leadership called 'unity, discipline, faithfulness,' the female rank and file searched for community, idealism and spirit."[29] Rose attempted to create community through the sending of laborers to labor colleges—as she had been sent before them—as well as establishing an all-female local in each of the shops she organized. By using music, singing, dances, and parties to encourage a feeling of unity among the workers, Rose did not just focus on bread and butter issues, for she knew that "her girls" needed to have feelings of camaraderie and sisterhood. Picnics, parades, events large and small were all part of Rose's strategies for developing a sense of community. She used food and drink to woo and keep workers happy in the movement. She knew that women wanted bread and they wanted roses.

Rose believed in, and demanded, democratic participation for her workers in the politics of their locals. In fact, she also demanded it for herself on the board, but was less successful in obtaining it there than she was at the grassroots level. Rose's brand of women's culture included educating other women to take power. She did not just pay lip service to this ideal; she implemented and activated it within every local she organized, by training the local women to take over the daily running of the offices and the union activities. This was most certainly a feminist activity.

Hers was a colorful style, one that used creativity to manipulate the media, including the radio and newspapers, to give her wide coverage. Needless to say this is one of the tactics that antagonized her more traditional male counterparts who felt that these were unimportant matters to which to attend. Or perhaps, as has been suggested, they were jealous of her charisma and popularity. Certainly it shows that the ILGWU leadership could not see beyond the confines of their previously constructed organizing tactics. Pesotta did not fit the norm of what they wanted from an organizer and vice president. Pesotta, as a woman, saw things with a female consciousness. The men on the board wanted another one of themselves, or they wanted a "good girl," not a woman who would argue with them and who fought for female workers' equality in power and decision making.

Compared with the male culture that surrounded her, Rose also had an openness in communication that was different. It was her style to talk with all of the workers about the politics and issues that were at hand. For her, information was power, and it was her goal to empower all those with whom she came in contact. Unfortunately, these were not the goals of the men who sat at the boardroom table. For them, empowering women workers was, at best, a marginal business, especially during the times when the unions themselves were trying to survive. Women were marginal to the work force during the time when Rose was at the height of her activities, and all her efforts, when seen in the context of male domination, made little sense to those in decision-making positions. This shows the classic male orientation of the GEB officers, who could little understand what Pesotta was talking about or even trying to do. After all, she posed a threat by training these women workers to take over their locals and to demand more representation on the GEB. Rose tried to create community, idealism, and spirit in a women's culture, but instead her efforts were viewed as troublesome, and she was labeled a "trouble-maker" rather than seen as what she actually was: someone breaking new and exciting ground in reaching large numbers of potential new recruits to the union. Additionally, she was doing all this in a uniquely female-centered and feminist manner, although she never used the word when speaking of herself. For this attempted breakthrough, Rose was viewed as a renegade. Clearly, this shows that the ILGWU was unable or unwilling to deal with a woman-oriented brand of organizing. It showed further the inability of the men to understand how to reach women workers, as well as their ambivalence about reaching these workers. What happened to Rose happened to other lone women vice presidents, like Fannia Cohn, before her. In fact, the men in power had no interest in women's equal participation.

Diane Balser has argued that there are several stages in the history of the relationship between women workers and the labor movement, and that each is accompanied by an improvement in women's conditions.[30] She believes that in the first, during early unionization, women were excluded from membership in all-male unions. In the early twentieth century, women began to join these unions and were included as permanent members; in the 1930s industrial unionization, women were finally organized and made a major step forward in working women's history.[31] During the current era, although still not in positions of decision making, women make up a far greater proportion than they did during Pesotta's era.

Using this framework, one might analyze Pesotta's position and experience as they apply to those stages. The ILGWU was at the stage of becoming more fully organized and had not yet learned about the need to integrate women fully within the structure. Dubinsky and the others were not yet conscious of the importance of women's power in their union. That awareness would have to come later, when women's rights were more at the forefront of the social agenda. Additionally, "high feminist content to female union struggles have usually been times when there was an active feminist movement even if it was separate from the working women's movement."[32] As we have seen, except for the Women's Trade Union League, during Pesotta's era, there was little feminist activity afoot to impact the ILGWU. It was the wrong era, historically, for a high feminist consciousness and for serious impact by women on the running of the union. Pesotta tried single-handedly to influence the GEB in a feminist and female-centered direction. She, alone, ahead of her time, tried to educate the "old men" to see the coming trends in organizing women. This, in fact, is what makes her so unusual and visionary in her approach. It is also what made her appear so difficult and like a trouble-maker.

Because Rose was one of the few women granted access to the seat of power, she was forced to try to accept the dominant male assumptions. There was little organized feminist support at the time, and she rarely joined feminist organizations, although she certainly aligned herself with progressive women's issues. Even though she had a tight support group, Rose was actually very much alone and felt it all of her organizing life. To fully understand this, one must look at the photos of events of the time, with Rose often the only woman in all the photographs that were taken. She was the lone woman in the GEB photos, the lone woman in the photos of various negotiations on strike committees, and the lone woman as an organizer speaking at rallies. This was the plight of the few women organizers allowed into positions of authority: to be, in fact, the voice lost in the wilderness of male administrators. Her style and personality made her even more alone: She failed to conform; she fought back. When fighting back became too difficult or looked impossible, she chose to run away from the patriarchs of the union rather than compromise any further. Rose knew what was happening to her and why. She was a woman alone, projecting women's culture and a woman's personality in an all-male society. For it, she was trivialized, marginalized, and ridiculed. In fact she was bound to fail. It is a wonder that she could go on for as long as she did. Had she been a man, the response to her would have been far different. Her power, strength, and outspokenness would have been considered normal and healthy. As a woman, she was only trouble.

Rose's life also illustrates the incompatible claims of anarchism and unionism. Many anarchists worked within the labor movement, but none climbed as far as Rose in the hierarchy of the unions. Her significance is, then, in observing the contrasting demands and learning how those claims could be reconciled. At times she spoke out as an anarchist on union matters, but was not supported. Often she spoke out as a unionist to the anarchists, and was not heard. In fact, it seems that although Rose valiantly attempted to be both an anarchist and a vice president, she eventually found that the conflict was too great. As hard as it was to be a woman in an all-male bastion, it was just as difficult to be an anarchist in an increasingly more bureaucratic and conservative institution such as a labor union hierarchy. The ILGWU alleged to be open to all workers, but it could not really deal with a gadfly anarchist, as it had earlier not been able to handle the Communists.

However, as an anarchist, Rose has significance because she is one of the more visible and outspoken of her generation. Although Rose did not convert many to the anarchist cause, nor did many become revolutionaries because of her efforts, she did reach countless numbers of people and was able to educate and help them to engage in critical thinking about their lives and working conditions. The anarchist cause did not grow because of Rose's work, but if her goal was, as she claimed, to do good for all humanity, then her efforts were effective: Rose helped improve working conditions for thousands of people; she was able to aid refugees; her life touched many; and she served as a catalyst for others to change. Perhaps this is not revolutionary anarchism, but it is certainly the humanistic and philosophic anarchism that she always espoused. In fact it may even have become, and certainly looked like, liberalism. Nonetheless, Pesotta identified her ideology with anarchism and the anarchists.

Beyond the historical implications of her life, Rose's life deserves a motivational and psychological analysis as well. Her life was an extremely difficult one, fraught with tension and loss. The major tensions seemed to revolve around her affiliations with men, beginning with her father and continuing through Kushnarev, Kasvan, Hapgood, Dubinsky, and, finally, Martin. Pesotta's conflict seems to focus on the tension between dependency and freedom; between power and domination. On the one hand, Rose adored and revered the important men in her life. At times she became quite dependent on them. Unfortunately, when this occurred, they attempted to control her, as did her father when he tried to force her into marriage. It was at these moments that Rose would choose to leave rather than lose the freedom she so sorely wanted. It definitely was a struggle for her, because the result of her freedom was a loneliness that continued throughout her entire life. She feared intimacy because she feared a loss of herself in such relationships. Pesotta wanted to be an equal, and ultimately she just could not be so in any of her significant relationships.

When Rose first rebelled, it was in a socially acceptable manner, as when she left home with passage paid for by her sister and in the company of her grandmother. Later, however, she chose a more flamboyant style of rebellion, as when she resigned from the union, giving a rousing speech to the entire GEB, returning to the sewing machine, and then writing a book exposing her situation. This was far from socially accept- able. Men tried to tame her, to turn her into an obedient daughter, a dutiful wife, or a woman cast in the image men desired her to be. Pesotta would have none of that. A fair analysis would be that her rebellion against restraints by the men in her life was a very political act. In both her personal life and her work, Pesotta was pioneering. She rebelled against all authority, particularly unjust authority, as she saw in her father and Dubinsky, most especially. Hers was a rebellion against an authority that included interpersonal male/female relationships. Rose was "un- lucky in love" because she refused to accept what was expected of wom- en who were "in love" in that era. She refused to become subservient or to be traditional. In other words, she rejected the gender role that was assigned to her. Actually, in this case, she lived her anarchism and her feminism pure and simple—fighting all who tried to constrain and re- strain her creativity, intelligence, and political dedication. To me that is anarchism at its best—not just being involved in revolutionary rhetoric, but actually living it in the day-to-day, in personal relationships.

Unfortunately, restlessness and discontent remained a never-ending theme for Rose as long as she lived. She worked hard, against many odds, and participated in many important historical events of her era. She had a people's historical perspective on such important situations as the Rus- sian Revolution; the Sacco and Vanzetti case; the radicalism of Emma Goldman and other anarchists; the rise of unionism, particularly the ILGWU and the CIO. She participated in labor colleges, the beginning of the New Deal, and the rise of Communism. Being in the throes of it all, she had something to say about it. These events had their impact on her, and she, too, influenced some of those events.

Rose Pesotta was one of the few women to write of these events, to leave such a wealth of documentation and to view it critically as well. For this we should be grateful to Rose and realize that the work she under- took fifty years ago is still work that must be done. Rose Pesotta died over twenty-five years ago, and still the issues with which she was dealing have contemporary relevance. Her life was filled with successes and failures. Hers was not an ideal life, but it was a significant one. She was an impor- tant woman and an absolute pioneer in her world. Rose was one of the countless radicals and labor organizers who were active from the turn of the century until the mid sixties. These people, many of whom have died or are now in their eighties or nineties, were fascinating individuals. There is much to be learned from these dedicated activists—lessons that will soon be lost to history. To Rose and her comrades, we give many thanks for the struggle and for carrying on. Her legacy is a powerful one, her lessons are useful ones, many of her goals have been realized, and perhaps one day the other hopes that she held to so firmly might be brought to fruition.

GLOSSARY

ADL	Anti-Defamation League of B'nai B'rith
AFL	American Federation of Labor—skilled workers
Anarchism	Social philosophy based on the liberty of the individual and the power of the collective
Bund	Jewish social democratic movement. Officially known as the General Union of Jewish Workers in Russia and Poland
CIO	Congress for Industrial Organization
CNT	Confederacion Nacional del Trabajo—Anarchist Trade Union in Spain
GEB	General Executive Board of ILGWU
Haskalah	Jewish Enlightenment
Histadrut	Labor Branch of Zionist Movement
ILGWU	International Ladies' Garment Workers' Union
IWW	International Workers of the World
JLC	Jewish Labor Committee
Mode O'Day	Sportswear company in Los Angeles where Rose made her last stand
Mother Earth	Emma Goldman's anarchist journal
Narodnya Volya	The People's Will movement in Russia
NIRA	National Industrial Recovery Act of 1933
NRA	National Recovery Administration formed to implement NIRA
Road to Freedom	Anarchist journal published 1924 to 1932
UAW	United Automobile Workers of America
Wobblies	Members of the IWW
Workmen's Circle (Arbiter Ring)	Mutual aid society
WTUL	Women's Trade Union League

ENDNOTES

Chapter 1. Early Life

1. Baum, Hyman, and Michel, *The Jewish Woman in America*, p. 56; Rischin, *The Promised City*, p. 24.

2. Howe, *World of Our Fathers*, p. 5.

3. Levin, *While Messiah Tarried*, p. 8.

4. Rischin, *The Promised City*, p. 39.

5. Pesotta, *Days of Our Lives*.

6. Ibid., chap. 2.

7. Interview with Dorothy Rubin Rotker.

8. Pesotta, *Days of Our Lives*, p. 20.

9. Interview with Esther Leibowitz.

10. Pesotta, *Days of Our Lives*, p. 101.

11. Leibowitz, interview.

12. Kessler Harris, "Draft on Rose Pesotta for ILGWU Archives," p. 1.

13. Pesotta, *Days of Our Lives*, p. 71.

14. Leibowitz, interview.

15. Pesotta, *Days of Our Lives*, p. 70.

16. Ibid., pp. 70–71.

17. The Bund was a Jewish Social Democratic organization that believed in fostering Jewish culture and Jewish autonomy within the European countries where they lived. They believed that Jewish workers should be a part of other socialist and labor movements; however, they further believed that there should be a separate organization. They were a politically sophisticated and fairly popular movement in the Ukraine and were officially known as the General Union of Jewish Workers in Russia and Poland. Howe, *World of Our Fathers*, p. 293.

18. Ibid., pp. 16–25.

19. Baum, *The Jewish Woman in America*, pp. 88–89.

20. Pesotta, *Days of Our Lives*, p. 181.

21. Ibid., p. 185.

22. Ibid., p. 217.

23. Ibid., p. 219.

24. Ibid.

25. Ibid., p. 221.

26. Ibid.

27. Ibid., p. 228.

28. Wexler, *Emma Goldman*, p. 15.

29. Goldman, *Living My Life*, p. 13; quoted in Wexler, *Emma Goldman*, p. 27.

30. Pesotta, *Days of Our Lives*, pp. 221–22.

31. Ibid., p. 223.

32. Howe, *World of Our Fathers*, p. 26.

33. Pesotta, *Days of Our Lives*, pp. 226–44.

34. Ibid., p. 233.

35. Ibid.

36. Ibid., p. 229.

37. Howe, *World of Our Fathers*, p. 58.

38. Ibid., p. 62.

Chapter 2. The New Life

1. Pesotta, *Days of Our Lives*, p. 245.

2. Rischin, *The Promised City*, p. 87.

3. Ibid.

4. Howe, *World of Our Fathers*, p. 145.

5. Ibid., p. 149

6. Ibid., p. 155.

7. Pesotta, *Days of Our Lives*, p. 247.

8. Howe, *World of Our Fathers*, p. 298.

9. For a full discussion of the historiography of the uprising of the twenty thousand, see Schofield, "The Uprising of the Twenty Thousand." See also Dubofsky, *When Workers Organize*, for earlier interpretations of the significance of this event, and Tax, *The Rising of the Women*.

10. Tax, *The Rising of the Women*, p. 234.

11. Baum, *The Jewish Woman in America*, pp. 151–52.

12. Kessler Harris, *Out to Work*, p. 152.

13. Kessler Harris "Where Are the Organized Women Workers."

14. Baum, *The Jewish Woman in America*, p. 147.

15. Robert Asher, private correspondence, Spring 1991.

16. Interview with Clara Rothberg Larsen.

17. Pesotta, *Bread upon the Waters* (reprint, 1987) p. 12.

18. Pesotta, "On Nursing and the Russian Revolution," n.d., Rose Pesotta Papers, New York Public Library, Box 35.

19. Ibid.

20. Paine, *Life and Death of Trotsky*, pp. 175–76.

21. Pesotta, "On Nursing."

22. Howe, *World of Our Fathers*, p. 310.

23. Feurlicht, *Justice Crucified*; Avrich, *The Haymarket Tragedy*.

24. Avrich, *The Modern School Movement*.

25. Ash, *Social Movements in America*, chap. 6.

26. Woodcock, *Anarchism*, p. 466.

27. Pesotta Papers, Diary, Box 35.

28. Kushnarev to Flynn—16 January 1920. Rotker Collection.

29. Kushnarev to Pesotta, 31 August 1920, Rotker Collection.

30. Avrich, *Anarchists in the Russian Revolution*, pp. 156–57.

31. Kushnarev to Pesotta, 30 December 1921, Rotker Collection.

32. Kushnarev to Pesotta, 19 December 1921, Rotker Collection.

33. Ibid., 26 May 1922.

34. Ibid., 31 January 1923.

35. Ibid., 14 October 1922.

36. Ibid., December 1923.

37. Ibid., February 1924.

38. Ibid., 18 April 1925.

39. Gordon, *Russian Civil War*, p. 240.

40. Ibid., pp. 212–13.

41. Pesotta, *Bread upon the Waters*, p. 15.

42. Charles Zimmerman quoted in Dubinsky and Raskin, *David Dubinsky*, p. 86.

43. Ibid., p. 88.

44. Pesotta, *Bread upon the Waters*, p. 17.

45. Joan Jensen, "Inside and Outside the Unions: 1920 to 1980," in Jensen and Davidson, *A Needle, a Bobbin, a Strike*, p. 186.

46. Pesotta, p. 17. For a full discussion of the civil war in the ILGWU, see Nadel, "Pinks versus Reds," and Gurowsky, *Factional Disputes within the ILGWU*.

47. Howe, *World of Our Fathers*, p. 338.

48. Dubinsky, *A Life with Labor*, p. 102.

49. Laslett, *Labor and the Left*, p. 128.

50. Ibid.

51. Brookwood was a residential college whose head was A. J. Muste. For a full discussion of womens' labor education, see Kornbluh and Frederickson, *Sisterhood and Solidarity*, and Wertheimer, *Labor Education for Women Workers*.

52. Marsh, *Anarchist Women*.

53. Pesotta speech given 27 February 1942, Pesotta Papers, Box 33.

Chapter 3. Sacco and Vanzetti

1. Woodcock, *Anarchism*, p. 466.

2. Isca, "Some Personal Recollections."

3. Paul Buhle, *Road to Freedom* vols. 1–8, 1924–32; (reprint, Westport, Conn.: Greenwood Reprint, 1970), introduction.

4. Avrich, *The Modern School*, p. 121.

5. Robert Asher, private correspondence, spring 1991.

6. Sacco and Vanzetti, *Letters* p. 344; Russell, *Tragedy in Dedham*, pp. 88–91; Avrich, *Sacco and Vanzetti*, pp. 192–93.

7. Sacco and Vanzetti, *Letters*, p. x.

8. Ibid., p. 51.

9. Ibid., pp. 44, 56, 65.

10. Ibid., p. 115.

11. Bartolomeo Vanzetti, *The Story of a Proletarian Life* (Boston: Sacco-Vanzetti Defense Committee, 1923; reprint, New York: Come! Unity Press, n.d.), p. 19.

12. Sacco and Vanzetti, *Letters*, pp. 217, 255.

13. Ibid., p. 207.

14. Avrich, *Sacco and Vanzetti*.

15. Sacco and Vanzetti, *Letters*, p. 207.

16. Ibid., p. 276.

17. Ibid., p. 212.

18. Pesotta, "The Sacco and Vanzetti Tragedy," 1927, 1939, 1947, Pesotta Papers, Box 25. This essay was written and rewritten a number of different times in commemoration of the execution of Sacco and Vanzetti. Excerpts were printed in various pamphlets and articles on the two. It is paraphrased here as the basis for most of this section of the chapter.

19. Valerio Isca, interview.

20. Pesotta, *Bread upon the Waters*, p. 229.

21. Russell, *Sacco and Vanzetti*, p. 35.

22. Pesotta, "Sacco and Vanzetti Tragedy."

23. Nicola Sacco to Rose Pesotta, 3 April 1927, Pesotta Papers, Box 1.

24. Bartolomeo Vanzetti to Rose Pesotta, 31 March 1927, Pesotta Papers, Box 1.

25. Ibid.

26. Pesotta, "Sacco and Vanzetti Tragedy,"

27. Interview with Leibowitz.

28. Ibid.

29. Russell, *Sacco and Vanzetti*, p. 91.

30. Vanzetti to Rose Pesotta, 31 March 1927, Pesotta Papers, Box 1.

31. Ibid., 22 May 1927.

32. Pesotta, "Sacco and Vanzetti Tragedy."

33. Interview with Larsen.

34. Pesotta, *Bread upon the Waters*, p. 328.

35. Pesotta, "Sacco and Vanzetti."

36. Pesotta, lecture at Atran House, 15 June 1961, Pesotta Papers, Box 33.

37. Interview with Hochman.

38. Sinclair, *Boston*, vol. 2, pp. 754–55.

Chapter 4. Labor Organizing: The Early Years

1. Foner, *Women and the American Labor Movement*, vol. 2, p. 256.

2. Carroll and Noble, *The Free and the Unfree*, p. 337.

3. Pesotta, *Bread upon the Waters*, p. 17.

4. Foner, *Women and the American Labor Movement*, vol. 2, p. 260.

5. Kessler Harris, *Out to Work*, p. 251.

6. Ibid., p. 259.

7. Stein, *Out of the Sweatshop*, p. 222.

8. Rayback, *A History of American Labor*, p. 318.

9. Kessler Harris, "Problems of Coalition Building," p. 125.

10. Foner, *Women and the American Labor Movement*, vol. 2, p. 279.

11. Pesotta, *Bread upon the Waters*, p. 1.

12. Kessler Harris, "Organizing the Unorganizable," p. 14.

13. James, *Notable American Women*, pp. 154–55 for discussion of Fannia Cohn, and pp. 631–33 for a discussion of Rose Schneiderman.

14. R. Cohen, *Fannia Cohn*.

15. Foner, *Women and the American Labor Movement*, vol. 2, p. 279. See also Schneiderman and Goldthwaite, *All for One*; and Kessler Harris, "Rose Schneiderman," pp. 160–84.

16. Dye, *As Equals and as Sisters*.

17. Waldinger, "Another Look at the ILGWU," p. 99.

18. Kessler Harris, "Organizing the Unorganizable," p. 20.

19. Milkman, "Organizing the Sexual Division of Labor," p. 125.

20. Thanks to Ruth Meyerowitz for her insights on women's lack of ambition. For further discussion, see *Twentieth-Century Trade Union Women: Vehicle for Social Change Oral History Project*, University of Michigan, nos. 9, 11, 27.

21. Cook, *Eleanor Roosevelt*, vol. 1, p. 371.

22. Roger Waldinger, "Another Look at the ILGWU," p. 99.

23. Pesotta, *Bread upon the Waters*, p. 21.

24. Ruiz, *Cannery Women, Cannery Lives*, pp. xiv, xvi, 123.

25. Kingsolver, *Holding the Line*.

26. Ibid., p. 5.

27. Pesotta, *Bread upon the Waters*, p. 125.

28. Ibid., p. 28.

29. Kessler Harris, "Problems of Coalition Building," p. 115.

30. Hall, "Disorderly Women."

31. Pesotta, *Bread upon the Waters*, p. 28.

32. Ibid., p. 51.

33. Pesotta to Emil Olay, 10 September 1934, Pesotta Papers, Box 1.

34. Kessler Harris, "Problems of Coalition Building," p. 115.

35. Ibid.

36. Bernstein, *The Turbulent Years*, p. 89.

37. Kessler Harris, "Problems of Coalition Building," p. 128.

38. Pesotta, *Bread upon the Waters*, chap. 6.

39. Bernstein, *The Turbulent Years*, p. 278.

40. Pesotta, *Bread upon the Waters*, p. 89.

41. Ibid., p. 101.

42. Ibid., p. 102.

43. Ibid.

Chapter 5. Labor Organizing: The Challenging Years

1. Howe, *World of Our Fathers*, p. 351.

2. Ibid., p. 353.

3. Pesotta, *Bread upon the Waters*, p. 111.

4. Ibid., p. 126.

5. Ibid., p. 159.

6. Ibid., p. 162.

7. Rose Pesotta to David Dubinsky, 5 June 1935, Dubinsky Papers, ILGWU Archives, Box 2.

8. Pesotta, *Bread upon the Waters*, p. 170.

9. Kessler Harris, "Draft on Rose Pesotta," p. 3.

10. Pesotta, *Bread upon the Waters*, chap. 19.

11. Ibid., chap. 22.

12. Rayback, *A History of American Labor*, p. 352.

13. Pesotta, *Bread upon the Waters*, p. 240.

14. Fine, *Sit Down*, pp. 91, 173.

15. Rotker, interview.

16. Pesotta, *Bread upon the Waters*, p. 252.

17. Ibid., chap. 24.

18. Ibid., p. 271.

19. Ibid., chap. 24.

20. Ibid., p. 274.

21. Ibid., p. 276.

22. Pesotta to Rae Brandstein, 16 July 1937, Pesotta Papers, Box 3.

23. Pesotta, *Bread upon the Waters*, p. 290.

24. Ibid., p. 298.

25. Pesotta, *Bread upon the Waters*, p. 316.

26. Ibid., p. 318.

27. *Boston Sunday Globe*, 24 December 1939, Dubinsky Papers, Box 134, Folder 2.

28. Kessler Harris, "Draft on Rose Pesotta," p. 3.

29. Gus Tyler, "Eulogy on Rose Pesotta," 9 December 1965, Clara Larsen private papers. Although these words were written years later, long after the period under discussion, I believe it is appropriate to quote here, because Tyler discusses Pesotta's organizing style and illustrates the esteem felt for Rose. It also exemplifies her leadership and strategies, which the author is here addressing.

30. Pesotta, speech given 15 January 1961, Pesotta Papers, Box 33.

31. Ibid.

32. Tyler, "Eulogy on Rose Pesotta."

33. Quoted in Pesotta to Hippolyte Havel, 19 February 1934, Pesotta Papers, Box 1.

34. Ibid.

35. Ibid.

36. Ibid.

37. Goldman as quoted in Porter, *Vision on Fire*, p. 317.

38. Pesotta to Yoffee, 31 May 1935, Pesotta Papers, Box 2.

39. Pesotta to Abe Bluestein, 11 March 1936, Pesotta Papers, Box 2.

40. Ibid.

41. Pesotta to David Dubinsky, 25 February 1938, and Pesotta to Fred Umhey, 10 March 1938, Pesotta Papers, Box 3.

42. Thanks to Amy Kesselman for help in clarification of this issue, summer 1991.

43. Pesotta to David Dubinsky, December 8, 1941 Dubinsky Papers, Box 2, Nos. 114, 12, File 1H.

44. Rose Pesotta to Dubinsky, 7 November 1939, Pesotta Papers, Box 3.

45. Ibid.

46. Pesotta, *Bread upon the Waters*, p. 96.

47. Ibid.

48. Rotker, interview.

49. Rose Pesotta to David Dubinsky, 30 September 1933, Pesotta Papers, Box 1.

50. Leibowitz, interview.

51. Larsen, interview.

52. General Executive Board Minutes 1933–44, Collection 16, ILGWU Archives.

53. Report and Record Report of General Executive Board to Twenty-Third Convention of ILGWU, 3 May to 15 May, 1937, p. 442, collection 16 ILGWU Archives.

54. First Quarterly General Executive Board, 21–25 June 1937, Collection 16, ILGWU Archives.

55. Pesotta, "Report to the General Executive Board in Atlantic City, June 15, 1942," Pesotta Papers, Box 17.

56. Larsen, interview.

57. Kessler Harris, "Problems of Coalition Building," p. 133.

58. Ibid., p. 123.

59. Gabin, *Feminism in the Labor Movement*, p. 8.

60. Ibid., p. 9.

61. Ibid., p. 22.

62. Ibid., p. 23.

63. Ibid., p. 25.

64. Ibid., p. 46.

65. Pesotta, *Bread upon the Waters*, p. 334.

66. Ibid., p.338.

67. Ibid., p. 365.

68. Ibid., p. 368.

69. Pesotta to Rae Brandstein, 9 August 1941, Pesotta Papers, Box 3.

70. Ibid., 15 August 1941.

71. Ibid., 12 December 1941.

72. Susan Adams to David Dubinsky, 22 March 1942, Pesotta Papers, Box 4.

73. Louis Levy to David Dubinsky, telegram, 10 February 1942, Dubinsky Papers, Box 114, File 1 G.

74. Adams to David Dubinsky, 22 March 1942, Pesotta Papers, Box 4.

75. David Dubinsky to Louis Levy, 10 February 1942, Dubinsky Papers, Box 114.

76. Dubinsky to Rose Pesotta, 8 December 1942, Dubinsky Papers, Box 114.

77. Cliff Gill to David Dubinsky, 22 February 1942, Dubinsky Papers, Box 114.

78. Ibid.

79. Levy to David Dubinsky, 8 February 1942, telegram, Dubinsky Papers, Box 114, File 1G.

80. Locals 266 and 384 letter to David Dubinsky, 9 February 1942, Dubinsky Papers, Box 114.

81. Resolution of Local 384 to Dubinsky, David Dubinsky Papers, Box 114, File 1 E. (n.d.)

82. Pesotta to David Dubinsky, 10 March 1942, Dubinsky Papers, Box 114, File 1 E.

83. Pesotta, *Bread upon the Waters*, p. 388.

84. Resolution of Local 384, Dubinsky Papers, Box 114.

85. Pesotta, "Testimonial Speech, February 27, 1942," given at the Park Manor Ballroom, Los Angeles, California, Dubinsky Papers, Box 114.

86. Sue Adams to David Dubinsky, 22 March 1942, Dubinsky Papers, Box 114.

87. Pesotta to Susan Adams, 10 June 1942, Pesotta Papers, Box 4.

88. Report of the General Executive Board of the ILGWU, Sixth Quarterly Meeting Minutes, 15–19 June 1942, Collection 16, ILGWU Archives.

89. Pesotta, Diary, 17 June 1942, Pesotta Papers, Box 15.

90. Ibid., 18 June 1941.

91. Ibid., 19 June 1942.

92. Pesotta to Susan Adams, 13 June 1942, Pesotta Papers, Box 15.

93. Pesotta to Melvin, 18 August 1942, Pesotta Papers, Box 4.

94. Pesotta to Rebecca, 1 December 1942, Pesotta Papers, Box 4.

95. Pesotta to Fannie, 18 August 1942, Pesotta Papers, Box 4.

96. Pesotta, "Resignation to the ILGWU," Dubinsky Papers, Box 134, Folder 2.

97. ILGWU Report and Record, twenty-fifth convention, 19 May–9 June 1946, Hotel Statler, Boston, p. 536, collection 16, ILGWU Archives.

98. Interview with Leibowitz; interview with Larsen.

99. Rose Pesotta to Emma Goldman, 23 September 1935, Pesotta Papers, Box 10.

100. Oral History Interview with Israel Breslow, 2 March 1983, ILGWU Archives.

101. Rose Pesotta to S. Zimmerman, 2 April 1936, Dubinsky Papers, Box 2.

102. Kenneally, *Women and American Trade Unions*, p. 157.

103. Ann Schofield, "Introduction," in Pesotta, *Bread upon the Waters*, p. xv.

104. Kessler Harris, "Organizing the Unorganizable," pp. 22–23.

105. Kessler Harris, "Problems of Coalition Building," p. 119.

106. Ibid., p. 133.

107. Ibid., p. 137.

108. Joan Jenson, "Inside and Outside the Unions," pp. 186–88.

109. Rose Pesotta to David Dubinsky, 13 December 1932, Pesotta Papers, Box 1.

110. Pesotta, *Bread upon the Waters*, p. 22.

111. Rose Pesotta to David Dubinsky, 6 February 1935, Pesotta Papers, Box 2.

112. Kessler Harris, "Problems of Coalition Building," p. 128.

Chapter 6. Political Work

1. Isca, "Some Personal Recollections," p. 1.

2. *Road to Freedom*, August 1925.

3. Pesotta, "Road to Freedom Camp," *Road to Freedom*, vol. 2, no. 11 (August 1926): 8.

4. *Road to Freedom* vol. 3, no. 8, 1 October 1926.

5. Ibid.

6. Ibid., vol. 3, no. 9, 1 November 1926.

7. Ibid.

8. Ibid.

9. Ibid., vol. 4, no. 7, January 1928.

10. Ibid., vol. 5, no. 6, February 1929.

11. Pesotta to Emma Goldman, 3 March 1934, Pesotta Papers, Box 10.

12. Sam Dolgoff, interview.

13. Darryl Baskin, "Introduction," *Freedom*, vols. 1 and 2 (1933–34).

14. *Freedom*, vol. 1, no. 5, 4 February 1933.

15. Leibowitz, interview.

16. Pesotta to Emma Goldman, 3 March 1934, Pesotta Papers, Box 10.

17. Goldman to Rose Pesotta, 6 April 1935, Pesotta Papers, Box 10.

18. Ibid., 31 January 1935.

19. Ibid.

20. Ibid., 23 June 1935.

21. Ibid.

22. Pesotta to Emma Goldman, 31 July 1935, Pesotta Papers, Box 10.

23. Ibid.

24. Ibid.

25. Goldman to Pesotta, 31 August 1935, Pesotta Papers, Box 10.

26. Ibid., 7 March 1935.

27. Pesotta to Emma Goldman, 23 September 1935, Pesotta Papers, Box 10.

28. Goldman to Rose Pesotta, 31 January 1935, Pesotta Papers, Box 10.

29. Pesotta to Emma Goldman, 3 March 1934, Pesotta Papers, Box 10.

30. Ibid.

31. Goldman to Rose Pesotta, 31 January 1935, Pesotta Papers, Box 10.

32. Pesotta to Emma Goldman, 25 August 1936, Pesotta Papers, Box 10.

33. Goldman as quoted in Porter *Vision on Fire*, p. 15.

34. Drinnon, *Rebel in Paradise*, p. 302.

35. Goldman to Rose Pesotta, 8 February 1937, Pesotta Papers, Box 10.

36. Pesotta, *Bread upon the Waters*, p. 313.

37. Mannin, *Women and the Revolution*, p. 137, quoted in Drinnon, *Rebel in Paradise*, p. 311.

38. Dorothy Rogers to Rose Pesotta, 23 February 1940, Pesotta Papers, Box 10.

39. Ibid., 26 April 1940.

40. Ibid., 14 May 1940.

41. Pesotta, "Speech at the Emma Goldman Memorial," 31 May 1940, New York Town Hall, Pesotta Papers, Box 33.

42. Ibid.

43. Flyer for Emma Goldman memorial, 31 May 1940, Pesotta Papers, Box 10.

44. Pesotta, "Speech at the Emma Goldman Memorial."

45. Leaflet, Vincent Ferrero and Domenick Sallito deportation case, Pesotta Papers, Box 36.

46. Isca, "Some Personal Recollections," p. 2.

47. Pesotta, *Bread upon the Waters*, p. 83.

48. Pamphlet, League of Mutual Aid, Pesotta Papers, Box 36.

49. Isca, "Some Personal Recollections," p. 3.

50. Pesotta, "On Political Parties," 1936, Pesotta Papers, Box 24.

51. Pesotta Papers, Box 24.

52. Pamphlet, Pesotta Papers, Box 38.

53. Ralph Fol to Rose Pesotta, 19 November 1940, Pesotta Papers, Box 3.

54. Pesotta to Frank Reel, 12 August 1940, Pesotta Papers, Box 3.

55. Eleanor Roosevelt to Rose Pesotta, 19 November 1940, Pesotta Papers, Box 3.

56. Pesotta to America Thatcher, 23 June 1941, Pesotta Papers, Box 4.

57. Pesotta to Lilly Sarnoff, 7 September 1942, Pesotta Papers, Box 4.

58. Ahrne Thorne to Elaine Leeder, personal correspondence.

59. Pesotta to America Thatcher, 23 June 1942, Pesotta Papers, Box 4.

60. Fanya Peisoty Bimbat, interview.

Chapter 7. Personal Life: Home, Friends, and Family

1. Marsh, *Anarchist Women: 1870–1920*, introduction.

2. Ibid., chap. 2.

3. Ibid., p. 167.

4. Information on the anarchist community, personal interviews with Clara Larsen, Lisa Luchovsky, and Abe and Selma Bluestein.

5. Thorne to Elaine Leeder, personal correspondence.

6. Pesotta to unknown recipient in Los Angeles, 18 January 1934, Pesotta Papers, Box 1.

7. Pesotta, diary, 6 September–6 October 1931, Pesotta Papers, Box 15.

8. Pesotta to unknown recipient, 18 January 1934, Pesotta Papers, Box 1.

9. Pesotta to Clara Larsen, 14 March 1950, and Pesotta to Horst Borenz, 3 February 1950, Pesotta Papers, Box 7.

10. Pesotta, diary, 6 September 1931 through 1936, Pesotta Papers, Box 15.

11. Ibid., 3 November 1931.

12. Pesotta, *Bread upon the Waters*, p. 136.

13. Pesotta, diary, 3 November 1931, Pesotta Papers, Box 15.

14. Ibid., 19 January 1935.

15. Thomas Smith to Rose Pesotta, 10 October 10, 1937, Pesotta Papers, Box 3.

16. Fol to Pesotta, 28 November 1939, Pesotta Papers, Box 3.

17. Paul Berg to Pesotta, 4 August 1935, Pesotta Papers, Box 2.

18. Marcaccio, *The Hapgoods*, preface.

19. Powers Hapgood to Pesotta, 30 April 1936, Pesotta Papers, Box 10.

20. Ibid., 28 June 1936.

21. Ibid., 26 August 1936.

22. Ibid.

23. Pesotta to Mary Donovan, 22 September 1936, Pesotta Papers, Box 10.

24. Mary Donovan to Pesotta, 25 August 1941, Pesotta Papers, Box 4. Clearly, Donovan remained distressed by the affairs.

25. Powers Hapgood to Pesotta, 24 September 1936, Pesotta Papers, Box 10.

26. Pesotta to Powers Hapgood, 29 September 1936, Pesotta Papers, Box 10.

27. Powers Hapgood to Pesotta, September 1936.

28. Powers Hapgood to Pesotta, 18 February 1937, Pesotta Papers, Box 10.

29. Ibid., 24 February 1937.

30. Ibid.

31. Ibid., 5 March 1937, Box 11.

32. Ibid., 30 May 1937.

33. Ibid., 8 June 1937.

34. Ibid., July 1937.

35. Ibid.

36. Ibid., September 1937.

37. Ibid., May 1938.

38. Pesotta to Powers Hapgood, 21 May 1938, Pesotta Papers, Box 11.

39. Ibid., 18 July 1938.

40. Powers Hapgood to Pesotta, 5 January 1941, Pesotta Papers, Box 12.

41. Ibid., 5 January 1941.

42. Pesotta, diary, 1 February 1942, Pesotta Papers, Box 15.

43. Pesotta to Rae Brandstein, 5 February 1949, Pesotta Papers, Box 6.

44. Ibid.

45. Pesotta to Al Desser, 11 February 1949, Pesotta Papers, Box 6.

46. Pesotta, "Tribute to Powers Hapgood," memorial speech given 8 February 1949, Indianapolis, Pesotta Papers, Box 24.

47. Heilbrun, *Writing a Woman's Life*, p. 92.

48. Ibid., p. 95.

49. Interview with Lisa Luchovsky.

50. Interview with Valerio Isca.

51. Pesotta to Isabel, 8 August 1953, Pesotta Papers, Box 8.

52. Interview with Jack Hochman.

53. Isca, interview.

54. Pesotta, diary, 3 November 1931, Pesotta Papers, Box 15.

55. Ibid.

56. Kessler Harris, "Organizing the Unorganizable," p. 22.

57. Pesotta, "In Memorium—Anna Sosnovsky Winocur," 10 May 1949, Pesotta Papers, Box 25.

58. Ibid.

59. Heilbrun, *Writing a Woman's Life*, p. 100.

60. Larsen, interview.

61. Heilbrun, *Writing a Woman's Life*, p. 98.

62. Pesotta to Clara and Christ Larsen, 18 December 1952, Pesotta Papers, Box 8.

63. Ibid.

64. For a full discussion of Mollie Steimer and the Abrams case, see Polenberg, *Fighting Faiths*.

65. Pesotta to Mollie Steimer, 26 February 1938, Pesotta Papers, Box 12.

66. Marsh, *Anarchist Women*, p. 38.

67. Pesotta to Mollie Steimer, 28 November 1939, Pesotta Papers, Box 12.

68. Pesotta to Jack Abrams, 8 December 1939, Pesotta Papers, Box 12.

69. Mollie Steimer to Comrades, 5 November 1941, Pesotta Papers, Box 12.

70. Mollie Steimer to Rose Pesotta, 30 January 1943, Pesotta Papers, Box 12.

71. Pesotta to Workers Defense League, 16 May 1962, Pesotta Papers, Box 8.

72. Leibowitz, interview.

73. Ibid.

74. Interview with Elias and Dorothy Rotker.

75. For an in-depth discussion of the role of women in the work force and women as professionals, see Kessler Harris's books *Women Have Always Worked* and *Out to Work*.

Chapter 8. From Organizer to Author to Rank and File

1. Pesotta to America Thatcher, 4 April 1943, Pesotta Papers, Box 5.

2. Pesotta, diary, Pesotta Papers, Box 16.

3. Luchovsky, interview.

4. Pesotta to Sue Adams, 15 October 1944, Pesotta Papers, Box 5.

5. *New York Post*, 7 December 1944, Pesotta Papers, Box 29.

6. *Justice*, 15 December 1944, Pesotta Papers, Box 29.

7. *New York Herald Tribune*, December 1944, Pesotta Papers, Box 29.

8. *Boston Globe*, Pesotta Papers, Box 29.

9. *Jewish Daily Forward*, 24 December 1944, Pesotta Papers, Box 29.

10. *Hatworker*, 12 December 1944, Pesotta Papers, Box 29.

11. Mark Starr to Pesotta, 6 December 1944, Pesotta Papers, Box 5.

12. Ibid.

13. Pesotta to Mark Starr, 10 December 1944, Pesotta Papers, Box 5.

14. Ibid.

15. Pesotta, diary, 17 August 1945, Pesotta Papers, Box 16.

16. Pesotta to Rebecca and Joe, 3 January 1945, Pesotta Papers, Box 5.

17. Pesotta to Dorothy, 21 January 1945, Pesotta Papers, Box 5.

18. Pesotta to Vincent Sherman, 10 December 1944, Pesotta Papers, Box 5.

19. Vincent Sherman to Pesotta, 14 February 1945, Pesotta Papers, Box 5.

20. Pen and Brush to Pesotta, 10 September 1945, Pesotta Papers, Box 6.

21. Pesotta to John and Sue Adams, 29 August 1945, Pesotta Papers, Box 5.

22. Pesotta to R. C. Beverstock, American Delegation, New Zealand, 19 June 1946, Pesotta Papers, Box 6.

23. Pesotta, report to Charles Sherman, 3 October 1946, Pesotta Papers, Box 6. Most of this section of chapter 8 is based on this memo.

24. Interview with Elias Rotker.

25. Pesotta to Charles Sherman, 3 October 1946, Pesotta Papers, Box 6.

26. Pesotta to Yelensky, 26 November 1946, Pesotta Papers, Box 6.

27. Ray Publishers to Pesotta, 14 January 1948, Pesotta Papers, Box 6.

28. Pesotta to Rae Brandstein, 22 February 1949, Pesotta Papers, Box 6.

29. Pesotta to Isadore Laderman, 5 May 1949, Pesotta Papers, Box 7.

30. Cohen, *American Jews*, p. 71.

31. Pesotta to Mollie Steimer, 23 May 1949, Pesotta Papers, Box 7.

32. Pesotta to Dorothy Rubin Rotker, 16 December 1949, Pesotta Papers, Box 7.

33. Pesotta, "They Know What They Want in Israel," June 1950, Pesotta Papers, Box 25.

34. Pesotta, "Women's Bureau Questionnaire Essay," 30 June 1950, Pesotta Papers, Box 25.

35. Kessler Harris, *Out to Work*, p. 301.

36. Ibid.

37. Ibid., pp. 304–5.

38. Ibid., p. 308.

Chapter 9. Epilogue

1. Pesotta to Bessie Robboy, 15 February 1961, Pesotta Papers, Box 8.

2. Ibid.

3. Pesotta to David Dubinsky, 13 March 1948, Pesotta Papers, Box 6.

4. Ibid.

5. Pesotta to *New York Times*, 6 August 1952, Pesotta Papers, Box 6.

6. Pesotta to *Freie Arbiter Stimme*, 6 March 1935, Pesotta Papers, Box 2.

7. Celia Gross to *Forward*, 20 July 1953, Pesotta Papers, Box 8.

8. Norman Thomas to Pesotta, 18 July and 23 July 1956, Pesotta Papers, Box 8.

9. Yelensky to Pesotta, 19 November 1946, Pesotta Papers, Box 6.

10. Margaret DeSilver to Pesotta, 3 May 1949, Pesotta Papers, Box 6.

11. Steimer to Pesotta, 17 June 1964, Pesotta Papers, Box 9.

12. Jewish Labor Committee Folder, Pesotta Papers, Box 9.

13. Pamphlet, 16 March 1964, Pesotta Papers, Box 9.

14. Pesotta, January 1960, Pesotta Papers, Box 36.

15. Emanuel Muravchik to Pesotta, 25 November 1964, Pesotta Papers, Box 9.

16. Pesotta, "Speech at Atran House," 15 January 1961, Pesotta Papers, Box 33.

17. Pesotta to Esther Liberman, 26 August 1963, Pesotta Papers, Box 9.

18. Invitation from Bernard Shane, 19 October 19, 1962, Pesotta Papers, Box 9.

19. Invitation from David Dubinsky, 8 May 1964, Pesotta Papers, Box 9.

20. Interview with Henoch Mendelsund.

21. Interview with Jack Hochman.

22. Pesotta to Hilda Adel, 11 August 1965, Pesotta Papers, Box 9.

23. Leibowitz, interview.

24. Larsen, interview; Luchovsky, interview.

25. Robert Gladnik to ILGWU, 3 December 1965, ILGWU Archives.

26. John Nicholas Beffel, Beffel Papers, New York University, Box 4.

27. Tyler, "Eulogy on Rose Pesotta," 9 December 1965, Clara Larsen private papers.

28. Asher, *Dorothy Jacobs Bellanca*, p. iv.

29. Kessler Harris, "Problems of Coalition Building," p. 129.

30. Balser, *Sisterhood and Solidarity*, p. 38.

31. Ibid.

32. Ibid., p. 32.

BIBLIOGRAPHY

Books and Articles

Alpern, Sara, Joyce Antler, Elisabeth Israels Perry, and Ingrid Winther Scobie, eds. *The Challenge of Feminist Biography: Writing the Lives of Modern American Women*. Urbana: University of Illinois Press, 1992.

Ash, Roberta. *Social Movements in America*. New York: Bobbs-Merrill, 1965.

Asher, Nina. *Dorothy Jacobs Bellanca: Feminist Trade Unionist 1894–1946*. Ph.D. diss., State University of New York, Binghamton, 1982.

Avrich, Paul. *An American Anarchist: The Life of Voltairine deCleyre*. Princeton, N.J.: Princeton University Press, 1978.

———. *The Anarchists in the Russian Revolution*. Ithaca, N.Y.: Cornell University Press, 1973.

———. *The Haymarket Tragedy*. Princeton, N.J.: Princeton University Press, 1984

———. *The Modern School Movement: Anarchism and Education in the United States*. Princeton, N.J.: Princeton University Press, 1980.

———. *The Russian Anarchists*. Princeton, N.J.: Princeton University Press, 1967.

———. *Sacco and Vanzetti: The Anarchist Background*. Princeton, N.J.: Princeton University Press, 1991.

Balser, Diane. *Sisterhood and Solidarity: Feminism and Labor in Modern Times*. Boston: South End Press, 1987.

Baum, Charlotte, Paula Hyman, and Sonya Michel. *The Jewish Woman in America*. New York: New American Library, 1976.

Bernstein, Irving. *The Lean Years: A History of the American Worker 1920–1933*. Cambridge: Riverside Press, 1960.

———. *The Turbulent Years: A History of the American Worker 1933–1941*. Boston: Houghton Mifflin, 1971.

Bookchin, Murray. *The Spanish Anarchists: The Heroic Years, 1868–1936*. New York: Harper Colophon Books, 1977.

Brandes, Joseph. "From Sweatshop to Stability: Jewish Labor between Two World Wars." *Yivo Annual of Jewish Social Science* (1976): 1–149.

Carroll, Peter N., and David W. Noble. *The Free and the Unfree: A New History of the United States*. New York: Penguin Books, 1982.

Cohen, Naomi W. *American Jews and the Zionist Idea*. KTAV Publishing House, 1975.

Cohen, Ricki. *Fannia Cohn and the International Ladies Garment Workers Union*. Ph.D. diss., University of South Carolina, 1976.

Cole, G. D. H. *Socialist Thought: Marxism and Anarchism: 1850–1890*. Vol. 2. London: Macmillan, 1957.

Cook, Blanche Wiesen. *Eleanor Roosevelt. Vol. 1. 1884–1933*. New York: Viking Press, 1992.

Cort, John C. "Trouble in Montreal." *Commonweal* (15 June 1945): 214–217.

Drinnon, Richard. *Rebel in Paradise*. Chicago: University of Chicago Press, 1961.

Drinnon, Richard, and Anna Maria Drinnon, eds. *Nowhere at Home: Letters from Exile of Emma Goldman and Alexander Berkman*. New York: Schocken Books, 1975.

Dubinsky, David, and A. H. Raskin. *David Dubinsky: A Life with Labor*. New York: Simon & Schuster, 1977.

Dubofsky, Melvyn. *We Shall Be All: A History of the IWW*. New York: New York Times Book Co., Quadrangle, 1969.

———. *When Workers Organize: NYC in the Progressive Era*. Amherst: University of Massachusetts Press, 1968.

Dubofsky, Melvyn, and Warren Van Tine, eds. *Labor Leaders in America*. Urbana: University of Illinois Press, 1987.

Dye, Nancy Schrom. *As Equals and as Sisters: Feminism, the Labor Movement, and the Women's Trade Union League of New York*. Columbia: University of Missouri Press, 1980.

Falk, Candace. *Love, Anarchy, and Emma Goldman*. New York: Holt, Rinehart & Winston, 1984.

Feurlicht, Roberta. *Justice Crucified*. New York: McGraw-Hill, 1977.

Fine, Sidney. *Sit Down: The General Motors Strike of 1936–1937*. Ann Arbor: University of Michigan Press, 1969.

Foner, Philip. *Women and the American Labor Movement*. Vol. 2: *From World War One to Present*. New York: Free Press, 1980.

Gabin, Nancy F. *Feminism in the Labor Movement: Women and the United Auto Workers, 1935–1975*. Ithaca, N.Y.: Cornell University Press, 1990.

Goldman, Emma. *Anarchism and Other Essays*. New York: Mother Earth, 1910. Reprint. New York: Dover Publications, 1969.

———. *Living My Life*. 2 vols. New York: Alfred A. Knopf, 1931. Reprint. New York: Dover, 1970.

———. *My Disillusionment in Russia*, 1922. Reprint. New York: Thomas Y. Crowell, 1970.

Gordon, Alban. *Russian Civil War: A Sketch for History*. London: Cassell, 1937.

Gurowsky, David. *Factional Disputes in the International Ladies Garment Workers Union 1919–1928*. Ph.D. diss., State University of New York, Binghamton, 1982.

Hall, Jacquelyn Dowd. "Disorderly Women: Gender and Labor History in the Appalachian South." *Journal of American History* (Fall 1986): 354–82.

Heilbrun, Carolyn G. *Writing a Woman's Life*. New York: Norton, 1988.

Howe, Irving. *World of Our Fathers: The Journey of East European Jews to America and the Life They Found and Made*. New York: Simon & Schuster, 1976.

Isca, Valerio. "Some Personal Recollections of Rose Pesotta." *Conorcorrente* (Boston, Winter 1966): 1.

James, Edward T., Janet Wilson James and Paul Boyer, eds., *Notable American Women: The Modern Period*. Cambridge Belknap Press of Harvard University, 1981.

Jensen, Joan, and Sue Davidson, eds. *A Needle, a Bobbin, a Strike: Women Needles Workers in America*. Philadelphia: Temple University Press, 1984.

Joll, James. *The Anarchists*. Cambridge: Harvard University Press, 1980.

Kenneally, James J. *Women and American Trade Unions*. Montreal: Eden Press, 1981.

Kessler Harris, Alice. "Organizing the Unorganizable: Three Jewish Women and Their Union." *Labor History* 7 (Winter 1976): 5–23.

———. *Out to Work: A History of Wage-Earning Women in the United States*. New York: Oxford University Press, 1982.

———. "Problems of Coalition Building: Women and Trade Unions in 1920's." In *Women, Work, and Protest*, edited by Ruth Milkman, 110–38.

———. "Rose Schneiderman and the Limits of Women Trade Unionism." In *Labor*

Leaders in America, edited by Melvyn Dubofsky and Walter Van Tine. Urbana: University of Illinois Press, 1987.

————. "Where Are the Organized Women Workers." *Feminist Studies* 3 (Fall 1975): 92–110.

————. *Women Have Always Worked*. N.Y.: Feminist Press, 1980.

Kingsolver, Barbara. *Holding the Line: Women in the Great Arizona Mine Strike of 1983*. Ithaca, N.Y.: ILR Press, New York State School of Industrial and Labor Relations, Cornell University, 1989.

Kornbluh, Joyce, and Mary Frederickson, eds. *Sisterhood and Solidarity: Workers Education for Women 1914–1984*. Philadelphia: Temple University Press, 1984.

Kropotkin, Peter. *Kropotkin's Revolutionary Pamphlets: A Collection of Writings by Peter Kropotkin*. Edited by Roger N. Baldwin. New York: Dover, 1970.

Laslett, John. *Labor and the Left: A Study of Socialist and Radical Influences on the American Labor Movement, 1881–1924*. New York: Basic Books, 1970.

Levin, Nora. *While Messiah Tarried: Jewish Socialist Movements, 1871–1917*. New York: Schocken Books, 1977.

Mannin, Esther. *Women and the Revolution*. New York: E. P. Dutton, 1939.

Marcaccio, Michael. *The Hapgoods: Three Earnest Brothers*. Charlottesville: University Press of Virginia, 1977.

Marsh, Margaret. *Anarchist Women: 1870–1920*. Philadelphia: Temple University Press, 1981.

Milkman, Ruth. "Organizing the Sexual Division of Labor: Historical Perspectives on 'Women's Work and the American Labor Movement.'" *Socialist Review* 49 (Jan.–Feb. 1980): 95–150.

————. *Women, Work, and Protest: A Century of U.S. Women's Labor History*. Boston: Routledge & Kegan Paul, 1985.

Miller, Martin. *Kropotkin*. Chicago: University of Chicago Press, 1976.

Nadel, Stanley. "Reds versus Pinks: A Civil War in the International Ladies Garment Workers Union." *New York History* (Jan. 1985): 50–72.

Paine, Robert. *The Life and Death of Trotsky*. New York: McGraw-Hill, 1977.

Pesotta, Rose. *Bread upon the Waters*. New York: Dodd, Mead, 1944. Reprint. Ithaca: ILR Press, New York State School of Industrial and Labor Relations, Cornell University, 1987.

————. *Days of Our Lives*. Boston: Excelsior, 1958.

Polenberg, Richard. *Fighting Faiths: The Abrams Case, the Supreme Court, and Free Speech*. New York: Viking Penguin, 1984.

Porter, David, ed. *Vision on Fire: Emma Goldman on the Spanish Revolution*. New Paltz, N.Y.: Commonground Press, 1983.

Rayback, Joseph G. *A History of American Labor*. New York: Free Press, 1966.

Rischin, Moses. *The Promised City: New York Jews, 1870–1914*. Cambridge: Harvard University Press, 1977.

Ruiz, Vicki L. *Cannery Women, Cannery Lives: Mexican Women, Unionization, and the California Food Processing Industry 1930–1950*. Albuquerque: University of New Mexico Press, 1987.

Russell, Francis. *Tragedy in Dedham*. New York: McGraw-Hill, 1971.

————. *Sacco and Vanzetti: The Case Resolved*. New York: Harper & Row, 1986.

Sacco, Nicola, and Bartolomeo Vanzetti. *The Letters of Sacco and Vanzetti*. Edited by Marion Frankfurter and Gardner Jackson. New York: Dutton, 1960.

Schneiderman, Rose, and Lucy Goldthwaite. *All For One*. New York: Paul Eriksson, 1967

Schofield, Anne. "The Uprising of the Twenty Thousand: The Making of a Labor Legend." In *A Needle, A Bobbin, A Strike: Women Needle Workers in America*. See Jensen and Davidson 1984.

Seller, Maxine. "Beyond the Stereotype: A New Look at the Immigrant Woman, 1880–1924." *Journal of Ethnic Studies* (Spring 1975): 59–70.

Sinclair, Upton. *Boston*. New York: Albert & Charles Boni, 1928.

Stein, Leon, ed. *Out of the Sweatshop: The Struggle for Industrial Democracy*. New York: New York Times Book Co., Quadrangle, 1977.

Tax, Meridith. *The Rising of the Women: Feminist Solidarity and Class Conflict 1880–1917*. New York: Monthly Review Press, 1980.

Waldinger, Roger. "Another Look at the ILGWU: Women, Industry Structure, and Collective Action." In Milkman, *Women, Work, and Protest*. See Milkman 1985.

Wertheimer, Barbara, ed. *Labor Education for Women Workers*. Philadelphia: Temple University Press, 1981.

Wexler, Alice. *Emma Goldman: An Intimate Life*. New York: Pantheon, 1984.

Woodcock, George. *Anarchism: A History of Libertarian Ideas and Movements*. New York: World, 1971.

Manuscript Collections

Boston Public Library. Sacco and Vanzetti Papers. Boston, Massachusetts.

Bund Archives. Located at 25 E. 78 Street, New York, New York.

Harvard University Law School Library. Manuscripts Division. Sacco and Vanzetti Papers. Cambridge, Massachusetts.

Indiana University. Manuscripts Department. Lilly Library. Powers Hapgood Papers. Bloomington, Indiana.

International Institute of Social History. Emma Goldman–Alexander Berkman Archives. Amsterdam, The Netherlands.

International Ladies' Garment Workers' Union Archives. David Dubinsky and Charles Zimmerman Papers. Labor Management Documentation Center, M. P. Catherwood Library, Cornell University, Ithaca, New York.

New York Public Library. Rose Pesotta Papers and Emma Goldman Papers. Rare Books and Manuscripts Division, Astor, Lenox and Tilden Foundations. New York, New York.

New York University. Tamiment Institution. John Nicholas Beffel Papers. New York, New York.

Radcliffe College. Arthur and Elizabeth Schlesinger Library on the History of Women in America. Emma Goldman Papers. Cambridge, Massachusetts.

University of Michigan. Labadie Collection. Ann Arbor, Michigan; *Twentieth-Century Trade Union Woman: Vehicle for Social Change Oral History Project*, 1978. Institute of Labor and Industrial Relations, University of Michigan—Wayne State University.

Wayne State University. Walter P. Reuther Library of Labor and Urban Affairs. The Archives of Labor History and Urban Affairs. John Nicholas Beffel Papers. Detroit, Michigan.

Journals and Reprints

Freedom. Vols. 1–2 (1933–34); Vol. 1, no. 5 (4 Feb. 4, 1933). Reprints. Westport, Conn.: Greenwood Reprint Corp., 1970.

Road to Freedom. Vol. 2, no. 11 (August 1926): Vol. 3, no. 8 (1 Oct. 1926); Vol. 3, no. 9 (1 Nov. 1926); Vol. 4, no. 7 (Feb. 1928); Vol. 5, no. 6 (Feb. 1929). Reprints of Vols. 1–8. Westport, Conn.: Greenwood Reprint Corp., 1970.

Private Interviews and Correspondence with the Author

Asher, Robert. Correspondence and conversations. Spring–Summer 1991.

Bimbat, Fanya, and Chaim Bimbat. Brooklyn, New York. Interview. July 30, 1987.

Bluestein, Abe, and Selma Bluestein. Croton-on-Hudson. Interview. September 3, 1983.

Dolgoff, Sam. New York Interview. 8 October 1983.

Hochman, Jack. New York, New York. Interview. 7 October 1983.

Isca, Valerio. New York, New York. Interview. 30 July 1987.

Kesselman, Amy. Correspondence and conversations. Spring–Summer 1991.

Larsen, Clara Rothberg. New York, New York. Interview, 7 October 1983.

Leibowitz, Esther. Workmen's Circle Home, Bronx, New York. Interview. 11 January 1984.

Luchovsky, Lisa. New York, New York. Interview. 21 November 1983.

Mendelsund, Henoch. New York, New York. Interview. 9 August 1983.

Monro, Barta Hapgood. Correspondence. January 1984.

Rotker, Dorothy Rubin, and Elias Rotker. Levittown, New York. Interview. 27 July 1987.

Thorne, Ahrne. Correspondence to Elaine Leeder, 5 December 1983.

Unpublished Manuscripts

Kessler Harris, Alice. "Draft on Rose Pesotta for ILGWU Archives." May 1979.

Rotker, D. collection, private papers.

Tyler, Gus. "Eulogy on Rose Pesotta," December 1965. C. Larsen private papers.

INDEX